MW00990696

BEST
HIKES
WITH
KIDS
ST. LOUIS
AND BEYOND

BEST HIKES WITH KIDS

KATHY SCHRENK

ST. LOUIS AND BEYOND

MOUNTAINEERS
BOOKS

To my favorite hiking buddies,
Arthur, Noah, Helen, and Nathan

MOUNTAINEERS BOOKS is the publishing
division of The Mountaineers, an organization founded in
1906 and dedicated to the exploration, preservation, and
enjoyment of outdoor and wilderness areas.

1001 SW Klickitat Way, Suite 201, Seattle, WA 98134
800-553-4453, www.mountaineersbooks.org

Copyright © 2018 by Kathy Schrenk
All rights reserved. No part of this book may be reproduced or utilized in any form, or
by any electronic, mechanical, or other means, without the prior written permission of
the publisher.

Printed in China
Distributed in the United Kingdom by Cordee, www.cordee.co.uk
First edition, 2018

Copyeditor: Pm Weizenbaum
Layout: Peggy Egerdahl
Series design: Jennifer Shontz and Mountaineers Books
Cartographer: Bart Wright, Lohnes+Wright

All photos by author unless noted otherwise.
Author photo on page 271: copyright © by Liz Schrenk, Something Blue Photography
    and Design, www.somethingblue-design.com
Cover photograph: *Hanging out at Klamberg Woods Conservation Area (see "Short
    Jaunts" sidebar in hike 13)* © Kathy Schrenk
Frontispiece: *A walk in the woods puts a smile on nearly everyone's face.* © Kathy Schrenk

Library of Congress Cataloging-in-Publication Data
Names: Schrenk, Kathy, author.
Title: Best hikes with kids : St. Louis and beyond / Kathy Schrenk.
Description: First edition. | Seattle, WA : Mountaineers Books, [2018] |
    Includes bibliographical references and index.
Identifiers: LCCN 2017036729| ISBN 9781680511024 (pbk) | ISBN 9781680511031
    (ebook)
Subjects: LCSH: Hiking for children—Missouri—Saint Louis
    Region—Guidebooks. | Family recreation—Missouri—Saint Louis
    Region—Guidebooks. | Saint Louis Region (Mo.)—Guidebooks.
Classification: LCC GV199.42.M82 S755 2018 | DDC 796.5109778/6—dc23
LC record available at https://lccn.loc.gov/2017036729

Mountaineers Books titles may be purchased for corporate, educational, or other
promotional sales, and our authors are available for a wide range of events. For
information on special discounts or booking an author, contact our customer service
at 800-553-4453 or mbooks@mountaineersbooks.org.

ISBN (paperback): 978-1-68051-102-4
ISBN (ebook): 978-1-68051-103-1

CONTENTS

NORTH AND WEST
OF ST. LOUIS

SOUTH OF ST. LOUIS

OVERVIEW MAP

161

70 JONESBURG

19

41
42 TROY
47
47
61

43

WENTZVILLE
44 70
45

79

100

28 29

3

94

ST CHARLES
ST PETERS
FLORISSANT
4

170

5 6
7 CHESTERFIELD
64

LAKE OF
THE OZARKS

OSAGE
BEACH
42 134
53
CAMDENTON
54
54
5
64
44
LEBANON

MISSOURI RIVER

46
47 48
8

49
50
94
51

9-11
12
13 15
14 19 16-18
20-23
24
25-27

270

64

UNION
59-60
65
50

62 61
63

64

30

ARNOLD
55
57
56
58

35
55

100

185
52

SULLIVAN
76
74
75
MERAMEC SP

MISSOURI

30

21

66

FESTUS
67

To Lake of
the Ozarks
44

77

68-69

DE SOTO

67

185

19

8

POTOSI

21

47

70

MARK TWAIN
NATIONAL
FOREST

8

78
PARK HILLS

FARMINGTON
32
NN

19

79

67

N

0   5   10
MILES

49

21
221

IRONTON
80
81 82 TAUM SAUK MTN SP
JOHNSON'S SHUT-INS SP

72

A QUICK GUIDE TO THE HIKES

Start here if you're looking for something specific, like waterfalls or spring wildflowers. These are the best of the best and will give hikers who are new to the area a good taste of what the region has to offer.

AUTHOR FAVORITES

- **Bluff View Park** (hike 15): A hike that's minutes from the subdivisions of West County, it nevertheless features a big view, a lot of wildlife, and a remarkable variety of natural environments.
- **Castlewood State Park, Lone Wolf and River Scene Trails** (hike 21): Along with one of the most spectacular views in the region, this hike also offers a beach and riverside trail with a jungle-like atmosphere in the summer.
- **Don Robinson State Park** (hike 64): This is a brand-new state park with unrivaled creek and cliff scenery.
- **Hawn State Park** (hike 72): One of the most rugged hikes in the region leads to a picturesque spot with rocks for scrambling and a pool created by Pickle Creek.
- **LaBarque Creek Conservation Area** (hike 63): The serene mixed forest includes a side trip to a pool and seasonal waterfall.
- **Pere Marquette State Park** (hike 28): Climb to one of the highest peaks in the area and enjoy river views from high above, plus bald eagles in winter if you're lucky.
- **Pickle Springs Natural Area** (hike 73): Packed with rock formations, waterfalls, scenic canyons, and vistas, this is an all-time favorite, and less than ninety minutes from St. Louis.
- **Piney Creek Ravine State Natural Area** (hike 37): This trail is worth the drive for unique rock formations, waterfalls, pools, and the finest samples of Native American art in the area.
- **Shawnee National Forest, Little Grand Canyon Trail** (hike 38): This path lives up to its name. Hike through two breathtaking canyons and then take in a view of the Big Muddy River and surrounding lands.

BEST BETS IN WINTER

- **Cahokia Mounds State Historic Site** (hike 31): There's little shade here, so nothing to block the warmth of the sun on a cloudless winter day. Plus, the trails aren't rocky, so there are fewer chances for slipping on ice.
- **Lone Elk County Park** (hike 23): Few steep sections make this less slippery than other nearby hikes, and the elk are out year-round.

Opposite: *Fall colors make for a dramatic scene at Hawn State Park, hike 72.*

Postcard-worthy views abound at Pickle Springs, hike 73.

- **Pickle Springs Natural Area** (hike 73): Ice formations add an extra treat to a hike that already has a lot of jaw-dropping sights.

BEST BETS IN SPRING

- **Babler State Park, Dogwood Trail** (hike 11): Not surprisingly, dogwood trees in this part of the park put on a glorious show in the spring.
- **Engelmann Woods Natural Area** (hike 51): The valley in the heart of this small park provides shady forest plus more open areas for a variety of wildflower environments.
- **Rockwoods Range** (hike 19): This area is known for its wildflowers, especially near the start of the hike and its creek.

BEST BETS IN SUMMER

- **Greensfelder County Park, Eagle Valley Trail** (hike 17): Plenty of shade on the Eagle Valley Trail makes this a great choice in the heat of summer.
- **LaBarque Creek Conservation Area** (hike 63): When it's extra-hot, head straight to the splash zone instead of hiking the whole loop. Just a quick scramble from the trail takes you to a series of pools for getting good and wet in the heat of Missouri summer.
- **Piney Creek Ravine State Natural Area** (hike 37): Splash in the pools of the first river crossing or farther along the loop near the rock art to cool off.

BEST BETS IN FALL

- **Castlewood State Park, Lone Wolf and River Scene Trails** (hike 21): The forest colors in the park and those across the Meramec River from this hike's signature viewpoint make it extra special in fall.
- **Klondike Park** (hike 50): Colorful trees across the river are the stars of this hike.
- **Shaw Nature Reserve** (hikes 59 and 60): Both hikes in this preserve feature views of fall colors across the prairies and the river.
- **Weldon Spring Conservation Area ("Lewis and Clark Trail")** (hike 48): The vista from this hike reaches across the Missouri River into St. Louis County, where the changing leaves of the trees make for a photo-worthy scene.

CAVES

- **Cliff Cave County Park** (hike 55): Look through the gate at the mouth of Cliff Cave and imagine Prohibition-era moonshiners hiding out here, protecting their wares.
- **Onondaga Cave State Park** (hike 77): Hike a picturesque trail above-ground, and then let a ranger show you the underground wonders. Tours are available.
- **Meramec State Park, Natural Wonders Trail** (hike 74): Peer into the mouths of three caves. You can also take a guided tour of Fisher Cave in this park.

STROLLERS AND WHEELCHAIRS

- **Al Foster Memorial and Rock Hollow trails** (hike 18): Start with a ride on the small-gauge railroad at the trailhead (runs on summer Sundays), and then push the stroller along these paved trails.
- **Creve Coeur Lake Memorial Park, Lake Trail** (hike 5): The path around Creve Coeur Lake is paved, passing through dense forests when it isn't hugging the lake.
- **Forest Park** (hikes 1 and 2): Both these hikes are paved and provide a tour of the most significant features of a nationally recognized urban park.
- **Meramec Conservation Area** (hike 76): This rare wilderness trail that's completely accessible to those with mobility issues includes a view of one of the area's many caves.
- **Queeny Park** (hike 12): A unique playground greets you at the start, with a variety of sights to discover on paved and gravel trails.

GREAT FOR JOGGING STROLLERS

- **Howell Island Conservation Area** (hike 8): Wide trails here accommodate jogging strollers on a forested island, and the trailhead is a short drive from Interstate 64 in Chesterfield.
- **Long Ridge Conservation Area** (hike 52): Wide forest roads at this secluded preserve make for a picturesque workout.

Kids often find crayfish in this pool at Hawn State Park, hike 72.

BREATHTAKING VIEWS

- **Bluff View Park** (hike 15): It's only a half mile on level terrain to the vista at Bluff View Park, where you'll see a pretty valley beyond the Meramec River.
- **Castlewood State Park, Lone Wolf and River Scene trails** (hike 21): A short but steep climb at the start of the hike provides quick rewards, with views across the Meramec River and a wide expanse of forest.
- **Pere Marquette State Park** (hike 28): The viewing platform atop McAdams Peak overlooks the Illinois River and miles of bottomland scenery along the Great River Road.

MOST SPECTACULAR WATERFALLS

- **Hickory Canyons Natural Area** (hike 71): This preserve includes two short hikes; the shorter one leads straight to a cliff with several trickling falls that combine into one after heavy rain.
- **Pickle Springs Natural Area** (hike 73): The waterfalls here flow over sheer cliffs along a hike that also includes fascinating rock formations and picturesque forests.
- **Taum Sauk Mountain State Park** (hike 82): The highest waterfall in Missouri flows from the state's highest point, making for a superlative hike.

FASCINATING HISTORY

■ **Cahokia Mounds State Historic Site** (hike 31): Discover the city of 20,000 that thrived 900 years ago just across the river from present-day St. Louis at this UNESCO-recognized World Heritage Site.

■ **Forest Park** (hikes 1 and 2): Learn about the early days of St. Louis through the St. Louis Art Museum, the Missouri History Museum, and landmark statues like *Apotheosis of St. Louis*.

■ **Piney Creek Ravine State Natural Area** (hike 37): Hike to one of the best examples of Native American wall art in the region, in the middle of a beautiful forest.

BEST OVERNIGHTS

■ **Cuivre River State Park, Lone Spring Trail** (hike 42): The backpacking site here is just minutes from the spring, perfect for filtering water during an overnight trip.

■ **Hawn State Park** (hike 72): Hike into the forest just past the rocky pools for some pretty camping spots, or stay at one of the designated sites along the Whispering Pines Trail.

■ **Lake of the Ozarks State Park** (hike 53): The backpacking destination deep in the forest of this state park provides a serene retreat from the constant action of "the Lake."

■ **Washington State Park, Opossum Track Trail** (hike 69): The backpacking site on this trail is also close to water, with a lot of space to spread out in a field surrounded by forest.

Even a three-year-old can make it through a rocky hike like Johnson's Shut-Ins, hike 80, with some rest stops and a good attitude.

INTRODUCTION

"Thousands of tired, nerve-shaken, over-civilized people are beginning to find out that going to the mountains is going home; that wildness is a necessity; and that mountain parks and reservations are useful not only as fountains of timber and irrigating rivers, but as fountains of life."

—John Muir, *Our National Parks*

When I was writing this book, I got a lot of confused looks. "Hiking . . . around here?" That's what people—even long-time residents—would ask. I assured them that, yes, indeed, there are countless trails through forests and up hills and along rivers all around them. The St. Louis region is full of state parks, county parks, wilderness areas, and nature preserves. They range from well-known trails with big views and big crowds in state parks to little-known paths in neighborhood parks and off-the-beaten-path conservation areas. Missouri does an amazing job of maintaining its state parks and has a vast network of conservation areas with hundreds of miles of trails waiting to be explored. St. Louis and St. Charles counties have incredible county parks that are in splendid natural settings, with ample trails that are well maintained and clearly marked. We're fortunate to have access to these wilderness experiences just a few miles from the strip malls and subdivisions of the suburbs. Across the Mississippi River, Southern Illinois has some of the most spectacular hikes in the Midwest.

And hiking in the St. Louis region is a year-round activity. Yes, there are some days in the winter when it's just too cold, and some afternoons in the summer when it's just too hot to safely hike. But if you plan ahead and watch the weather forecast, you can hike fifty-two weeks a year. My rule in the winter is that if it's 30 degrees or warmer and not raining, we hike. Kids rarely seem to be bothered by the cold, as long as they have sufficient layers. In winter there are plenty of sunny weekend days that are perfect for hiking. The temperatures are low and the days are short, but the views are broader, since the trees don't have any leaves to block sight lines. Remarkable animals, such as bald eagles, are easier to spot (see the "Bald Eagle Viewing" sidebar in hike 29 for more information about viewing bald eagles). And there's something special about being the only group of hikers in a wintry forest when the trees are leafless and their true, hauntingly beautiful form is revealed.

In summer I've been known to get my kids up at 6:00 AM to get a hike in, if the forecast calls for temperatures above 85. But keep in mind that heat seems to bother young kids more than cold does, sapping their energy quickly. When you do manage to get them outside in the summer, reward them with shaded trails so rich with plant life that they resemble exotic jungles (the River Trail at Meramec State Park, hike 75, comes to mind) in shades of green that are so vibrant they almost seem unreal or spots where they can splash in a creek to cool off, like La Barque Creek Conservation Area, hike 64.

The weather tends to be the most pleasant in spring, when wildflowers decorate the trailsides like jewels on a crown, and in fall when the trees turn all shades of warm colors. So, get outside as much as you can when the weather is nice, but remember that you can do it year-round with a little planning.

When you start exploring the trails of the St. Louis area, you'll quickly find, as I did, that there's more than you imagined—so much to explore that it would take years to hike every trail. And you'll find some that are so wonderful that you'll want to go back again and again. You may even find some truth to John Muir's sentiment that going into the wilderness is really going home.

WHY HIKE WITH KIDS?

If you're reading this book, you probably don't need much convincing that hiking is good for mind, body, and soul. But if you're trying to entice a reluctant partner, remind them of some of the benefits.

The American Academy of Pediatrics recommends that children get at least an hour of physical activity a day. For some kids, that quota gets met during school recess periods and physical education classes. But kids don't necessarily have PE every day, and weekends are another story. Homework loads, extracurricular activities, and the distractions of electronic devices mean that most kids (and adults) have to consciously make time for exercise. With the increased incidence of childhood obesity, it couldn't be more important. Besides preventing disease, exercise strengthens bones and muscles and develops motor skills. Hiking in particular is good for coordination, because it requires kids to adjust their gait based on the terrain and to navigate obstacles like rocks and roots. Most kids will respond better to the command to "get some exercise" when it involves exploring the woods. And while you're not going to get a serious cardio workout when you hike with little kids (unless you're carrying them), all adults aside from the most serious amateur athletes will get some physical benefit from a walk in the woods.

Research at Stanford University and elsewhere has shown that hiking improves mood. Researchers even found that walking in the woods decreases the chance of future depressive episodes significantly more than walking in an urban area. But most of us don't need scientists to tell us hiking is good for us; few things are as perfect for clearing the head as a favorite hiking trail, even if it's not a lung-busting climb up a rocky peak. A short stroll in the woods exposes us to fresh air and sunshine, both perfect antidotes to a bad mood.

Taking kids hiking means raising the next generation of conservationists, teaching them that it's up to every outdoor enthusiast to care for the natural spaces they love. Even if you don't align politically with the Sierra Club or the "green" movement, you likely agree that preserving wild spaces benefits everyone. In Missouri, a politically conservative state, 80 percent of voters voted in favor of extending a sales tax that benefits parks and preserves in the November 2016 election. This decision shows an incredible commitment to open spaces. The state is adding parks and conservation areas every year. Kids who grow up hiking will continue to value these spaces that benefit the earth and all the creatures on it, including humans.

Many hikes offer a chance to spot a reptile or amphibian, like this toad.

Tips for Hiking with Kids

Your kids aren't always going to be gung ho about hiking; sometimes they may be outright hostile to the idea. I have one son who loves to hike and is even enthusiastic about carrying fifteen or twenty pounds of gear for an overnight backpacking adventure. His brother, however, complains mightily every time we tell him it's time for a hike, and he celebrates when the weather forces us to cancel. Once he's actually on the trail, his attitude usually improves, thanks to some of the tricks I've learned over the years.

Bolster kids' enthusiasm for the hike before you go with information about the trail—from this book or from your own memories: "Last time we hiked there, we saw a turtle!" If your child is not excited about hiking, frame the outing a different way. If they like to go for a picnic, or a rock scramble, just change the name. "Today we're going for a picnic!" Take the focus off the walk, but be clear that the whole family is going on an outdoor adventure. The most crucial part of getting your kids to hike is actually getting them out to the trailhead. If you make it clear from an early age that hiking is an activity your family does on a regular basis, you'll all experience more success and happiness on the trail.

Poems, fairy tales, and your own made-up stories can help pass the time on hikes. Many of the kids I hike with enjoy making up their own stories as a group; someone starts a tale with one sentence and the next in line adds to it, and so on. This activity can keep the group occupied for miles.

Food is important for every hike, and you can add motivation by mixing in special treats. Because my kids love candy, we allow only a few select kinds in the house, to keep consumption under control. But we have a stash of "special"

Exploring a creek at Powder Valley, hike 26

candy in the hiking backpack to use for bribes. Toddlers and preschoolers are especially easy to bribe: "I'll give you a lollipop if you walk to that tree!" or "You can have a piece of chocolate if you take another hundred steps!"

My favorite way to keep kids happy on hikes is to invite their friends. It's amazing how much complaining happens on a hike with only one family. But if you add another family with at least one kid in roughly the same age range, then like magic the hike seems to get shorter and the climbs easier for everyone involved.

Hiking at Every Age

No kid is too young to hike. There are carrying slings and harnesses built for the tiniest newborns; if your baby can leave the hospital, you can take him or her on a hike. The hikes in this book can be enjoyed by people of all ages. Parents who are used to rigorous hikes can take an infant or even a large toddler on all but the most rugged trails in a carrier. All the hikes described here will be of interest to kids and adults, but the trail descriptions are aimed at families with kids through age 10.

Infants

When you're hiking with a newborn, the hardest part is getting out the door, and the benefits are mostly for the adults, but those can be huge. The effort of packing up the diaper bag and making sure baby is clean and fed pale in comparison to the pleasures of walking through the forest with baby strapped to your chest. Plan ahead to have all your gear ready (see "Gear" below for tips on what to bring) long before it's time to hit the trail. Once you're ready to go, there is a wide and ever-growing variety of slings, packs, and wraps that make carrying a tiny baby easy. Parents' clubs and online used-item forums can be a great source for secondhand carriers, if you want to try out a few. Doctors encourage new moms to walk for exercise and to help combat post-partum depression. I remember the intense sense of relief I felt when my first baby (now twelve years old) was just a few weeks old and I got out into the woods with him. I was overwhelmed with being a new mom and exhausted from sleep deprivation, and the smell of the woods, the fresh air, and the sun spilling through the branches was a salve to my jangled nerves. Just make sure to check with your doctor before going on a long or strenuous hike, because healing from childbirth can take time.

Babies

These kiddos are starting to crawl and eat solid food, but are usually still happy to be carried in a front pack or backpack. This may be the age where they are the most portable. Be sure to add snacks to the gear list. Pouches of pureed food make this easier than ever, and you can even buy reusable pouches and fill them with your own puree.

Toddlers

This age can be the most challenging, in a lot of different ways. Toddlers are starting to walk, or perhaps have been for many months. However, they might not want to be told that "it's time to go for a hike!" even if they'll enjoy it once they get out there. At this stage, parents might have to be patient and acknowledge that they may not be able to hike many miles with their little one. This is where a stroller with rugged tires can come in handy. Several hikes in this book, like the one at Creve Coeur Lake (see hike 5), offer a trip into the woods on a paved path. Some hikes have dirt trails that are wide and level enough for strollers (see "Great for Jogging Strollers" in "A Quick Guide to the Hikes" for suggestions). Sometimes the only way to get a kid on the trail is by pushing him or her in a stroller. While this means they aren't getting exercise, they are getting fresh air, and the caregiver is experiencing some all-important exercise and a change of scenery from the usual indoor play.

Preschoolers

Once they get good at walking on their own, some children will be able to hike for miles. Then those same kids might backslide and decide they're tired after twenty steps. This is the time to invest in either a soft carrier or a sturdier child carrier, a hard-frame backpack for carrying a preschooler. Take your child with you to a local outdoor gear store for help with fitting. Again, be patient. Kids may change their feelings about hiking from one day to the next. Just when you think your daughter is a hiking pro and can handle a 3-mile hike without being carried, she decides she hates hiking, or she wants to be carried the whole time. Or she wants to be carried for ten minutes, then walk for ten minutes, and so on. Just keep soldiering on.

There are views for miles at Taum Sauk Mountain State Park, hike 82.

Grade-Schoolers

By the age of five, most kids will start to be able to really hike without whining much or needing to be carried. Skill levels vary widely, of course. This is the age when having friends along for the journey starts to become the most important. Ask other families with kids close in age to join you. See if your child has a favorite friend in school, and ask that family to come along. If that doesn't work, look online for local hiking groups. Chances are good that other families are out there looking for hiking companions as well.

KNOW BEFORE YOU GO

This section will help you prepare for any hike. If you've never set foot on a trail before, start here. Even if you're an experienced hiker, it's a good idea to review the basics.

Gear

From the Ten Essentials to what to wear to the type of kid carrier to use, parents face a lot of choices when packing for a hike. With a little planning and preparation, you can keep your children (and yourself) comfortable and safe.

The Ten Essentials

Every time you get ready for a hike of any length, your first move should be to grab the Ten Essentials, a handy list developed by The Mountaineers. This checklist is recognized by most outdoor experts and outfitters as the minimum you should have with you on every outdoor adventure, no matter how short.

Save yourself a lot of time and frustration by keeping these items in a designated hiking bag or backpack, or in a small sack that you can throw in the kid carrier.

1. **Navigation:** A detailed topographic map isn't necessary for most day hikes, but at the very least, bring this book or a printed map of the park or trail you plan to hike. A compass and a phone with GPS are also a good idea.

2. **Headlamp:** Even if you are leaving first thing in the morning, keep a small flashlight or headlamp in your hiking bag (also useful for peeking into caves!).

3. **Sun protection:** Everyone, youngsters and adults, should wear a wide-brimmed hat and sunglasses and apply sunscreen on all exposed skin, even in winter or on cloudy days.

4. **First aid:** Buy a packable first-aid kit at the drugstore or, more economically, purchase your own supplies and assemble a kit. While you're at it, make a larger one that you can keep in your car. Search online for first-aid kit checklists. Don't forget toilet paper and a sanitary shovel (see "Potty Time on the Trail" later in the Introduction for more on relieving oneself outside). I also like to carry an extra pair of hiking boot laces; they cost about $3 and take up almost no space, and hiking with a broken boot lace could result in a lot of painful blisters.

5. **Knife:** Your implement can be as simple as a basic pocket knife or as versatile as a multiuse tool and repair kit.

6. **Fire:** A signal fire in the event of getting lost or injured can be a lifesaver—literally. Keep waterproof matches and fire starter (this can even be lint from your dryer) in your bag.

7. **Shelter:** Carry along a lightweight, waterproof shelter for the worst-case scenarios: someone is injured, or there's a freak blizzard (unlikely in Missouri), or you're hopelessly lost. Outdoor stores sell thin but warm emergency "space blankets" that roll up to the size of a can of soup and weigh almost nothing. Adding a couple to your pack is sufficient, unless you're setting out on a 10-mile trek.

8. **Extra food:** Bring at least one more granola bar, apple, or serving of trail mix per person than you think you'll need. No matter how short the hike, someone will ask for an extra snack at some point, and then everyone will want some.

9. **Extra water:** Always, always, always bring water: at least one bottle per person. Invest in a reservoir system (a bladder that you carry in a backpack attached to a long straw) for when your crew's hikes get longer and you need more water, or if your kids are motivated to drink more water by having access to the straw at all times.

10. **Extra clothes:** Unless it's so hot that you're worried about heat exhaustion (see "Heat and Cold" later in the Introduction), bring one more layer than you think you'll need. Pick lightweight fabrics like fleece to keep from adding too much weight to your pack. A good fleece from a local outdoor outfitter will last for years, and it's easy to find used ones for kids who will outgrow them quickly. Consider adding extra socks to your gear bag in case of a stream crossing or puddle jumping.

A NOTE ABOUT SAFETY

Safety is an important concern in all outdoor activities. No guidebook can alert you to every hazard or anticipate the limitations of every reader. Therefore, the descriptions of roads, trails, routes, and natural features in this book are not representations that a particular place or excursion will be safe for your party. When you follow any of the routes described in this book, you assume responsibility for your own safety. Under normal conditions, such excursions require the usual attention to traffic, road and trail conditions, weather, terrain, the capabilities of your party, and other factors. Keeping informed on current conditions and exercising common sense are the keys to a safe, enjoyable outing.

—Mountaineers Books

Clothing

Layers are key to comfort on any hike. Comfy, roomy pants or shorts work best, especially pairs with pockets, so kids can carry their own snacks and trash. A short-sleeve T-shirt makes a good base layer, topped with a fleece jacket or sweatshirt. Keep a rain jacket or warmer coat in the backpack for more extreme weather. Avoid cotton if the weather forecast calls for any rain or if you expect to sweat—once cotton is wet, it wicks heat away from the body, which can prove dangerous.

Footwear

Most kids will do fine with sneakers on short hikes. If you find that your family does a lot of hiking, it makes sense for their comfort and safety to invest in some boots. Kids' boots are cheaper than those for adults, and kids often outgrow them before they wear out, so they can get a lot of use by being passed down to multiple kids. Wool hiking socks are ideal for keeping feet warm in winter and cool in summer.

Kid Carriers

There are two basic kinds of carriers you can use to tote those who can't make it the whole way on their own. The first is a soft carrier, such as a sling or a tailored fabric pack. These are for babies and the smallest toddlers; check the manufacturer specifications for weight limits. The second kind is a hard-frame backpack that kids can ride in for as long as an adult is willing to carry them.

A Few Extras

To help make for a smooth hike with little ones, think about some fun extras beyond the safety basics. A camera is high on the list. If you trust your child to handle your smartphone, great. If not, you can buy small point-and-shoot cameras that are resistant to water, sand, and being dropped from high places. Binoculars are fun for spotting wildlife and taking in grand views. Magnifying glasses are also useful. Some kids love to have a book or laminated card in hand to identify birds, butterflies, flowers, and other flora and fauna. Experiment to see what kinds of accessories get your kids excited about getting on the trail.

Leave No Trace

"Take only pictures, leave only footprints" should be every hiker's motto. Few things are worse than having an idyllic forest stroll soured by a plastic bottle or grocery bag cluttering the landscape. Now is the time to teach kids the importance of keeping trash where it belongs. To lessen the chance of food wrappers blowing in the wind, encourage your kids to wear pants or a jacket with pockets when they hike. For extra credit, bring a plastic shopping bag and pick up any trash you see on the trail—just remind kids not to pick up anything gross, like cigarette butts, or dangerous, like pieces of glass.

Discourage kids from trying to take home rocks or sticks, and do not let them pick flowers. Remind them that the forest needs those sticks to grow new trees and plants, and they need to leave the flowers for everyone to enjoy.

Finding Your Way

Most of the parks and preserves highlighted in this book have a website from which you can print helpful maps of the trails. And most have well-marked trails with signs and blazes to ensure that you stay on the right path. As a result, carrying a map and compass may not always seem necessary, but it's a good habit to instill when children are starting out.

Getting the kids involved with routefinding and orientation will help give them a sense of purpose and ownership of the outing. You can let kids carry a copy of the map during the hike and point out trail junctions and landmarks

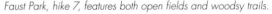
Faust Park, hike 7, features both open fields and woodsy trails.

on the map as you hike past them. Ask your little hiker if she can figure out what direction you're walking using the map or the compass.

Most of the hikes in this book are very well signed. Where they're not, I've noted that with a warning about a "tricky junction" or similar wording. Missouri State Parks, in particular, are very good about marking the trails with blazes, which are usually plastic squares nailed to trees. Typically each trail in a park will have its own color; this is noted at the trailhead and on the park map.

If you're interested in teaching your family about orienteering, check with local outdoor retail stores, some of which offer classes to get adults started quickly with a map and compass. Local orienteering clubs will let you put your skills to the test. It's fun to practice using a compass, plus you get outside, and meet and learn from other outdoors lovers.

Trail Hazards
Hiking may be the safest way to enjoy the outdoors, but dangers exist any time you venture out your front door. Being prepared and informed is the best way to stay safe and healthy on the trail.

Ticks
Ticks seem to scare people away from hiking more than bears, snakes, or other wildlife. Ticks are a fact of life on trails in most of the United States, but they shouldn't stop you from enjoying nature. The good news is that ticks in this region are much less likely to carry diseases like Lyme than are the ticks found along the East Coast. But it's still a good idea to avoid them.

Ticks can't jump or fly; they only crawl. So they hang out on a leaf or blade of grass and wait for a host—human or animal—to brush against the foliage and let them catch a ride. Then they can tuck in for a meal of mammal blood. These dastardly bugs can detect exhaled carbon dioxide, body odors, vibrations, and changes in light, which is how they know where to wait for an unsuspecting host. For the highest level of protection, use a four-pronged approach:

- Treat clothing and gear, including footwear and hats, with a permethrin spray, which you should be able to buy at a hardware or department store or online. Make sure to follow all the directions on the bottle. Once you spray your gear, the chemical will remain and repel ticks for several washings. I've found this to be the most successful method for avoiding tick bites; if you do only one thing to repel ticks, spray your boots and socks with permethrin.
- Wear long pants tucked into your boots, and a shirt tucked into your pants. Don't forget the wide-brimmed hat, since ticks can drop onto heads from trees.
- Use insect repellent with DEET on exposed skin—again, read the directions and warnings.
- Stay on the trail.

I do some of these, but not all (I just hate hiking in long pants during the summer, so I make sure my socks and shorts are treated with permethrin).

Hanging out on the Johnson's Shut-Ins Trail, hike 80

No matter what you do, you still might get bitten. Once you get home, do a thorough check of everyone. If you find one dug in, look for tips and tricks for removal with a quick online search. Pulling it out with tweezers is the most common technique. Make sure to have tweezers and some alcohol wipes (to clean the site of the bite after removal) in your first-aid kit. Watch for symptoms of Lyme disease, although it is rare in this region according to the Centers for Disease Control and Prevention. And if you hike with a dog, make sure the dog is up to date on tick treatments, which are topical treatments you can buy over the counter. These cause ticks to die after they bite, so you still need to check the dog for ticks to keep it from bringing ticks into the car or house.

Bears

Campers and park rangers are spotting black bears in increasing numbers in the Ozark region and the counties south of St. Louis. Black bears were reintroduced in Arkansas in the 1960s after settlers in the 1800s decimated the species. Their populations have been increasing, with bears moving farther north every year. Black bears are much smaller and less aggressive than brown or grizzly bears. Human interaction with black bears almost never ends in injury to the humans. (Grizzly bears were found as far east as Kansas before Anglo-American settlers came west, but now US grizzly habitat is confined to the northern Rocky Mountains.)

The Missouri Department of Conservation (MDC) is carefully tracking black bear populations in the hope that management practices will help

Deer are a common sight on many of these hikes.

humans and bears coexist. They've captured, tagged, and released dozens of bears in southern Missouri. At the time of this writing, the MDC estimated that there were about 300 bears living in the part of the state south of Interstate 44, where many of the hikes in this books take place.

Check the MDC website, https://mdc.mo.gov, to learn all about the extensive bear research program, and call or email them if you have concerns or questions. The best way to stay bear-safe is to keep kids in sight while hiking in bear country. If you see a bear, first, consider yourself lucky to have spotted one of these incredible animals. Then, respect the bear's need for personal space, remain calm, and detour widely or slowly back up. Avoid eye contact, which the animal may interpret as a threat. Keep kids close to you.

Exercise extra caution if you see cubs or a sow with them. Be sure to report your sighting to the MDC, noting the time, day, location, and appearance of the bear.

Snakes

Snake sightings on the trail are not uncommon, but always exciting. Missouri and southwest Illinois share five species of venomous snake: copperhead, cottonmouth, western pygmy rattlesnake, massasauga rattlesnake, and timber rattlesnake. The most common venomous snake in Missouri is the copperhead. All are members of the pit viper family. Pit vipers have a pit between the eye and nostril on each side of the head.

The best way to avoid surprising a snake is to stay on the trail. Always keep a safe distance, unless you have experience identifying snakes. Instruct kids to observe snakes from a distance. Snakebites are rare, however, and fatalities from snakebites, even more so. But if someone does get bitten by a snake, get them to the hospital as soon as possible.

Hunting

If you spend enough time in MDC preserves and hiking areas, you will notice that you're sharing the space with hunters. Although hunting is allowed in all the conservation areas—though not in state parks—it's strictly controlled by season and type of firearm. Most of the hunting seasons happen in fall and winter, with hunters prohibited from firing guns or bows close to trails. Occasional "controlled hunts" will close trails, but those instances are always posted on the website and at the trailhead. If you're concerned about hiking during hunting season, search https://nature.mdc.mo.gov for the conservation area you plan to visit, and call the MDC contact number listed on the website.

Heat and Cold

Water is important year-round, but especially in summer. Remind kiddos to drink frequently when the weather is warm. Check the heat index (a measure of perceived heat based on temperature and humidity), which can be found on weather sites or phone apps, before you go out; if the index is above 90 degrees Fahrenheit, consider choosing an easier hike than what your group is used to.

Know the signs of heat exhaustion and heatstroke. Of the two, heat exhaustion is less severe and can be treated at home. The symptoms include fatigue, nausea, headache, achiness, weakness, and dizziness. Get the patient drinking

For some kids, collecting and playing with sticks is one of the best parts of hiking.

cold water and into air-conditioning. Avoid excessive exercise for a while. Follow up with the doctor.

Heatstroke is life threatening, requiring immediate medical care. Look for shortness of breath, blood in urine or stool, convulsions, and very fast or slow heartbeat, in addition to the symptoms mentioned for heat exhaustion.

On the other end of the spectrum, cold can be a threat during winter. Check the forecast; if the windchill is below 20, consider hiking on a different day to avoid frostbite. If the windchill factor is merely cold and not arctic—say, in the upper 20s—cover as much skin as possible and wear several layers. A ski mask is a good idea; you can even get ones with a breathable panel that covers nearly your whole face. If anything starts to feel numb, get back inside.

Kids tend to be more averse to heat than cold. If it's chilly but the sun is out, most kids (and adults) will be fine if they layer up, and after a good ten or fifteen minutes on the trail they'll be shedding a layer or two.

Potty Time on the Trail

No matter how short the hike, or how much you cajole them to use the bathroom before leaving the trailhead, someone will have to relieve themselves on the trail at some point.

Boys, of course, can pee standing up. But that doesn't mean they'll be eager to pee outside. Some boys prefer a tree to a toilet any day, but others are more anxious about the outdoor experience. Try to get them to practice as much as possible, either in the backyard, if that's feasible, or on the trail.

Things are considerably tougher for girls. Moms can show their daughters how to squat or share a YouTube video about how to relieve yourself without getting pee all over your boots and clothes. I like to use a urinary directional device. There is a lot out there, but my favorite is a flexible, specially shaped funnel that you press against your body while you urinate to allow you to pee standing up.

Going number-two is another issue. Make sure you have some toilet paper and your sanitary trowel. Move away from the trail, avoiding any body of water by at least 100 feet. After digging a hole six inches deep, just squat and aim. Sticks are handy for covering everything up. Pack out used paper in a separate bag.

SUGGESTIONS?

I've hiked all these trails and checked the routes, directions, and driving instructions. But conditions change, old trails fall into disrepair, and new trails are built. If you notice any discrepancies in trail descriptions or have any suggestions for future editions, please write to me in care of Mountaineers Books at the street address listed on the copyright page or mbooks@mountaineersbooks.org.

HOW TO USE
THIS BOOK

Most of the hikes in this guide are located in and around St. Louis City and County. Those in Illinois will be noted in the directions and on the corresponding map. With the exception of a few noted in the "Great Getaway" sections, the hikes are an hour or less from the city. They vary from unique state parks north of the city to urban parks to Ozark region hikes showcasing some of the most spectacular treks in the Midwest. The hikes are geared toward kids up to age 10. None are longer than 5 miles. Use the difficulty ratings (explained below) to decide which hikes are best for your group.

The hikes are divided into four areas: In and Around, close to the city; East, in Illinois; North and West, for outlying areas including St. Charles County; and South, for those hikes south of Interstate 44.

Each hike is preceded by two brief summaries, "Before You Go" and "About the Hike." These summaries contain valuable information to help you decide whether this is the right hike for your crew on that day, and how to prepare for it.

BEFORE YOU GO
This section includes four categories of information.

Map: This line lists where to find the most relevant map for the hike. Almost all of these hikes have good maps available online; just type the name of

Hike father, hike son.

MAP LEGEND

⑤	Interstate highway	⊤⊤	Bench
②	US highway	■	Building of interest
N ⑤③⓪	State route or highway	⌂	Campground (backpacking)
1230	County road	▲	Campground (established)
-●-	Main trail	→	Direction of travel
·········	Continuation of main trail	↦	Gate
········	Other trail	↶	Good turnaround point
═══	Paved road	℗	Parking
⌗⌗⌗	Gravel road	℗	Alternate parking
-⌗-	Bridge	▲	Peak or mountain
-⊣⊢-	Underpass or tunnel	⊕	Playground
⊢⊢⊢⊢	Railroad	⊗	Splash zone
·-··-·	Powerline	⊜	Shelter
	Body of water	⊼	Picnic table
──	River or stream	•	Point of interest
	Park, forest, or wilderness area	⓪	Restroom or privy
	Wetlands	ⓣ	Trailhead
⟋	Waterfall	ⓥ	Viewpoint

the park or preserve in your browser. Usually the first listing will be the main page for the park, with a link to a map of the whole park. Missouri State Parks web pages also offer more detailed maps of each specific trail. Where maps are not available at the park entrance or trailhead, bring this book, a photocopy of the particular hike, or a printout from the website.

Contact: The agency responsible for the trail is listed here, with contact information in the Resources. More information is usually available online, or you can call a ranger if you have questions; web addresses and phone numbers are also listed in Resources.

GPS: Coordinates for this book were drawn from online mapping services, including Google Maps and CalTopo; they're based on the WGS84 datum (which both mapping programs use) and are formatted as decimal degrees. Enter the coordinates into your mobile device if you like to get directions this way.

Notes: Here you'll find important topics for the hike, like road issues and bathrooms. If fees aren't mentioned, entrance to the park or preserve is free. To avoid disappointment, be sure to double-check for changes in hours and possible trail closures.

ABOUT THE HIKE
This section summarizes several key details to orient you to a particular hike.

Seasons: Every season in St. Louis allows a different hiking experience. As long as you're prepared, you can hike almost any time. In this section of the

KEY TO ICONS

Each hike includes icons that highlight significant features.

 Accessible: Some or all of the hike is accessible for wheelchairs and strollers.

 Bike path: The hiking trail or a connecting trail is good for family bike rides.

 Dog-friendly: The trail allows leashed dogs and is well suited to bringing your dog along.

 Wildflowers: Spectacular wildflowers are on display in spring and summer.

 Historic site: Landmarks along the trail, or a museum at the trailhead, offer insights into the area's human past.

 Interpretive trail: Signposts along the trail or special brochures offer extra information about the natural or historical environment.

 Forest: All or part of the hike leads you through forest.

 Splash zone: Along the hike or near the trailhead you'll find a good spot for splashing and cooling off on a hot day.

 Waterfall: The hike features a waterfall.

 Wildlife: There's a good chance of seeing animals from the trail.

hike summary, you can see when each hike is at its best. Hikes that are fun in summer have shade. Those that are fun in winter have big views or a chance to see dramatic icicles hanging off cliffs.

Difficulty: Every kid is different, so it's up to you as the caregiver to decide what they can handle. Each hike is labeled with one of five difficulty rankings, based on distance, elevation change, and how smooth or rocky the trail surface is. Some shorter hikes can have high difficulty rankings because of tricky stream crossings or trail sections that resemble a rock scramble more than a trail.

- **Easy:** These hikes are suitable for any age and ability level and often are stroller-friendly.
- **Easy to moderate:** With these you'll have a little more elevation gain or slightly rougher trail than easy hikes.
- **Moderate:** These hikes are still suitable for small children, but the going may be slow as the terrain gets rougher and the climbs get steeper.
- **Moderate to difficult:** These hikes are good for more experienced young hikers, or little ones with a strong parent willing to carry when needed.
- **Difficult:** You'll encounter a lot of elevation change and difficult terrain with plenty of roots and rocks along these trails; they are best for experienced hikers who can walk 2–3 miles of a moderate hike without resting much, or parents who are fit enough to carry children on steep climbs and over rough terrain.

Length: Here the distance is noted, as well as the type of hike, which is either round-trip or loop.

Loops
When I describe a loop trail, I try to put an exciting feature like a waterfall or splash zone in the second half of the hike as a motivator. If the really good stuff is at the beginning of the hike, you're more likely to have whiny bored kids at the end. When there's something to look forward to, you can tell them it's "just a little farther" to the big attraction.

GETTING THERE
The driving directions listed for each hike begin at the nearest reference point, whether a major highway exit or intersection or a town. Roads are paved unless otherwise specified. For a few hikes, directions are given for families coming from St. Louis and for those coming from Illinois. Where hikes are accessible by public transportation, the nearest stop is listed.

ON THE TRAIL
The hike description guides you from the trailhead to the destination and back, mile by mile. All major junctions and features are described, with suggestions for great rest stops, picnic areas, side trips, and more.

Opposite: A big, partially hollow tree offers a little hiker a fun hideout.

IN AND AROUND THE CITY OF ST. LOUIS

1 FOREST PARK: WEST

BEFORE YOU GO
   MAP On park website and at visitor center
   CONTACT Forest Park Forever
   GPS 38.643564° N, -90.283461° W
   NOTES Wheelchair and stroller accessible except for avoidable section in Kennedy
      Forest; bathrooms and water fountains throughout park

ABOUT THE HIKE
   SEASON Fall, winter, spring
   DIFFICULTY Easy
   LENGTH 3.7 miles loop
   HIGH POINT 590 feet
   ELEVATION GAIN 330 feet

GETTING THERE

From Interstate 64 (known locally as "40") in St. Louis, exit at 36A-36B for South Kingshighway Boulevard and turn right (north). Drive 0.9 mile on Kingshighway, and then turn left (west) on Lindell Boulevard. Drive 1 mile, and turn left (south) on DeBaliviere Circle into the park. Halfway around the circle, turn right on Lagoon Drive and then in 0.1 mile turn left (east) on Grand Drive. The Dennis & Judith Jones Visitor and Education Center is in 0.8 mile on the left; parking is on the right.

A fox on the trail in Kennedy Forest, Forest Park

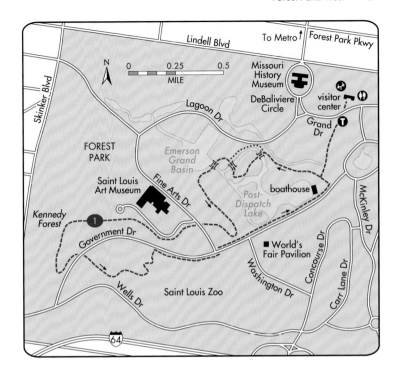

Both MetroBus 90 and the Forest Park Trolley stop at the Missouri History Museum, which is just northwest of the visitor center. The Forest Park MetroLink stop is across the street from the museum.

ON THE TRAIL

Forest Park is one of the great public open spaces in the country, in the tradition of New York City's Central Park and San Francisco's Golden Gate Park. At 1300 acres, it is larger than the marquee parks in Manhattan and the City by the Bay—in fact, it's so large that two hikes in this book take place here! This hike showcases some of the most well-known and scenic features in the park's western half.

Start with a tour of the visitor center: pick up a map, talk to a volunteer, or browse the gallery of photos. The building has a lot of information about the park and museums, tours, and wildlife on the park grounds. There's also a café and a playground.

Head south past the tennis courts, and after a quarter mile turn right (west) onto the gravel path. Walk along Post-Dispatch Lake—which you can explore by paddleboat—and toward the Emerson Grand Basin. At 0.5 mile, turn left (west) across the white suspension bridge to Picnic Island, because what kid doesn't love a bridge? If you have a dog with you, though, avoid this particular bridge, since its metal-grate surface is hard on paws. Instead, take the slightly longer way to the right along the lake. At 0.7 mile, leave the island by crossing another bridge, and turn left to enjoy the view of the Saint Louis Art Museum and its iconic *Apotheosis of St. Louis*, which served as a symbol of St. Louis until the Gateway Arch was completed in 1965. This statue of King Louis IX—twenty-one feet high and sitting atop a twenty-foot concrete stand—rules over Art Hill, which is crammed with sledders on wintry weekend afternoons.

Make a sharp left at the base of Art Hill to head southeast on a path that takes you past Wildlife Island, not accessible by bridges because it's reserved for wildlife. Next, at 1 mile, take a sharp right and head uphill. Turn left (southwest) just before the parking lots, and cross Fine Arts Drive to follow the paved path that leads behind the art museum, curving to the right along the way.

At mile 1.7, turn left (south) into Kennedy Forest. Set aside right from the park's beginning in 1876, these 60 acres form a woodland park within a park, making it an ideal place for birding and wildlife viewing. In 2016, Forest Park Forever and AmeriCorps undertook a significant effort to revitalize a ten-acre portion of the forest by removing invasive nonnative species, such as honeysuckle, and by increasing populations of native flora and fauna. Watch for interpretive signs about the project and evidence of the honeysuckle removal in the open forest floor. At mile 1.9, turn left through the forest, and then cross Government Drive.

Within Kennedy Forest a series of switchbacking trails and bridges, known as the boardwalk, features signs identifying tree species and other information about the trees and their surroundings. At mile 2.3, head downhill along these paved trails. After about a third of a mile, come out of the woods near the zoo's north parking lot. At this point there's a short, steep, gravel path with some steps, so if you're using a wheelchair or less rugged stroller, return 0.2 mile

A PARK WITHIN A PARK: THE (FREE) SAINT LOUIS ZOO

A familiar refrain about St. Louis is that it's "a great place to raise kids." Not least among the reasons is the plethora of free museums and attractions, and topping the list is the Saint Louis Zoo. It's considered one of the best zoos in the world because of its quality exhibits and commitment to conservation and education. In 2016 it was named the top free attraction in the United States by *USA Today*, and in 2014 was ranked the fourth-best zoo in the world by TripAdvisor.

Admission to the zoo is always free, and includes indoor exhibits like the reptile and primate houses, plus outdoor features like the polar bear and elephant exhibits. There's a fee for parking in the attached lots, but you can find parking on the surrounding streets in Forest Park for free. Some activities in the zoo, like the sea lion show and the train, require a fee.

back to Government Drive, and walk 0.4 mile northeast along the sidewalk to the zoo.

Turn right (east) on the sidewalk along Government Drive past the Saint Louis Zoo, which is considered one of the top zoos in the country—and does not charge an admission fee! After about a quarter of a mile, cross Government Drive at Fine Arts Drive, and keep walking on the path on the north side of the road, with Post-Dispatch Lake now on your left. At mile 3.4, turn left (north) to go past the boathouse and retrace your steps to the visitor center.

2 FOREST PARK: EAST

BEFORE YOU GO
MAP On park website and at visitor center
CONTACT Forest Park Forever
GPS 38.643564° N, -90.283461° W
NOTES Wheelchair and stroller accessible; bathrooms and water fountains throughout park

ABOUT THE HIKE
SEASON Fall, winter, spring
DIFFICULTY Easy
LENGTH 2.6 miles loop
HIGH POINT 525 feet
ELEVATION GAIN 240 feet

GETTING THERE
From Interstate 64 (known locally as "40") in St. Louis, exit at 36A-36B for South Kingshighway Boulevard and turn right (north). Drive 0.9 mile on Kingshighway, and then turn left (west) on Lindell Boulevard. Drive 1 mile, and turn left (south) on DeBaliviere Circle into the park. Halfway around the circle, turn right on Lagoon Drive, and then in 0.1 mile turn left (east) on Grand Drive. The Dennis & Judith Jones Visitor and Education Center is in 0.8 mile on the left; parking is on the right.

Both MetroBus 90 and the Forest Park Trolley stop at the Missouri History Museum, which is just northwest of the visitor center. The Forest Park MetroLink stop is across the street from the museum.

ON THE TRAIL
Take a walk on the wilder side of Forest Park while staying close to some of the busiest and fanciest neighborhoods in the city. This side of Forest Park features a lot of trees, fields of wildflowers, and flowing streams, plus homes and rest stops for thousands of birds.

This hike starts in the same place as the Forest Park: West hike (hike 1), at the visitor center, which is full of information about the park, its museums, and its history. There's also a café and a fun playground.

Once you're done at the visitor center, head east on the sidewalk on the south side of Grand Drive. Looking south across the cricket field, you see the grandstands of the Muny, St. Louis's famous outdoor musical theater, where more than 350,000 people view seven different musicals each summer.

As you walk along Grand Drive, on the left is the former location of a controversial monument to the Confederate soldiers of the Civil War. The thirty-two-foot granite structure stood as a testament to Missouri's status as a divided border state for 102 years until it was removed in June 2017.

At 0.4 mile, cross Grand Drive to the path that winds past the fish ponds, which were used more than 100 years ago for breeding and harvesting fish to feed city dwellers. Now the ponds are run by the Missouri Department of Conservation for wildlife management and education. Here the path splits to offer a paved route for those using wheels, running parallel to a gravel route for those on foot. At mile 0.7, the path recrosses Grand Drive and continues through a tranquil forest, an interesting juxtaposition to the high-rises of the hospital district and Central West End looming just past the east edge of the park.

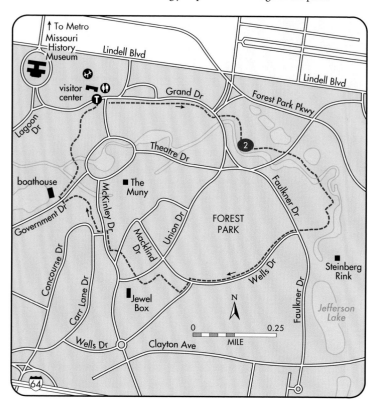

Kids enjoy water play even in the winter; these children are using sticks to break up ice at the edge of a pond in Forest Park.

Next the path curves to the south past Steinberg Skating Rink, a favorite winter gathering place, where the large rink is open every day. At 1 mile, take the path to the right. For 0.1 mile the surface is gravel, but is packed and even. Cross Jefferson Drive and continue on Wells Drive, where there is no sidewalk. Here the only options are the mowed grass or the street, but traffic is minimal along this stretch. At mile 1.5, turn left to stay on Wells Drive, and immediately turn onto the paved path to the right that heads into the forest. To your left stand the stately pillars and somber benches of the Korean War Memorial, a worthwhile side trip. Just past the memorial is the Jewel Box, a floral display house with a very modest admission fee and special flower shows around holidays.

Staying on the path, cross Union Drive and move through a lovely and fragrant evergreen forest. The path crosses the Muny parking lot entrance and then McKinley Drive, where it then curves downhill to the right through a deciduous forest. At mile 2.1, cross Government Drive and turn right, passing the driveway to the boathouse, where you can rent a paddleboat or grab a bite to eat. Turn left onto the paved path, which takes you north past the tennis courts and back to the visitor center.

3 COLUMBIA BOTTOM CONSERVATION AREA

BEFORE YOU GO
MAP On park website
CONTACT Missouri Department of Conservation
GPS 38.813972° N, -90.126076° W
NOTES Accessible to confluence view deck; bathrooms and water at visitor center; check website for closures after heavy rains

ABOUT THE HIKE
SEASON Year-round
DIFFICULTY Easy
LENGTH 3.2 miles roundtrip
HIGH POINT 460 feet
ELEVATION GAIN 270 feet

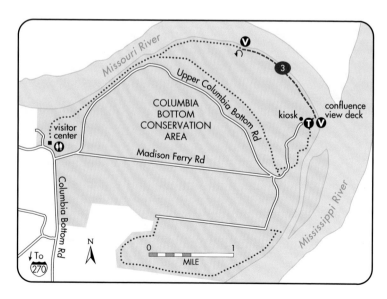

Exploring along the Mighty Mississippi

GETTING THERE

From Interstate 270 in northern St. Louis, take exit 34 for Riverview Drive and turn left (north). In 2 miles, Riverview Drive becomes Columbia Bottom Road. Continue for 1 mile, and turn right onto Madison Ferry Road. In 3 miles, turn right on Upper Columbia Bottom Road, which ends in 0.9 mile at the trailhead parking lot.

ON THE TRAIL

This hike begins at a superlative site: the confluence of the two longest rivers in the country and the beginning of one of the most important journeys in the nation's history.

Here the Missouri River flows into the Mighty Mississippi. And here is where Lewis and Clark began their journey of discovery after President Jefferson directed them to map the way west on the Missouri, when the nation was less than fifty years old. It's a hugely significant natural area, too: many birds, but most significantly the nation's symbolic bald eagle, make stopovers here.

Start your hike at the east end of the parking lot, at the easternmost point of the conservation area. A large, low kiosk decorated with beautiful mosaics is the first thing you see. Read the interpretive signs with or to your kids; they tell some of the stories of Lewis and Clark and even the explorers who came before them. Note the pole in the middle of the kiosk; it shows the water levels during major floods of the last several decades. The top of the pole towers over even the tallest person and is a reminder of how devastating the 1993 flood was.

The signed trail starts at the confluence view deck. Look for trail signs that point you left into the forest. The trail is sandy, with a different feel than the forest duff of higher ground. Towering walnut trees grow all over these woods, but here a bramble of low shrubs, branches, and woody debris surrounds you. This is, of course, due to the low floodplain. This trail was underwater as recently as December 2015, when heavy rains caused flooding across the region. The conservation area was closed for weeks, with a huge effort needed to clear the trail and clean up trash and other debris left behind when the water receded.

The trail hugs the Missouri River for about 2.6 miles. At 0.4 mile, END NO HUNTING ZONE signs appear. Hunters are prohibited from hunting within one hundred feet of all trails and roads, but if you're concerned about hiking here during hunting season, check the MDC website for Columbia Bottom Conservation Area.

The Missouri River, your companion throughout this hike, is 2341 miles long. It begins in western Montana, traveling through seven states on its way to St. Louis. Ask your kids to picture the source of the river in the high Rocky Mountains (there is some debate as to the exact start of the river) of Montana and its journey through the Great Plains. See if they can name some animals that aren't found in the wild in the St. Louis area that might occupy the land around the river in other states. (Hint: buffalo.)

The trail continues relatively flat along the river's edge. Watch for a lot of different birds, including bald eagles, especially in winter. At mile 1.6, stop for a good view across the rivers and the lowland areas to Alton, Illinois, and the Clark Bridge, a suspension bridge that spans the Mississippi about four miles north of where you're standing. This is a good turnaround point for an easy 3-mile walk, but the trail continues for several more miles if the kids are feeling energetic; it's 2.5 miles from here to the visitor center.

4 ST. STANISLAUS CONSERVATION AREA

BEFORE YOU GO
MAP On park website and at trailhead
CONTACT Missouri Department of Conservation
GPS 38.811495° N, -90.394923° W
NOTES Short section near parking lot is accessible for strollers and wheelchairs; bug spray is a must in spring and summer; no bathrooms or water at trailhead

ABOUT THE HIKE
SEASON Year-round
DIFFICULTY Easy to difficult
LENGTH 1.4 miles loop
HIGH POINT 680 feet
ELEVATION GAIN 380 feet

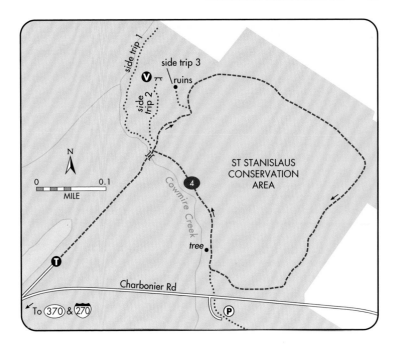

GETTING THERE

From Interstate 270 in northwest St. Louis, take exit 23 (McDonnell Boulevard) and turn left (north) on Howdershell Road. In 2 miles, turn left onto Riverwood Estates Boulevard. Drive 1 mile, and then turn left onto Charbonier Road for 1 mile. The parking lot is on the left.

ON THE TRAIL

St. Stanislaus Conservation Area offers an interesting change from most parks and preserves. Its trails are steep, rugged, and largely unsigned, which makes them feel like an adventure for hikers. Bring your map, compass, and GPS receiver (or phone with an app) if you have one. If you dislike uncertainty and prefer signed intersections, this may not be the hike for you. Combined, the side trips add another 1.1 miles to the hike distance.

Start down the path heading northeast from the parking lot. Stay on this paved path for 0.2 mile before crossing a bridge over picturesque Cowmire Creek. Just past the bridge is a three-way intersection; to the left is the first of three fun optional trips. Walk about a quarter of a mile along the creek through a forest of mostly persimmon. These trees are easy to spot by their bark, which looks like it's been split by an axe, dividing the bark with a lot of deep fissures. Persimmon fruit ripen in the fall; it's perfectly fine to pick some to take home, or eat them on the trail. Make sure they are ripe (the skin will be slightly soft), or you'll be in for a sour surprise.

After the persimmon-tree side trip, retrace your steps to the three-way intersection. Go up the center path, and then take an immediate left for side trip 2. It ascends very steeply for just under a tenth of a mile and then evens out somewhat before reaching a bench 0.2 mile from the intersection. The bench looks west over forest and fields. It's an impressive vista and a good place for a breather.

Returning to the trail junction, turn left onto the main trail. In just a few steps, take another left to explore side trip 3, a short 0.1-mile walk to the foundation of an old building. This is part of the remnants of a seminary that used this area for a retreat. After you check out the ruins, retrace your steps and turn left onto the main trail. The trail here is wider and mostly level as it winds through thick forest for about a third of a mile. Pass between two low columns that are rounded on top, and turn right through a line of trees, then right again, and continue about 100 yards across a field to a narrow trail. At this point the trail goes steeply downhill.

At mile 1 on the main loop, turn right just before the trail meets Charbonier Road. A bit farther on, glimpse a path that leads across the road to the left, to another parking lot for the conservation area. Turn right to walk under the limbs of a huge dead sycamore that sticks out in summer with its absence of leaves. From here the trail follows the creek back to the junction near the bridge; turn left and retrace your steps to the parking lot.

5 CREVE COEUR LAKE MEMORIAL PARK: LAKE TRAIL

BEFORE YOU GO
MAP On park website
CONTACT St. Louis County Parks and Recreation Department
GPS 38.714125° N, -90.478860° W
NOTES Accessible to wheelchairs and strollers; bathrooms and water at several spots

ABOUT THE HIKE
SEASON Fall, winter, spring
DIFFICULTY Easy
LENGTH 3.75 miles loop
HIGH POINT 535 feet
ELEVATION GAIN 450 feet

GETTING THERE
From Interstate 270 in western St. Louis County, take exit 17 for Dorsett Road and turn left (west). Drive 1.5 miles, and turn right (north) onto Marine Avenue. Drive 0.5 mile, and turn left into the parking lot at the lakefront.

The paved path at Creve Coeur Lake is a good choice on rainy days.

ON THE TRAIL

Creve Coeur Lake is a very popular destination for walkers, joggers, bikers, and paddlers of all ages. It's easy to get to and provides a good workout for anyone, whether you're pushing your kid in a stroller, carrying her on your back, letting him walk, or a combination. With enough snacks, water, and encouragement (a.k.a. bribes), walkers of all ages can complete the gentle 3.75-mile loop.

The Lake Trail is so popular, in fact, that you might want to opt for a different trail, like Bootleggers Run (hike 6), also in Creve Coeur Park, on weekends when the weather is nice. In spring and summer, some bicyclists treat it like a raceway, and it can be scary for little kids to have them whiz by at 25 miles per hour. Save this one for a wet day when dirt trails will be sloppy or for a chilly winter afternoon.

Start your hike on the southeast side of the lake. There are plenty of parking spots here. In the summer you can rent a paddleboard or kayak for a fun on-water outing on the 320-acre lake. Head north to walk the trail around the lake counterclockwise. The trail is sandwiched between Marine Avenue and

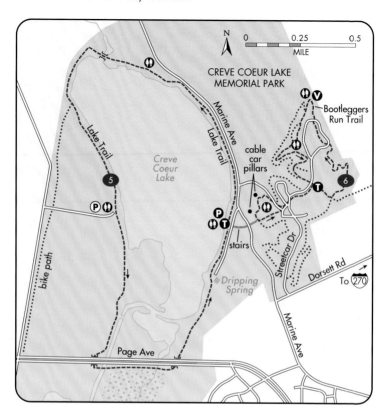

the lake for the first mile. Across the road glimpse another section of Creve Coeur Park that contains a disc golf course. Up the hill are playgrounds and the Bootleggers Run Trail.

At mile 1, take advantage of year-round bathrooms, plus vending machines. Continue on the path as it veers west along the northern edge of the lake. Cross a wooden bridge at mile 1.25, and get a view to the right of the building that houses the local rowing club. Creve Coeur Lake was one of the venues when St. Louis hosted the Olympic Games in 1904, and this building was constructed for that purpose (see "West County Resort" sidebar). Here find a bit of shade as the path moves a few extra feet away from the lake so trees line both sides of the trail. At mile 1.4, reach a junction to a bike path that connects to western neighborhoods. Stay to the left to walk along the lake.

Pass another parking option near the soccer fields at mile 1.9. Just beyond the fields, enter the wildest portion of the trail. The woods and marshy areas here host thousands of migrating birds, plus snakes and rodents. If you're lucky, you may spot a river otter.

The trail jogs to the right a bit at mile 2.6, and then takes a sharp left just after going through the Page Avenue underpass. This area is often marshy, providing additional opportunity for wildlife viewing. At mile 3, the trail takes another sharp left, again crossing under Page Avenue. This final stretch is one of the most scenic parts of the trail, with trees framing the view of the lake and a lush growth on the cliff extending up to the right.

At mile 3.5, there's a spot for one last break and a pretty waterfall at Dripping Spring. From here it's a short quarter-mile walk back to the parking lot.

6 CREVE COEUR LAKE MEMORIAL PARK: BOOTLEGGERS RUN TRAIL

BEFORE YOU GO
MAP On park website
CONTACT St. Louis County Parks and Recreation Department
GPS 38.717384° N, -90.470942° W
NOTES Seasonal water and bathrooms around park

ABOUT THE HIKE
SEASON Year-round
DIFFICULTY Easy to moderate
LENGTH 2.6 miles loop
HIGH POINT 660 feet
ELEVATION GAIN 350 feet

GETTING THERE
From Interstate 270 in western St. Louis County, take exit 17 for Dorsett Road and turn left (west). Drive 1.5 miles. Turn right (north) onto Streetcar Drive. Drive 0.7 mile. Pass tennis courts and immediately turn right into the large gravel parking lot.

ON THE TRAIL
For thousands of West County residents, the Bootleggers Run Trail is practically their backyard, but thick forests here give hikers a feeling of isolation.

WEST COUNTY RESORT

Creve Coeur Park has a fascinating history. In the mid-1800s, it became a prime leisure destination for people in the city of St. Louis, with multiple rail lines bringing vacationers to the resorts around the lake. In 1904, the park hosted some of the events for the 1904 World's Fair and Olympics. After that its popularity declined, and it became a haven for gangsters and moonshiners. By the end of Prohibition in 1933, the park was all but overrun with mobsters. But in 1945, Creve Coeur Lake Memorial Park became the first St. Louis County Park.

Many hikes that are good for families also make for a nice outing with dogs.

In winter, leafless trees allow remarkable views to the north and west, clear to the Missouri River. Year-round, hikers can enjoy lessons about this park's fascinating past.

This double-loop hike starts in the southeast corner of the parking lot. Watch for the trailhead sign and walk downhill to the southeast. At mile 0.1, take a sharp left to stay on the loop portion of the trail. Watch for mountain bikers all along this trail; it's popular with cyclists and was laid out and built by Gateway Off-Road Cyclists and their volunteers.

Continue downhill through dense forest of oak, walnut, and sycamore. Looming to the right at mile 0.3 is the elevated mound built for one of the train lines that served the park in the 1800s. Today it's a path to the subdivision west of the park. Next, the park enters a series of tight switchbacks that make the grade easy as you head downhill. This continues until mile 0.5, when the trail dips into a wash and then starts going up in elevation.

Cross Streetcar Drive at mile 0.8, and head through the forest nestled in the middle of the driving loop. Cross the road again, turn left, and come around a sharp bend at mile 1.1. Stop here for a few minutes to take in the view over Creve Coeur Lake and the Missouri River beyond.

The trail hits an unsigned junction at mile 1.3; take a left here instead of going right, which will take you down the hill and along a few curves. By 1.5 miles, return to the road. (This is a good place to bail out if some of you are feeling tired; the parking lot is less than a tenth of mile from here.) To continue on to the second loop of the hike, walk southwest along the road toward a ropes course facility. At mile 2, watch for the trail sign for Bootleggers Run Trail and go right (west). Follow this bend in the trail around the top of the bluff to take in the view, and watch for the big concrete bases of pillars that supported a cable car track down to the lake during the 1904 World's Fair. (See "West County Resort" sidebar.)

Continue around the bend. (By 2.1 miles, if the kids have enough energy to play at the lake, descend the Creve Coeur Lake Memorial Park Staircase all the way down to the lake area for a 0.3-mile down-and-back side trip.) Complete the hike by climbing just a handful of steps back up to the road and close to your car. Cut back through the area around the ropes course and continue along the road to the parking lot.

7 FAUST PARK

BEFORE YOU GO
MAP On park website
CONTACT St. Louis County Parks and Recreation Department
GPS 38.665466° N, -90.539764° W
NOTES Trails inaccessible for wheelchairs and strollers; bathrooms near playground

ABOUT THE HIKE
SEASON Fall, winter, spring
DIFFICULTY Moderate
LENGTH 1.75 miles loop
HIGH POINT 645 feet
ELEVATION GAIN 130 feet

GETTING THERE
From Interstate 64 (known locally as "40") in Chesterfield, take exit 19B to State Route 340 (Olive Boulevard) north. Drive 1.2 miles and turn left on Faust Park Drive to enter the park. Turn right into the parking lot and continue to the northeast end of the parking lot, farthest from the Butterfly House. (This area of the parking lot is quieter than the area closer to the park entrance, but still allows you to start and end your hike near the playground and bathrooms.)

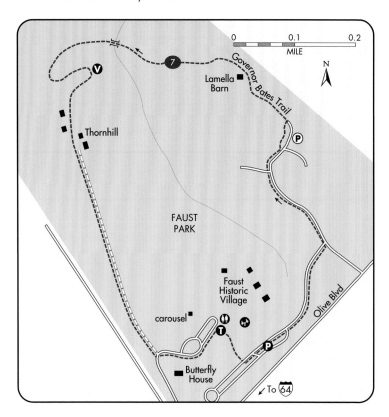

St. Louis MetroBus 91 stops on Olive Boulevard about a quarter mile from the park.

ON THE TRAIL

Faust Park, a county park, has a number of unique attractions for the nonhiker, yet still holds rewards for those who wander into its modest yet scenic wilder areas.

Start by exploring the Faust Historic Village, which offers tours on select weekends and has a festival with docents in period costume at the end of September. Then head southeast to the parking area, and turn left (northeast) on a sidewalk alongside the parking area, parallel with Olive Boulevard. In a quarter mile take a left and follow the one-lane road, past several county parks department buildings. Turn left through a parking lot at 0.4 mile, and find a sign indicating the start of the Governor Bates Trail.

The trail heads past Lamella Barn, of interest to architecture historians because of its half-dome roof. At 0.6 mile, the trail heads steeply downhill. Kids and adults alike will find the walking easier on the legs by cutting a zigzag pattern across the trail. Signposts along this section offer tree identification and fascinating tidbits about the species and what their wood has been used for, such as the ash trees that make baseball bats.

The trail crosses a bridge at 0.85 mile and then heads uphill, in a quarter mile coming upon a vista that offers a view of the valley you just hiked through. In winter you can see across the forest to the Missouri River bottom.

In another tenth of a mile enter Thornhill, a national historic site. This was the home of Missouri's first governor, Frederick Bates. The estate buildings give a sense of what it was like to live on this remote frontier more than 200 years ago. The estate gives occasional tours.

Continue down the gravel road toward the busy center of the park, passing the historic carousel at 1.5 miles, which was originally part of an amusement park in Forest Park. When the amusement park burned down in 1963, the carousel survived largely undamaged, and eventually was installed here. At 1.6 miles, walk past the Butterfly House, which is worth a stop for its climate-controlled dome that houses thousands of butterflies. It's operated by the Missouri Botanical Garden. Your car awaits just a few steps southwest.

For operating hours and costs of the carousel and historic sites, visit the Parks and Recreation part of the St. Louis County website, www.stlouisco.com. To learn more about the Butterfly House, visit www.butterflyhouse.org.

The nonvenomous garter snake is a common sight along trails in the region.

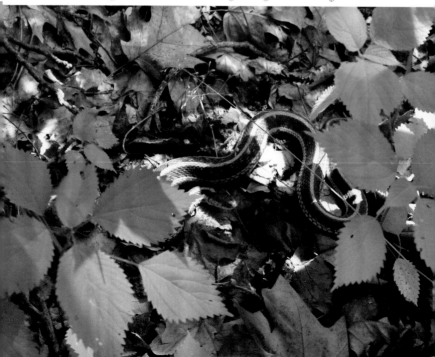

8 HOWELL ISLAND CONSERVATION AREA

BEFORE YOU GO
MAP On park website and at trailhead
CONTACT Missouri Department of Conservation
GPS 38.664423° N, -90.675467° W
NOTES Trails are accessible for jogging strollers; trail approach is underwater after heavy rain, or when the Missouri River is above sixteen feet; no water or bathrooms at trailhead

ABOUT THE HIKE
SEASON Year-round
DIFFICULTY Easy to moderate
LENGTH 3.9 miles loop
HIGH POINT 520 feet
ELEVATION GAIN 70 feet

GETTING THERE
Eastbound: From the intersection of Interstate 70 and Interstate 64 (US Highway 61) at Wentzville, drive 13.7 miles southeast on I-64 and take exit 14 onto Chesterfield Airport Road. Drive 0.5 mile, and turn right onto Olive Street Road. In 1 mile, Olive Street Road becomes North Eatherton Road. Continue 0.7 mile west to the area entrance.

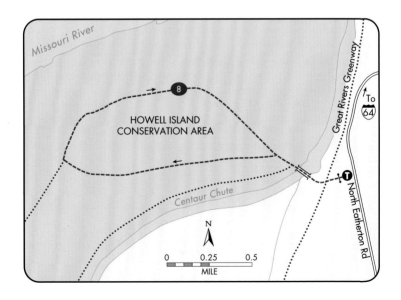

The land bridge leading to Howell Island

Westbound: From St. Louis, take I-64 (known locally as "40") westbound, and take exit 16 onto Long Road. Turn right (west) on Chesterfield Airport Road. Drive 2 miles, and then turn left at Olive Street Road. In 1 mile, Olive Street Road becomes North Eatherton Road. Continue 0.7 mile west to the area entrance and parking lot.

ON THE TRAIL

Howell Island is a unique suburban getaway—a literal island surrounded by the waters of the Missouri River and a wide creek called Centaur Chute. Families with kids of all ages can enjoy a flat walk through the forest; the trail is wide and level enough that caregivers can push jogging strollers along the nearly 4-mile trail.

Howell Island is named for the town of Howell, one of several that were taken over by the federal government for the war effort in 1940. The government purchased 20,000 acres in the Weldon Spring area to build a munitions plant. Despite their protests, hundreds of families were moved from the farming communities on the northwest side of the Missouri River. Munitions testing bunkers can still be spotted at August A. Busch Memorial Conservation Area (hike 47).

Today, Howell Island is known for mushroom hunting, birdwatching, and wide paths perfect for families. Just across the Missouri River from Howell Island is Weldon Spring Conservation Area (hike 48), home of the popular Lewis and Clark trails. If you've hiked there, ask your kids to think about how different that trail feels. What makes these trails unique?

From the parking lot, head west through the gate onto the wide access road. In 0.2 mile, turn northwest along the trail to cross the wide concrete causeway that links the mainland to the island. Watch for cyclists pedaling by on the Great Rivers Greenway trail. At 0.4 mile, take the second left. The path is wide enough for a vehicle or even two, so let the kids spread out and take in the forest on either side.

At mile 1.6, acres of open field appear on the left. Some conservation areas, including this one, lease land to farmers who plant crops, so you're likely to see corn or soybean plants sprouting in spring or summer. During high-water years, there is no planting.

Turn right at the junction at 2.1 miles, just past the field, and continue on a similar track. By 2.3 miles, the forest gets more dense, with a variety of older trees, including sycamore and cottonwood. Ask kids to guess how tall the tallest tree in this forest is.

The forest becomes more open again at 3.4 miles, just before reaching the loop junction. Turn left to retrace your steps across the causeway to the parking lot.

9 BABLER STATE PARK: HAWTHORN TRAIL

BEFORE YOU GO
MAP On park website and at visitor center
CONTACT Missouri State Parks Department
GPS 38.615919° N, -90.706669° W
NOTES Trail inaccessible for wheelchairs and strollers; bathrooms and water at parking lot

ABOUT THE HIKE
SEASON Year-round
DIFFICULTY Easy to moderate
LENGTH 1.3 miles loop
HIGH POINT 808 feet
ELEVATION GAIN 240 feet

GETTING THERE
From Interstate 64 in St. Louis (known locally as "40"), take exit 16 for Long Road. Drive 0.8 mile south, and turn right onto Wild Horse Creek Road.

MEET BABLER STATE PARK

The land for Babler State Park was donated by a prominent St. Louis family in 1934. This was a prescient decision, since, as you'll see during your drive to the park, the suburban sprawl of subdivisions and strip malls has pushed up against its borders. Now the park is available as a close-by retreat.

Just a short drive for everyone in the St. Louis region, it makes for great day trips. There are many short trails and plenty of opportunities for longer hiking trips, plus a trail for biking. A visitor center presents detailed exhibits about the natural history of the area that will fascinate everyone from toddlers to adults. With a spacious campground, playgrounds, and a swimming pool, it's a good candidate for a close-to-home weekend getaway. An Outdoor Education Center includes cabins for scouting groups.

Drive 3.1 miles, and turn left onto State Route 109 south. In 0.75 mile, turn right onto Babler Park Drive, and in 1.5 miles turn right onto Guy Park Drive. Follow this past the visitor center, and in 1.5 miles turn left onto Theodore Martin Drive. Drive 1.4 miles, past signs for the Outdoor Education Center, and park near the Alta Shelter on the right side of the road. The trailhead is across the road.

ON THE TRAIL

Hawthorn is the shortest trail in Dr. Edmund A. Babler Memorial State Park (more commonly referred to as simply "Babler State Park"), but shows off a different variety of geologic scenery than other parts of the park. It's also a good length for inexperienced hikers and doesn't have a great deal of elevation change.

Start at the trailhead just southwest of the Alta Shelter parking lot. The Hawthorn Trail is blazed in yellow. Head straight across the brown-blazed Equestrian Trail that rings the park. In about a tenth of a mile the Hawthorn Trail splits. Turn right and follow the trail slightly downhill and into the forest. You might see small areas cordoned off with fence and tape where naturalists are trying to restore the native trees of this part of the park. Continue through the forest along the northeast side of this ridge that showcases the wilder west side of Babler.

At 0.5 mile the trail gets steeper and rockier, and at 0.6 mile reach a rocky outcrop above a cliff that drops to Wild Horse Creek Road. Listen for the creek bubbling below, and spy a charming view of the ranches in the valley to the west. And keep an eye on inattentive young hikers to make sure they don't get too close to the edge.

After the vista, the trail turns to the left and heads southeast. At mile 0.7 the trail's interesting geology becomes obvious. Watch for the trees to open up to a glade, another area that park rangers are trying to restore. The drier, hotter southwest winds of this section of the ridge keep the plants sparser and expose

Birdwatching and other nature activities keep kids engaged at the Babler visitor center.

the underlying rock. Point this out to kids, and try to get them to figure out why the south-facing side of the ridge looks different from the north-facing side.

From here the trail meanders up and down, with some sections steeper and rockier than others. Watch the trail signs at mile 1.2 when you get back to where the trail splits, and follow the yellow blazes up a short rise back to the road.

10 BABLER STATE PARK: VIRGINIA DAY TRAIL

BEFORE YOU GO

MAP On park website and at visitor center
CONTACT Missouri State Parks Department
GPS 38.617141° N, -90.689606° W
NOTES Trails inaccessible for wheelchairs and strollers; bathrooms and water at
visitor center

ABOUT THE HIKE

SEASON Year-round
DIFFICULTY Easy to moderate
LENGTH 15 miles loop
HIGH POINT 800 feet
ELEVATION GAIN 390 feet

GETTING THERE

From Interstate 64 in St. Louis (known locally as "40"), take exit 16 for Long Road. Drive 0.8 mile south, and turn right onto Wild Horse Creek Road. Drive 3.1 miles, and turn left onto State Route 109 south. In 0.75 mile, turn right onto Babler Park Drive, and in 1.5 miles turn right onto Guy Park Drive. Drive about a half mile to the visitor center parking lot.

ON THE TRAIL

This fun and easy trail for hikers of all sizes is a good introduction to 900-acre Babler State Park, officially named Dr. Edmund A. Babler Memorial State Park. Before or after this hike, kids love to hit the visitor center with its hands-on puzzles and building blocks, fish tanks, and a live (nonvenomous) snake. A theater here shows educational films about the state parks. The trail is named for Virginia Day, a volunteer naturalist who spent some of the last years of her life working in the park to share her love of nature.

From the visitor center parking lot, carefully cross the street and look for the trailhead sign on the other side of the circular drive. The trail immediately enters dense forest. Walk slightly downhill into the valley for glimpses of the

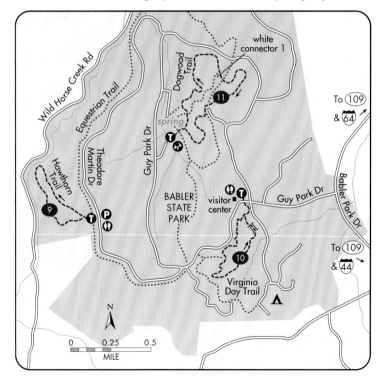

Babler State Park's short but varied trails offer adventures for even the littlest hikers.

old-growth hardwood forests that make this park such a treasure so close to the St. Louis area.

At 0.1 mile the trail splits. Head to the right and go deeper into the woods of predominately oak and hickory, past a connector trail back to the trailhead. From here, proceed on mostly level terrain with mild ups and downs. In spring and summer, the tree canopy is high above and makes for a dense covering and ample shade on warm days. Watch for a trail junction at 0.7 mile, where another connector path provides the opportunity to explore more of the park's trails on future hikes.

Soon after the junction, the trail goes slightly uphill and jogs to the left, turning back toward the visitor center. At mile 1, the trail dips into a valley where it wanders along a pleasant creek for a time. Encourage kids to take note of the types of trees in the various parts of the forest, with differing varieties growing near the creek and higher up on the ridge.

At mile 1.3, the trail crosses a small creek at a wooden bridge and then heads uphill. At 1.4 miles, turn right where the loop ends and go uphill, retracing your steps to the trailhead.

11 BABLER STATE PARK: DOGWOOD TRAIL

BEFORE YOU GO
> **MAP** On park website and at visitor center
> **CONTACT** Missouri State Parks Department
> **GPS** 38.622667° N, -90.697982° W
> **NOTES** Trails inaccessible for wheelchairs and strollers; bathrooms and water available seasonally near trailhead

ABOUT THE HIKE
> **SEASON** Year-round
> **DIFFICULTY** Moderate
> **LENGTH** 2.25 miles loop; 2.5 with side trip to spring
> **HIGH POINT** 725 feet
> **ELEVATION GAIN** 250 feet

GETTING THERE

From Interstate 64 in St. Louis (known locally as "40"), take exit 16 for Long Road. Drive 0.8 mile south, and turn right onto Wild Horse Creek Road. Drive 3.1 miles, and turn left onto State Route 109 south. In 0.75 mile, turn right onto Babler Park Drive, and in 1.5 miles turn right onto Guy Park Drive. Follow this past the visitor center, and in about 0.6 mile veer right to stay on Guy Park Drive. In 1 mile, turn right into the parking lot for the playground and the trailhead.

ON THE TRAIL

Babler State Park (officially named Dr. Edmund A. Babler Memorial State Park) has numerous roads, buildings, and other development, but the Dogwood Trail sits in the heart of the park and feels remote. In the summer especially, when the leafy cover of trees, including oak, redbud, and, of course, dogwood, is thick along the trail, hikers could easily imagine being in the middle of nowhere instead of close to the suburban sprawl of St. Louis County. Though not very long, this trail provides a variety of natural environments, from hardwood mixed forest to drier, rockier hilltops. The playground at the trailhead makes for a fun diversion once the hike is done.

From the playground and parking lot, head north at the sign for the trailhead. Stay to the left for the Dogwood Trail, which is blazed in green. As with almost all Missouri State Park trails, this one is well-marked with blazes in the form of plastic squares nailed to trees. Keep those in sight, and you should have little difficulty staying on the Dogwood Trail.

The Dogwood Trail crosses the white-blazed connector trail #1 at mile 0.15, and the loop begins at 0.25 mile. Turn left and soon cross the connector trail again. At 0.75 mile you have the option of visiting a spring, by taking the trail to the left. This quarter-mile (there-and-back) side trip is worth a look; kids

Downed trees across the trail present extra challenges for little legs.

can even crawl under overhangs at a "cave" at the mouth of the spring and splash in the stream on warm days.

Continue on the Dogwood Trail uphill for about a tenth of a mile. Take a couple more small ups and downs, along with a right bend.

Next the trail is shared with the connector trail #1 for about a tenth of a mile. With a moderate uphill trek of about two-tenths of a mile, reach the highest point of the hike at 1.4 miles. Here you can see a bit more of the park through the trees to get a sense of what a spacious oasis this is.

Continue downhill, watching for the flowering dogwood trees that this trail is named for, which come alive with pink-purple blooms in the spring. Cross the Equestrian Trail at 1.6 miles. Reach the start of the loop at 2 miles, and turn left to return to the parking lot.

12 QUEENY PARK

BEFORE YOU GO
MAP On park website
CONTACT St. Louis County Parks and Recreation Department
GPS 38.607401° N, -90.491517° W
NOTES Accessible for most strollers; portions may flood after heavy rain; bathrooms
and water seasonally near playground and year-round at museum

ABOUT THE HIKE
SEASON Year-round
DIFFICULTY Easy
LENGTH 2 miles loop
HIGH POINT 550 feet
ELEVATION GAIN 120 feet

GETTING THERE

From Interstate 270 in western St. Louis, take exit 9 to Manchester Road (State Route 100) west. Drive 2.5 miles, and turn right (north) onto Weidman Road. In 0.75 mile, turn right (east) onto Queeny Park Drive. Proceed about 0.5 mile to the main parking lot on the left, across from the playground.

ON THE TRAIL

Queeny Park provides miles of trails right in the heart of busy west St. Louis County. Paved paths allow parents with even lightweight strollers, and kids with the littlest legs, to stroll past lovely gardens. Some of the rougher trails meander through forest. You can jump off to any of the paths from this part of the park, which features a unique playground and indoor ice-skating complex. Allow some extra time for kids to explore the one-of-a-kind playground; they'll love climbing up the sides of stone pyramids and descending ladders into tunnels. (Grown-ups have been known to enjoy these features as well.)

Queeny is also home to Missouri's Native Tree Trail; check out the park website before you go and print out a map that will help you and your kids identify up to twenty-two native trees, depending on the length of your hike. On that trail, you learn how the trees are used commercially and what uses they have in home landscaping.

DOG-LOVERS' PARADISE

Queeny Park is home to the Museum of the Dog, which houses a collection of art devoted to, yes, dogs. It also hosts "dog of the week" get-togethers for owners and fans of specific breeds. Check the schedule and find other information about the museum at www.museumofthedog.org.

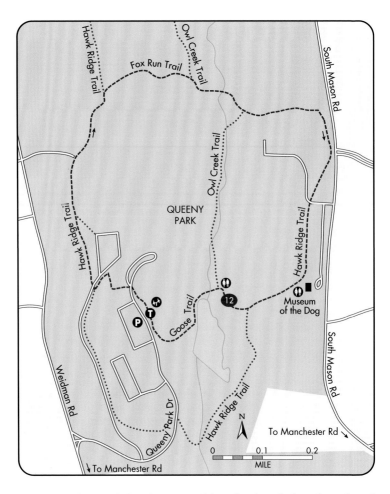

Once you've rounded up the younger hikers, head north along the park road and take the winding uphill trail just past the parking lot through the trees. Emerge from the forest alongside another parking lot. Wind your way west, and at 0.2 mile turn right (north) at the Hawk Ridge Trail, which is paved here.

This section of the trail is easy for kids of all sizes. A sign describes the surrounding forest, including oaks and maples estimated to be more than 200 years old. Queeny Park began as part of the estate of the late Mr. and Mrs. Edgar M. Queeny. Mr. Queeny was a former head of Monsanto Chemical Company, founded by his father. It became a park in 1970.

Wide paths make Queeny Park good for big groups and strollers.

Leave the Hawk Ridge Trail at 0.6 mile, turning right (east) onto the Fox Run Trail. (For a hike of up to 4 miles, continue straight on Hawk Ridge.) The half-mile Fox Run Trail, a gravel track, runs east to west across the park through the mixed hardwood forest. Almost all strollers can handle this terrain. The trail heads downhill, dipping into the wash in the middle of the park through a forest of oaks and maples. Kids enjoy hunting for the tiny frogs that can be found along the trail here in spring and summer. At mile 0.9, the Owl Creek Trail joins the Fox Run Trail for 0.1 mile.

The Fox Run Trail ends at 1.2 miles, on the eastern edge of the park. Here, reenter the most popular part of the park, sharing the trail with hikers, joggers, and dog-walkers. Turn right to rejoin the Hawk Ridge Trail going south, as it parallels South Mason Road. At 1.6 miles, go past the equestrian staging area and the Museum of the Dog (see "Dog-Lovers' Paradise" sidebar).

Turn right (northwest) on the Owl Creek Trail at 1.7 miles, noting that there are bathrooms here, and then immediately left (west) onto the Goose Trail to head back across the creek, then up the hill and through some woods behind the ice-skating rink to the playground.

13 ROCKWOODS RESERVATION: ROCK QUARRY TRAIL

BEFORE YOU GO
   MAP On park website
   CONTACT Missouri Department of Conservation
   GPS 38.565218° N, -90.668438° W
   NOTES Inaccessible for strollers and wheelchairs; bathrooms and water at
      education center

ABOUT THE HIKE
   SEASON Year-round
   DIFFICULTY Moderate
   LENGTH 2.25 miles loop
   HIGH POINT 795 feet
   ELEVATION GAIN 200 feet

GETTING THERE

From Interstate 44 in Eureka, take exit 264 for State Route 109 north, and drive 4 miles. Turn left (west) onto Woods Road and take an immediate right (north) onto Glencoe Road. Drive 1.4 miles to the education center parking lot.

ON THE TRAIL

Rockwoods Reservation has been part of the rich network of parks in the St. Louis area for eighty years, because civic leader and construction baron A. P. Greensfelder made parks preservation a priority. You might recognize his name from other parks he helped preserve, such as nearby Greensfelder

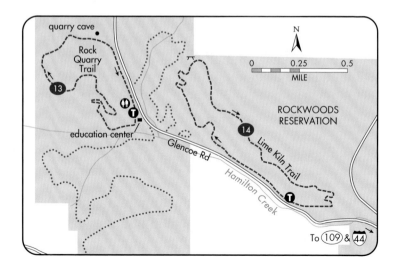

Hiking under the tree canopy at Rockwoods Reservation

County Park (hikes 16 and 17), and the recreation complex at Queeny Park (hike 12).

A truly special place, Rockwoods Reservation comprises 1800 acres, with 12 miles of trails close to the ever-growing suburban populations of west St. Louis County. It's on the fringe of the Ozarks region, and hiking just a mile into the park's woods feels like being deep in the wilderness.

The Rock Quarry Trail leads hikers along a wide, level trail amid a forest of oaks, dogwoods, and sycamores to a manmade cave, a remnant of the quarry operations that took place here decades ago. It's a great hike for anyone, but is an especially good alternative for novice hikers who want to try something easier than the difficult Lime Kiln Trail (hike 14), which is also located in Rockwoods Reservation.

Start from the Conservation Education Center parking lot and head west into the woods. The trail starts with several steep switchbacks, then heads more gradually uphill through forest and past rocky outcrops. Wildflowers decorate the patches of the dirt around these jagged displays during summer. After 0.5 mile, the trail reaches a wide plateau and a junction. The forest is a bit thinner here, allowing wider views that give some sense of the surrounding hills and forest.

Keep left (northwest) at the junction to stay on the Rock Quarry Trail. Take time to look down occasionally, and you might spot tiny toads, funnel-shaped spider webs, millipedes, and all kinds of wildflowers. The trail continues west and north on fairly level ground through thick forest, where the shade canopy keeps the trail comfortable even on warmer summer days. The trail continues

SHORT JAUNTS CLOSE TO HOME

You don't have to drive far or hike for hours to get a refreshing shot of nature. Our region is dotted with small parks that feature short trails. Many of them are easy to get to, so you can get a quick hike in after school or in between weekend activities. Here are three of the best.

Bluebird Park, Ellisville: Bluebird Park has all the facilities of a major suburban park, like an aquatic center, playgrounds, meeting space, and picnic tables. It also has some lovely trails that lead downhill into a dense forest. The park is adjacent to Klamberg Woods Conservation Area, which is about 67 acres and has 0.6 mile of trails. To get there, drive west on Manchester Road from the town of Ballwin, then south on Kiefer Creek Road for a half mile. Park near the playground at the back of the parking lot and take the trails downhill. Some of the trails are paved.

Beckemeier Conservation Area, Chesterfield: This area is just down the road from Faust Park but has a wilder side than that busy park (which is home to a historic village, a carousel, and the Butterfly House). Beckemeier is all forest, with a loop trail of about a half mile that has great views of the Missouri River, especially in winter. From Interstate 64 (US Highway 61) in Chesterfield, turn north on Olive Boulevard and drive north 2.4 miles, then turn left into the parking lot. The trail heads toward the river from the parking lot, going downhill toward the river and then coming back up to form a loop.

Phantom Forest and Bittersweet Woods, Des Peres: Right in the middle of the subdivisions just west of Interstate 270 are two parcels totaling 23 acres, with about a mile of trail between them. Start in Phantom Forest, so named because the man who donated the land was an illustrator of the *Phantom* comic series. After hiking through Phantom Forest, find a trail of about 100 yards that connects to Bittersweet Woods. From I-270, take the Dougherty Ferry exit west 1.2 miles and turn right (north) on Barrett State Road. In 0.4 mile turn right into the parking lot.

to be wide, level, and graded, making it easy for kids. Then around mile 1.25, the trail descends a series of steps, dropping about 100 feet in less than a quarter mile. Let kids take their time so they aren't worried about tripping. Soon enough there will be an exciting area to explore.

Just past the stairs is one of the remnants of the quarrying that was done here in the 1800s and 1900s. From the main trail it looks like a cave. Take the short side trail about 100 feet down across the wash to explore the enclosure dug out of the rock. Beams from support structures, metal pipes, and a furnace from the quarry operations give a glimpse into the practices of these long-ago uses of the land before it was established as a park in 1938.

Once your kids have had their fill of the cliffs and outcroppings, head down the trail toward Glencoe Road. The trail continues through a forest that features some ancient, fat sycamore trees. Reach Glencoe Road at 2 miles. Then hug the road the last quarter mile back to the parking lot. If there's time, check out the education center's exhibits on the local trees, plants, and wildlife; sometimes it even has ranger programs and live animals on display.

14 ROCKWOODS RESERVATION: LIME KILN TRAIL

BEFORE YOU GO
MAP On park website
CONTACT Missouri Department of Conservation
GPS 38.558124° N, -90.651975° W
NOTES Inaccessible for wheelchairs and strollers; bathrooms and water at education center a mile away

ABOUT THE HIKE
SEASON Year-round
DIFFICULTY Moderate to difficult
LENGTH 2.75 miles loop
HIGH POINT 720 feet
ELEVATION GAIN 380 feet

GETTING THERE
From Interstate 44 in Eureka, take exit 264 for State Route 109 north, and drive 4 miles. Turn left (west) onto Woods Road and take an immediate right (north) onto Glencoe Road. The trailhead parking lot is about a half mile up on the right.

ON THE TRAIL
Rockwoods Reservation is one of a string of preserves in west St. Louis County that's remarkable for its vast areas of natural beauty so close to the sprawling suburbs of a Midwestern city. Hundreds of thousands of people live within a short drive of this lovely spot that offers a taste of Ozark wilderness. Rockwoods Reservation is known for its variety of plant and animal life from rocky ridges to verdant river bottoms, as well as the popular winter Maple Sugar Festival.

As soon as you get out of your car, notice a huge, crumbling lime kiln—thus the trail name. The seventy-foot-tall structure is a remnant of the area's history of use in cement and lime mining and manufacturing.

Take the Lime Kiln Trail loop clockwise, heading left (northwest) from the kiln along Hamilton Creek. Inlets trickle across the trail at some spots, and kids can take some time to splash and hunt for tadpoles or frogs in this area. The stream and trail run between the road and some gently rising cliffs here, providing a mellow warm-up to the more difficult hiking ahead.

The huge lime kiln at Rockwoods Reservation

After about a half mile, the trail begins to climb gently at first, then more steeply over a series of switchbacks through some thin forest. It begins to get rocky at 0.6 mile as it climbs up the hill, so hikers need to use caution as the footing gets interesting. As the trail heads north and west, away from the road, it also becomes rockier and feels more remote. This section helps give Rockwoods its reputation as a spot to experience the Ozarks without driving to southern Missouri.

The trail undulates over and around the steep slopes and valleys thick with a variety of hardwood trees. At mile 1, the trail jogs northeast into thicker forest, up a rise, and over another hill.

At the top of the hill, a bench at 1.3 miles provides a rest station and a view across the valley during winter, when leaves don't obstruct the view. For the next half mile, the trail is flat and level, meandering through a lovely deciduous forest, shaded in the late spring and summer. At 2.2 miles the trail begins to descend, becoming steep and rocky again. Watch for a rocky outcropping on the right where you can just see Hamilton Creek below in the winter. Take your time descending, and check out the variety of trees here, from pawpaws to maples and oaks. The trail reaches the elevation of the creek at 2.5 miles, and evens out for an easy stroll back to the parking lot.

Note: The Rockwoods Reservation Conservation Education Center contains exhibits on local history, plants, and animals. To visit, drive past the Lime Kiln trailhead for approximately a mile on Glencoe Road.

15 BLUFF VIEW PARK

BEFORE YOU GO
MAP On park website
CONTACT Wildwood Department of Parks and Recreation
GPS 38.548492° N, -90.620727° W
NOTES Inaccessible for wheelchairs and strollers; no bathrooms or water

ABOUT THE HIKE
SEASON Year-round
DIFFICULTY Easy for overlook hike; moderate to difficult for 5-mile hike
LENGTH 1 mile roundtrip to overlook; 5 miles roundtrip to Al Foster Trail
HIGH POINT 665 feet
ELEVATION GAIN 130 feet for 1-mile hike;
420 feet for 5-mile hike

GETTING THERE
From Interstate 44 in Eureka, take exit 264 for State Route 109 north, and drive 3 miles. Turn right on Old State Road, and drive 0.5 mile to the park entrance. Turn right into the park entrance, and drive 0.2 mile to reach the large oval parking area with picnic tables in the center.

From Manchester Road in Ellisville, turn south on Old State Road. Stay on Old State Road for 3.5 miles, and turn left into the park entrance. Drive 0.2 mile to reach the large oval parking area with picnic tables in the center.

ON THE TRAIL
Bluff View Park is hidden away off State Route 109 near Eureka. It offers one of the nicest trails in the area with the Bluff View Trail, yet it has flown under most hikers' radar so far. Here you'll enjoy some spectacular scenery in near solitude. Since this is a roundtrip trail rather than a loop, you can choose

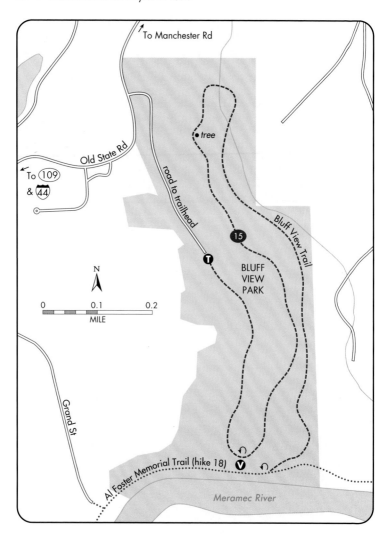

between an easy hike of 1 mile to an overlook and back or a hike of as many as 5 miles in picturesque forest.

Like many nearby parks and trails, Bluff View owes most of its dramatic vistas and lush scenery to the Meramec River. From its start, the trail heads directly south to the eponymous bluff view over the Meramec and the valley below.

Head south on the trail from the parking lot, and almost immediately reach a fork. Take the dirt path to the left. The forest is a dense, deep green in the summer here, immersing hikers in nature. Watch for wildlife of all kinds: box turtles, deer, millipedes, even barred owls. There are never any guarantees when it comes to spotting wildlife, but I've seen more here on one hike than on a dozen other hikes combined.

After about a tenth of a mile, pass through the remnants of a stone gate. The path is wide and flat here, so allow your eyes to wander and take in the tree canopy, which is so thick that it's possible to walk through in a steady rain and feel barely a drop. At mile 0.3 the forest opens up to a series of glades. Take some time to check out the view over the Meramec Valley to the south. Be sure to keep little ones close, as the drop over the cliff is steep. Note the stone and concrete foundations; there was once a home here that enjoyed the remarkable view over the river. In the 1970s, this land was donated to the Humane Society of the United States and was used to shelter animals for a time before it was sold to the state of Missouri.

From the overlook, walk east along the bluffs for a short distance; watch along here for the rare native yucca, which can produce spectacular blooms in the summer. When the path starts to turn to the left and leaves the view behind, turn around to keep the hike to just 1 mile, or continue along the path to lengthen your journey.

The view across the Meramec River is a highlight of Bluff View Park.

As you continue, the forest quickly becomes dense and verdant again, with a lot of shade. At 0.7 mile there's a gentle uphill, and over the next quarter mile the forest thins a bit. Show your hikers the intriguing hollowed-out stump, an old skeleton of a tree, at mile 1.2.

Over the next half mile, the terrain becomes rockier and the trail undulates up and down over stream crossings. Be sure to watch for wildlife in this section; there are some residences nearby, but it's quiet enough here that deer and even an occasional owl may stay close enough for hikers to enjoy at length.

The forest here is especially lush, taking on that vivid, almost fluorescent green that is so remarkable in Midwestern summers. Luckily, the thick tree canopy makes the forest temperature bearable on all but the hottest days.

At mile 1.9, watch for a big, old, gnarly tree on the left, with its several arms reaching out in all directions. Reach the end of the Bluff View Trail at mile 2.5, where it meets the Al Foster Memorial Trail (hike 18), which runs for 5.5 miles along the Meramec River. This is a roundtrip hike, so retrace your steps to go back to the parking lot.

16 GREENSFELDER COUNTY PARK: BEULAH TRAIL

BEFORE YOU GO
MAP On park website
CONTACT St. Louis County Parks and Recreation Department
GPS 38.535772° N, -90.670241° W
NOTES Inaccessible for wheelchairs and strollers; pit toilet near trailhead at Beulah Shelter

ABOUT THE HIKE
SEASON Year-round
DIFFICULTY Moderate
LENGTH 2 miles loop
HIGH POINT 870 feet
ELEVATION GAIN 230 feet

CHAMPION MULE

The Beulah Trail is named for a mule named Beulah, who was donated to the St. Louis County Parks and Recreation Department and lived at Suson Park in South County for twenty years. In 1971, she won the title of World's Champion Riding Mule at the National Show of the American Donkey and Mule Society. At the same show, she was judged "best mule on the grounds." After her championship, she appeared twice on the cover of the monthly magazine of the American Donkey and Mule Society, *The Brayer*, which is still in publication today.

Once kids get their hiking legs, it can be hard for adults to keep up.

GETTING THERE

From Interstate 44 in Eureka, take exit 261 (Allenton Road and Six Flags). From the exit ramp, turn right (north) onto Allenton Road. About a quarter mile from the freeway be careful to keep all the way to the left to stay on Allenton Road and avoid entering the Six Flags parking lot. Drive about one mile to Scenic Loop Road and turn right (east). After about one mile, turn right into the trailhead parking lot.

ON THE TRAIL

Greensfelder County Park is one of three parks, including Rockwoods Range and Rockwoods Reservation, that, strung together, make a trail network nearly fifteen miles long over 5200 acres in central west St. Louis County. The park offers a lot of activities for kids, big groups, equestrians, and more, including campgrounds and a nature center. This trail, tucked away in the less traveled northeast corner of the park, makes for a secluded experience.

This park was named for A. P. Greensfelder, a civic and business leader in the 1930s, who helped preserve this park, as well as Rockwoods Reservation. He kept a weekend home in Rockwoods Range, just southwest of Greensfelder County Park.

The trail does not have any very steep sections, but the terrain has a lot of rocks and trees that can make it tough for the littlest legs. It is almost totally

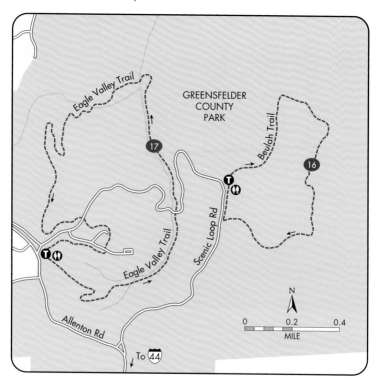

shaded, making it a good choice for summer hiking. Start your hike at the edge of the parking lot closest to the Beulah Shelter and turn left to do the loop clockwise. Immediately enter a dense forest of oak, maple, and hickory. The track narrows and widens along the way and in a quarter of a mile starts into a gentle downhill. Sharp switchbacks take you gradually down into a creek valley.

At mile 0.8 the trail crosses a streambed that rarely contains water. This section of the trail has a number of dens for wildlife made of leaves, sticks, and other debris; keep your distance but see how many kinds of animals the kids can think of that might have homes here. The next half mile features a very gradual climb back up from the creek, with a few rock piles and outcrops that climbers are interested in exploring. If the rock scrambling looks too nerve-wracking, mile 1.3 also offers a downed tree that holds worlds of interest. Some sections of the trunk are on the ground, inviting kids to scramble on top. Another section rests a few feet above the ground, at an angle from the broken stump to the ground twenty or thirty feet away. Kids find this symmetry irresistible and tromp off the trail to examine the wood for as long as you'll let them. At mile 1.6, watch for a sign that guides you to stay on the trail and avoid the deer trail. The rest of the trail is a level walk back to the parking lot.

17 GREENSFELDER COUNTY PARK: EAGLE VALLEY TRAIL

BEFORE YOU GO

MAP On park website
CONTACT St. Louis County Parks and Recreation Department
GPS 38.530121° N, -90.683656° W
NOTES Trails inaccessible for wheelchairs and strollers; bathrooms and water available seasonally at trailhead; trail is popular with equestrians

ABOUT THE HIKE

SEASON Year-round
DIFFICULTY Moderate to difficult
LENGTH 3.6 miles loop
HIGH POINT 910 feet
ELEVATION GAIN 650 feet

GETTING THERE

From Interstate 44 in Eureka, take exit 261 (Allenton Road and Six Flags). From the exit ramp, turn right (north) onto Allenton Road. About a quarter mile from the freeway be careful to keep all the way to the left to stay on Allenton Road and avoid entering the Six Flags parking lot. Drive about two miles and park in the trailhead parking lot.

ON THE TRAIL

This almost completely shaded hike is a great choice for a hot summer day. It's beautiful year round, with wildflowers in the spring and a lot of color in the fall, and in the winter the leafless trees make for easier wildlife spotting and observation of geologic features. Eagle Valley Trail presents many ups and downs and a variety of scenery to keep everyone interested. There are numerous beautiful trails at this 1734-acre park, but this one provides a wonderful sampling of what the park has to offer in less than 4 miles.

From the parking lot, follow signs for the Eagle Valley Trail downhill and straight ahead, and then at 0.1 mile turn right to start your hike on the Eagle Valley loop. You are immediately surrounded by a dense, mixed oak forest. At first you can meander gently downhill, but the trail gets steeper as you go. A series of tight switchbacks starts around mile 0.3, as the trail drops steadily into a valley. Watch for the trail to get more rooty and rocky here.

The forest thickens as you hike deeper into the valley. The path widens along the creek at mile 0.7. Stay straight at the trail junction at mile 0.9, and at mile 1.2 cross Scenic Loop Road; watch for the blue Eagle Valley Trail signs. Here the trail becomes level and flat for a bit as you continue strolling beside the creek. Around mile 1.5, notice fences and boards that equestrians use for horse jumping and agility.

As you get farther into the valley, watch for exposed rocks along cliffs. The valley is also rich with wildlife and sprinkled with wildflowers in the spring. At mile 1.7, turn left at the trail junction and sign. The trail remains flat as it meanders through the valley, veering this way and that with the creek.

Good buddies make the trail all the sweeter.

At mile 2.1, stay left to keep on Eagle Valley Trail. The trail starts to go up-hill here and gets steep at times. Use the occasional breather to take in the view to the left (east) and behind you.

Reach the top of the hill at mile 2.4. This is a somewhat tricky section of trail; the signs can seem to point downhill and to the right toward an unmaintained trail, but make sure to turn left and go up the hill.

On this section of the trail you approach the horse trail parking lot, so watch for equestrians, and remember to yield by keeping all hikers to the right side of the trail. Continue to follow the signs for the Eagle Valley Trail past the equestrian parking and campground before returning back to the trailhead parking lot.

18 AL FOSTER MEMORIAL AND ROCK HOLLOW TRAILS

BEFORE YOU GO

    MAP On park website

    CONTACT Wildwood Department of Parks and Recreation or St. Louis County Parks and Recreation Department

    GPS 38.543750° N, -90.624568° W

    NOTES Most trails accessible to wheelchairs, all trails accessible to strollers; porta-potties at trailhead

ABOUT THE HIKE

    SEASON Year-round

    DIFFICULTY Easy

    LENGTH 3 miles roundtrip

    HIGH POINT 560 feet

    ELEVATION GAIN 300 feet

GETTING THERE

From Interstate 44 in Eureka, take exit 264 for State Route 109 north, and drive 3 miles. Turn right onto Old State Road and immediately take another right onto Washington Avenue. Drive 0.2 mile on Washington Avenue, which turns into Grand Street. Park at the end of the road or at the trailhead parking lot.

ON THE TRAIL

The Al Foster Memorial Trail is part of a series of trails maintained by several agencies working together to provide a trail system that travels through a diverse set of environments. The result is a recreational playground that makes nature accessible to suburbanites. Popular with cyclists, it's also a treat for hikers and kids in strollers. The trail is named for Al Foster, a journalist and historian who was known for helping keep the Meramec River clean and free-flowing.

This hike starts at the site of the Wabash, Frisco, and Pacific Railroad, a small-gauge track on which a steam engine tows cars full of excited kids every Sunday during the summer. (For more information, check out www.wfprr .com.) The miniature railroad track and the trail are close together for much of the hike.

From the end of Grand Street, walk through the gate and follow the signs to head left (northeast) onto the Al Foster Trail and the Rock Hollow Trail toward Castlewood State Park. (In addition to this hike, a couple of side trails to the right are worth a short jaunt. The one to the overlook goes over a bridge, past some picturesque cliffs, and to a view across the river.)

Where these two trails merge, enjoy a lovely walk along the Meramec River. This is near where Hamilton Creek, one of the most ecologically diverse bodies of water in the area, meets with the Meramec, making this an area with fascinating views across the flowing river and into forests on all sides of the creek

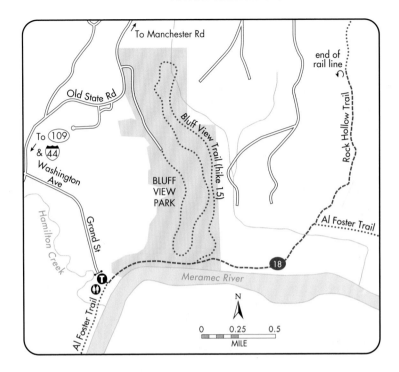

and river. Around mile 0.3, get a close-up view of dramatic cliffs that rise up from the river.

At mile 0.5, the trails pass by Bluff View Trail (hike 15), another beautiful hike. Continue along the Al Foster and Rock Hollow trails past stands of evergreen trees. Watch for several spots where there are gaps in the brush and you can scoot down the embankment to the river, offering kids a chance to splash if you're willing to let them.

At 1 mile, continue up the hill to the left on the Rock Hollow Trail. (The Al Foster Trail continues to the right for several miles down the river.) The Rock Hollow Trail is wide and paved, but provides the sense of being deep in the forest. Ascend through a narrow canyon. The last half mile of pavement gets steep as it approaches the northern trailhead at Ridge Meadows Elementary School in Ballwin, where the WFP Railroad line ends. Continue as long as you like before turning around, but if you turn back here, you'll have gone about 1.5 miles, making your total trip 3 miles by the time you get back to the parking lot.

Opposite: *Impressive cliffs line the Al Foster Trail.*

19 ROCKWOODS RANGE

BEFORE YOU GO
   MAP On park website and at trailhead
   CONTACT Missouri Department of Conservation
   GPS 38.504109° N, -90.702262° W
   NOTES Inaccessible for strollers and wheelchairs; no bathrooms or water

ABOUT THE HIKE
   SEASON Year-round
   DIFFICULTY Difficult
   LENGTH 3.5 miles loop
   HIGH POINT 780 feet
   ELEVATION GAIN 490 feet

GETTING THERE
From Interstate 44 in Eureka, take exit 261 for Six Flags and turn right (north). Make an immediate left (west) on Fox Creek Road. Drive 1.3 miles, and turn left into the parking lot.

ON THE TRAIL
In the wilds of Wildwood, Rockwoods Range is the southernmost in a string of parks and preserves that offer a family-fun alternative to the chaos and expense of the big amusement park just off Interstate 44. A short drive from most of the St. Louis area, the rugged Green Rock Trail offers a taste of the Ozarks in its hills, rocky outcrops, and valleys. The beauty of this place will fill you with wonder, so close is it to the thrill rides and highway and yet so secluded.

Carefully cross Fox Creek Road to reach the trailhead directly across from the parking lot; it's identified by a large wooden sign. The full trail actually goes all the way to the northwest corner of Rockwoods Range, rambles 7 miles through Greensfelder County Park (hikes 16 and 17), and continues on to the visitor center at Rockwoods Reservation, known for its towering lime kiln (hike 14) and popular winter Maple Sugar Festival. Rockwoods Range, like Greensfelder County Park, was preserved in part by the efforts of A. P. Greensfelder, a businessman and civic leader, in the mid-twentieth century.

Start on the trail by veering left to follow a tributary of Fox Creek through a lovely, shaded valley. It's a narrow, rocky trail, so take your time and enjoy your surroundings: oak and sycamore forest, splashable pools and puddles carved out by the stream, mossy rocks, and seasonal wildflowers. At 0.4 mile, the trail and creek are one and the same for about 20 feet; then hike sharply uphill for about a tenth of a mile. Walk along a ridge for another tenth of a mile before entering a stand of flowering dogwoods.

Next the trail jogs west, reaching the park boundary at mile 1.1, then circling east around a ridge, ambling peacefully across land that remains much as it has been for centuries. The Missouri Department of Conservation calls this area a transition zone—it's less rocky than the Ozarks but has the same type of

The Green Rock Trail starts with a pleasant stroll along the creek.

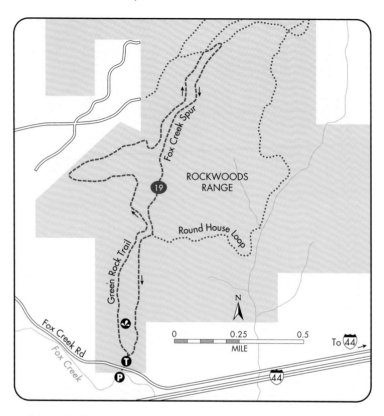

undulating landscape and dense forest, consisting of a mix of deciduous and evergreen trees. Around 1.7 miles, the wilderness spell is broken for a bit, as a rural neighborhood bordering the preserve comes into view. Shortly after it disappears, turn right (northeast) at the junction with the Fox Run Trail, mile 1.8. In just under a tenth of a mile reach another junction. Make a sharp right (southeast) here to switch to the Fox Creek Spur trail.

This section of the trail is wide, so it allows horses and mountain bikes. It goes gently but steadily downhill and makes for a quicker return to the trailhead than the Green Rock Trail. Watch out for footing that is muddied and damaged by horse traffic and, of course, for equine land mines. Along this stretch, also notice many fine examples of Missouri's only native evergreen, the shortleaf pine.

At 2.9 miles, arrive at the junction of the Fox Creek Spur and Green Rock trails. Stay to the right and take this about a half mile back to the trailhead, again enjoying the gentle downhill, shade from the mixed forest, and wildflowers.

20 WEST TYSON COUNTY PARK

BEFORE YOU GO
    MAP On park website and at trailhead
    CONTACT St. Louis County Parks and Recreation Department
    GPS 38.511488° N, -90.586483° W
    NOTES Inaccessible for wheelchairs and strollers; bathrooms and water
      at parking lot

ABOUT THE HIKE
    SEASON Year-round
    DIFFICULTY Difficult
    LENGTH 2.75 miles loop
    HIGH POINT 820 feet
    ELEVATION GAIN 460 feet

Rock scrambling at West Tyson County Park

GETTING THERE

From Interstate 44 in Eureka, take exit 266 to North Outer Road. Go north to stay on North Outer Road. Drive 0.2 mile and take the first right at the sign for West Tyson. Veer right 0.1 mile after you enter the park, and take the road to its end at a parking area just past the bathrooms.

ON THE TRAIL

West Tyson County Park is easy for most families in the greater St. Louis region to get to and offers a huge variety of trail types and distances. On the Flint Quarry Trail you'll find steep climbs, rocky outcrops, and rough trails that will keep everyone's interest.

From the parking lot, spy the trailhead to the right of the service road, marked with green signs that show a rock falling from a hill. The trail starts steep and rocky, so be prepared to take it slow if you're hiking with very small hikers. A variety of trees, including maples, oaks, and cedars, provide shade as you enter a narrow canyon with scenic rocky outcrops.

The trail veers right at mile 0.2, and the woods get even more dense and lovely, with plenty of evergreens dotting the forest. Watch for the sharp left turn in the trail at mile 0.3, and continue around a bend and up the hill. After 0.75 mile, the trail opens out to a small clearing with a bench and a view over the valley to the southeast. This is a great spot to rest and take some photos.

The trail continues across a ridge through a cedar forest. At mile 0.9, notice a fence on the right that separates West Tyson Park from the Tyson Research Center, a facility owned and operated by Washington University for studying ecological systems. After heavy rains, keep watch for a variety of colorful and strangely shaped mushrooms. The trail is mostly level along this pretty stretch, with just a few ups and downs. The trail meets with the Chubb Trail at a picnic table at 1.25 miles, making another great spot for a break and a snack. Turn left (south), and the Chubb Trail and Flint Quarry Trail will be one and the same for nearly a mile more.

At mile 1.5, watch for a sharp right turn and a sign that reads OLD TRAIL CLOSED; DO NOT USE. Follow the arrow to stay on the established trail, which

CENTURIES OF PARK HISTORY

West Tyson County Park has a fascinating history dating back hundreds of years to the Native Americans who mined flint for their weapons and tools. In fact, all of the flint artifacts found at Cahokia Mounds State Historic Site, about forty miles east of West Tyson in Illinois, can be traced back to this site. Observant hikers may notice shallow depressions along the trails where the early Native Americans did surface mining.

In 1940, the federal government purchased 2400 acres that included West Tyson and Lone Elk county parks. The land was used to store and test ammunition during World War II and the Korean War.

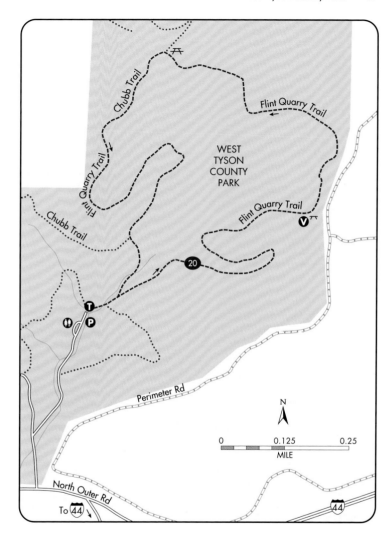

is relatively level until mile 1.9, when it returns to rocky steepness. At mile 2.2, the Chubb Trail continues straight while the Flint Quarry Trail turns left downhill; watch your footing, since this section can be slippery. After a tenth of a mile the trail levels out into the lovely valley where your hike started. Turn right when you get to the pavement, and retrace your steps back to the parking lot.

21 CASTLEWOOD STATE PARK: LONE WOLF AND RIVER SCENE TRAILS

BEFORE YOU GO
MAP On park website, at trailhead, and at park headquarters
CONTACT Missouri State Parks Department
GPS 38.549987° N, -90.540162° W
NOTES Inaccessible for wheelchairs; pit toilets at trailhead

ABOUT THE HIKE
SEASON Year-round
DIFFICULTY Difficult
LENGTH 2.5 miles loop
HIGH POINT 680 feet
ELEVATION GAIN 630 feet

GETTING THERE
From State Route 141 in Ballwin, take Big Bend Road west 3 miles to Ries Road and turn left (south). Drive 1 mile, and then turn left (east) on Kiefer Creek Road. In half a mile, pass the park office and stop at the trailhead parking lot 0.4 mile farther along on the right. If this lot is full, park in the lot across the street.

ON THE TRAIL
This spectacular hike offers incredible views and a broad diversity of environments. Because of this and its proximity to the constantly growing population of west St. Louis County, it's often very crowded on sunny weekends. If you can, try this one during the week or when imperfect conditions keep less hardy hikers indoors.

Castlewood has a long history as a spot for recreation. The train tracks that run along the river (and still carry Amtrak trains from St. Louis to Kansas City) brought loads of St. Louisans to this country retreat in the early 1900s. It was a wild time, with a huge hotel at the top of the bluff, dance halls, and parties on the beach. As many as 10,000 revelers were here some weekends. It's much quieter now, though still popular, and continues to be a beautiful place to enjoy nature.

From the information kiosk at the edge of the parking lot, head straight uphill; it's a tough start but there's a quick payoff with the views at the top of the bluff just 0.3 mile in. After about 0.2 mile on the wide gravel path, short side trails begin appearing to the left that lead to views across the bluffs. You can check these out or wait till you get to the top, where there are benches and a viewing platform built out over the cliff.

The trail offers views across the Meramec River valley, woods, and the cliffs below. Keep young children close, as there are many tempting rock outcrops with steep drops. Enjoy the views, but don't forget to appreciate the mixed pine and deciduous forest to the right of the trail.

Castlewood State Park is famous for this view across the Meramec River.

Just past the bluffs the River Scene Trail continues to climb up through the forests; the Lone Wolf Trail goes to the right. Stay left along the bluffs and switch to the River Scene Trail. Follow the signs to stay on the hiking trail rather than joining one of the bicycle trails. At 0.6 mile, the trail makes a winding descent. As you move downward, make sure to follow the trail toward the right—do not use the straight-ahead steep trail, which is closed to prevent erosion (though the sign sometimes gets knocked down). Along this portion of the trail, notice old foundations that were part of the resorts that brought visitors here in the early part of the twentieth century.

At 0.8 mile the trail becomes a series of nearly 200 stairs. Watch your step as you head down, down, down the hill. At the bottom of the stairs, let the kids discover a tunnel under the railroad track, which leads to the Meramec River. Today these tracks carry freight trains, but 100 years ago they brought vacationers from the city to stay at the aforementioned resorts. Take a break here, and scramble down the wash to explore the gravel shore. Observant explorers could find small crabs, lizards, and snakes here.

From mile 1 at the river's edge, walk east between the river and the railroad track. This portion of the trail can feel jungle-like in the summer, with branches meeting high above and creating another sort of tunnel for hikers. If you're a tree enthusiast (and who isn't?), check out the pawpaw trees and massive old sycamores. Be careful after heavy rains, as this area can get muddy and boggy.

At mile 1.5, go straight at the junction to continue to walk east on the white connector trail to Kiefer Creek Road. Turn left (north) at 1.9 miles to follow the trail (which parallels the road) back to the parking lot. To the right are open playfields and a playground. Northwest of the playground parking lot is a wide, shallow section of the creek that provides a good spot for splash play after a warm hike.

22 CASTLEWOOD STATE PARK: GROTPETER TRAIL

BEFORE YOU GO
MAP On park website
CONTACT Missouri State Parks Department
GPS 38.552574° N, -90.542898° W
NOTES Inaccessible for strollers and wheelchairs; pit toilets just past trailhead

ABOUT THE HIKE
SEASON Year-round
DIFFICULTY Moderate
LENGTH 3 miles loop
HIGH POINT 695 feet
ELEVATION GAIN 590 feet

GETTING THERE
From State Route 141 in Ballwin, take Big Bend Road west 3 miles to Ries Road and turn left (south). Drive 1 mile, and then turn left (east) on Kiefer Creek Road. In 0.2 mile the park office is on your right. Park there or in the parking lot just a few hundred feet away.

Common blue violet

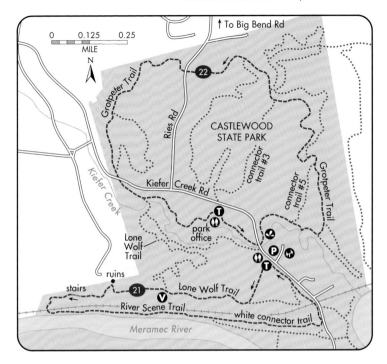

ON THE TRAIL

Grotpeter Trail isn't one of the marquee hikes at busy Castlewood State Park, but that's part of its charm. It doesn't have the big sweeping views of the river valley that Lone Wolf and River Scene trails do (hike 21). But it also doesn't have the traffic of those trails, which can get downright crowded on temperate weekends. Instead, it offers a meandering walk through quiet, verdant forest, gentle ups and downs across sloping valleys, and connector trails that let you bail early if someone in the group runs out of steam.

The hike starts at the parking lot just east of the park office. From your car, walk through the mowed field to the equestrian parking lot, and then carefully cross Kiefer Creek Road to the Grotpeter trailhead at mile 0.2. The trail proceeds slightly uphill at the start, with a gentle climb above Kiefer Creek. After that, the path evens out and ambles through a dense forest providing plenty of shade, though the trail is still wide and smooth. (The first opportunity for a shortcut comes at mile 0.35: if you don't mind some steep uphill stretches, leave the trail and head north at connector trail #5 to cut out about a third of a mile.) Continuing on Grotpeter, enjoy a pleasant forest stroll through dogwoods, sycamores, and oaks.

At mile 1.3, turn right at a signed junction with connector trail #3 to stay on the Grotpeter Trail. (If you're ready to head back to the parking lot, go straight south and take connector #3 for a direct 0.4-mile path to the park office.) Past this point the Grotpeter Trail gets even wider and the hiking is easy. At 1.8 miles, however, cross Ries Road (carefully, as there are no yield signs and the curves and hills make it a blind crossing for cars), and then the trail gets steep and rocky. It descends for 0.2 mile to a footbridge over a seasonal stream. Climb back uphill for a third of a mile, and watch for a bench on a ridge at 2.1 miles, where you can see almost to the river when winter has stripped the trees of leaves.

Head down the hill and recross Kiefer Creek Road at mile 2.7. Shortly after that, at the unnamed connector to the Lone Wolf Trail (hike 21), is a great place for creek play on a hot day. After that, it's just a third of a mile to the parking lot, along the creek and around a naturalized field on the edge of the tree-lined creek. At the heart of the park, this area makes it obvious why Castlewood is so popular. From here you can observe its variety of creek pools, river scenes, and gateways to climbs up the hills to grand vistas. Enjoy the stroll along the creek and meadow as you continue back to the park office.

23 LONE ELK COUNTY PARK

BEFORE YOU GO
    MAP On park website and at visitor center
    CONTACT St. Louis County Parks and Recreation Department
    GPS 38.531066° N, -90.543246° W
    NOTES Dogs prohibited; inaccessible for wheelchairs and strollers; bull elk can be
      more aggressive during mating season in September and October; bathrooms
      and water at visitor center

ABOUT THE HIKE
    SEASON Year-round
    DIFFICULTY Moderate
    LENGTH 3 miles loop
    HIGH POINT 650 feet
    ELEVATION GAIN 310 feet

GETTING THERE
From Interstate 44 in Valley Park, take exit 272 for State Route 141 and turn right (north). Immediately north of the freeway, turn left (west) onto Outer Road West. Drive 2 miles, and follow the signs to Lone Elk County Park. Turn left to continue on Lone Elk Park Road for 0.6 mile. Continue following the signs and stay left, traveling counterclockwise around the lake. Turn left on Elk Hollow Road for parking and the visitor center.

ON THE TRAIL
This hike has something for everyone: dense forests, views of the park's central reservoir, and, of course, wildlife. It also has a strange history: during both World War II and the Korean War, the site was used to test and store ammunition. Between the wars, herds of elk and bison were established,

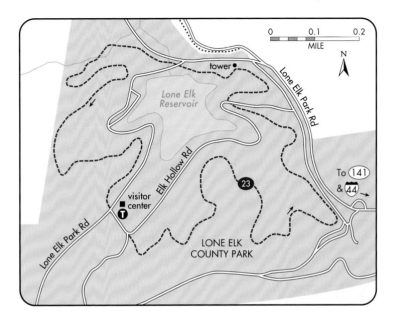

but then eliminated when the Korean War again necessitated the land's use for military purposes. One elk—which gave the park its name—was missed when the rest of the herd was evicted. In the 1960s, St. Louis County acquired part of the land and brought six elk from Yellowstone National Park. Now you can hike alongside some of the largest mammals native to North America, right here in St. Louis County.

After the hike you can drive past a herd of bison, acquired by the parks department from the Saint Louis Zoo in the 1970s, in a separate section of the park. Be sure to leave your dog at home when you visit Lone Elk—pets are prohibited, even in cars. The elk here are generally docile and thousands of people hike at Lone Elk every year without incident. But use common sense: if elk appear aggressive (bellowing or staring at your group), turn around if you must in order to keep a safe distance. Never walk through the middle of a herd or get too close to any individual elk.

The hike starts from the visitor center. Find the post with the bison symbol at the southeast end of the parking lot to locate the trail. Like most of the hike, this segment is characterized by gentle ups and downs. The forest is mixed and not too dense, so make sure to stay alert and look around as you walk so you don't miss any elk sightings. In moist seasons, watch for a wide variety of mushrooms growing on logs, in between grasses, and under shrubs. They come in all shapes and patterns: some look like orange blobs while others appear in neat rows, like an army of fan shells marching across a fallen trunk (see "Myriad Mushrooms" sidebar).

In this and other areas of the park, you might see signs encouraging extra caution during elk mating season. Mating usually takes place during September and October, and bull elk can be especially aggressive and territorial, particularly if they are with a group of cows. Maintain a respectful distance.

The trail turns toward the lake at 0.7 mile, and the forest opens up. Here especially, be on the lookout for deer and elk; the big animals are often seen sitting quietly not far from the trail. At 1.2 miles, the trail comes close to Lone Elk Park Road, and hikers can see a cement tower that was used as a base for target practice during the wars.

Around mile 1.7, the trail crosses Elk Hollow Road and heads into denser forest. One benefit to the large population of deer here, as well as elk, is the relative absence of poison ivy; they love to munch on the vines, reducing the chance of getting a rash from the plant's nasty oil. Despite that, stay on the trail to avoid ticks. From here, the loop continues to meander through the forest and along Park Road and the northeast edge of the park. This section has a more lush feel, with small creeks running down to the reservoir, and likely sightings of wildflowers in the spring. After crossing Park Road at mile 2, follow the ridgeline, with trees offering plenty of cooling shade. Around mile 2.8, the trail heads downhill toward Park Road again; cross the road to return to the parking lot.

In some circumstances, it is OK to view elk close-up; just don't walk through the middle of a herd or get too close to any individual elk.

MYRIAD MUSHROOMS

Mushroom hunting is tremendously popular in Missouri. You know it's spring when you see people wandering in and out of the woods carrying little sacks, eyes downward in search of their favorite fungus. Parks and preserves are rife with varieties known for their tastiness, like morels and chanterelles. (The area is also home to a lot of poisonous varieties, so make sure you have an expert with you if you decide to forage for mushrooms.) Hunting for edible mushrooms is allowed in parks and preserves, as long as you follow the rules of the park and the ethical mushroom hunting guidelines agreed upon by local mushroom groups.

Even if you don't plan on eating any of the forest's meaty mushrooms, spotting them is a joy in itself. There is an incredible variety of colors and shapes in the mushroom world, rivaling spring's wildflowers in their visual delights.

- **Chanterelles:** These edible mushrooms are in the vase or trumpet category of mushrooms. They can be bright yellow or dark red. They are especially common under oaks.
- **Morels:** Probably the most popular edibles, these aren't much to look at unless you're a mushroom hunter, and then they'll inspire the kind of awe usually felt by gold miners at the sight of a sparkly glint in a stream. They are usually only a few inches tall and grayish, with a bulbous tip lined with ridges and pits in often intricate patterns. A similar mushroom, called a false morel, has been known to be so poisonous that it can cause death, so again, don't dine on morels without an expert to help with your hunting.
- **Chicken of the Woods:** When most of the spring wildflowers have faded, seeing a bright orange splotch of color deep in the woods is a special treat. When this happens, you might be spotting chicken of the woods. This is another edible mushroom much sought after by foragers. It's usually fan shaped and can grow up to a foot wide.
- **False Turkey Tail:** You're likely to see these mushrooms more often than any other on the trail. They aren't large on their own but grow in groups of hundreds on downed trees. When you see rows of fan-shaped brown or gray fungi on a log, it's probably false turkey tail.
- **Jack-o-Lantern:** This is another type of bright orange mushroom that grows in groups at the base of trees. It's poisonous to eat, but it's safe to take a small sample home and into a dark room for a surprise—it glows in the dark!

The Missouri Department of Conservation has published a book called *Missouri's Wild Mushrooms* by Maxine Stone that details how to find the mushrooms; it even has recipes. If you really want to get into mushrooms, look up the local chapter of the Missouri Mycological Society.

24 FOREST 44 CONSERVATION AREA

BEFORE YOU GO
 MAP On park website and at trailhead
 CONTACT Missouri Department of Conservation
 GPS 38.529269° N, -90.513140° W
 NOTES Inaccessible for strollers and wheelchairs; area used heavily by horses;
  porta-potty at trailhead

ABOUT THE HIKE
 SEASON Year-round
 DIFFICULTY Easy to moderate
 LENGTH 2.4 miles loop
 HIGH POINT 690 feet
 ELEVATION GAIN 530 feet

GETTING THERE

From Interstate 44 in Valley Park, take exit 272 for State Route 141 and turn left (south) onto SR 141. Immediately turn right (west) on Lambert Drury Drive. Drive 0.1 mile, and turn right (west) on Meramec Station Road. Drive 0.8 mile, turn left (south) on Hillsboro Road, drive 0.4 mile, and turn right into the parking lot just past the Kraus Farms Equestrian Center.

Being closer to the ground lets kids spot all kinds of cool stuff that adults miss.

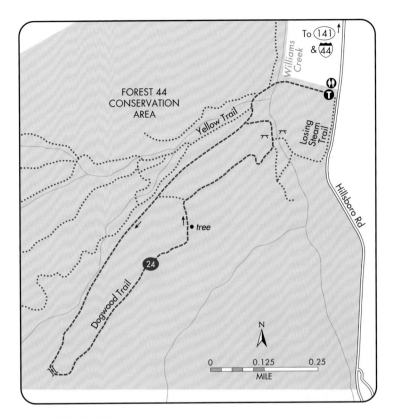

ON THE TRAIL

Forest 44 Conservation Area is great for beginning hikers. It feels like an adventure, with its rocky creek crossings, wide meadows, and dense forests. Only one short section is steep, so most kids should be able to make the full loop with a little help.

This area of the county is packed with parks and trails on both sides of busy Interstate 44. And for good reason: geologists mark this area as the very northeast edge of the Ozark region, so it contains plants and animals typical of areas farther south in Missouri. It was once part of a 10,000-acre cattle ranch and contains several springs that feed Williams Creek.

From the north end of the parking lot, head west, away from Hillsboro Road. The trail is flat and wide in the first half mile, alternating between gravel and grass. At 0.1 mile turn left at a drainage ditch, and then make two more lefts in the next 200 feet, crossing another drainage ditch in between, to stay on the Dogwood Trail. Avoid the trails named for colors (red, blue, yellow, etc.), which are designated horse trails. Finally, at about 0.3 mile, a sign points both ways to the Dogwood Trail loop; turn right to travel counterclockwise. From here on out, you'll be on hiking-only trails, so no more worrying about stepping on one of the equestrian land mines.

This section of the trail continues level and relatively easy for all ages. On your right is a meadow, and to the left the forest stretches up the hill. Watch for many varieties of wildflowers in the meadow. At 0.6 mile, reach the junction with a cutoff trail for a shorter loop, a good place to bail if anyone's feeling tired. At 1 mile, enter the forest of mature trees. This portion of the trail, still wide and flat, showcases a variety of species, including dogwood, redbud, oak, and hickory. Continue through the woods to mile 1.3, where you cross a short bridge and then veer left heading uphill. The forest is not dense here, so sometimes it can be hard to spot the trail; watch for signs pointing to the Dogwood Trail to stay on the path. The trail is steep for about a quarter mile and then begins to go downhill gently at mile 1.4. Around mile 1.7, watch for a huge tree on the right that sticks out because of its long limbs, burls, and bumps that look like arms, eyes, and lips. In springtime, find yourself surrounded by spectacular displays of the flowering dogwood trees.

Near the end of the loop, find a bench on a platform just above the creek. When the water is low, you can choose to take a right turn here, switching to the Losing Stream Trail, and cross the creek. Come up from the creek bed near another bench on the opposite side, to take a slightly different path back to the parking lot. It all depends on how wet you want to get your feet. If you choose not to cross the creek, continue up the Dogwood Trail a few hundred feet and turn right to retrace your steps to the parking lot.

25 RUSSELL E. EMMENEGGER NATURE PARK

BEFORE YOU GO
MAP On park website
CONTACT Missouri Department of Conservation
GPS 38.547012° N, -90.432699° W
NOTES A short loop near parking area is paved and accessible for strollers and wheelchairs; bathrooms and water near trailhead

ABOUT THE HIKE
SEASON Year-round
DIFFICULTY Moderate to difficult
LENGTH 1.2 miles loop
HIGH POINT 635 feet
ELEVATION GAIN 340 feet

GETTING THERE
From Interstate 44 at Kirkwood, take exit 277A for Geyer Road and turn left (north). Drive 0.7 mile on Geyer, and turn left onto Cragwold Road. Continue 1 mile, past Powder Valley Nature Center and across I-270. At the T, turn left

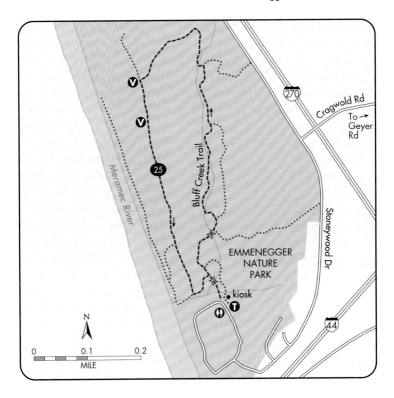

(south) onto Stoneywood Drive. Drive 0.5 mile to its end at the Emmenegger Nature Rock parking lot.

ON THE TRAIL

Emmenegger Nature Park borders both I-270 and I-44, so it's in easy reach for a short hike after school or on the weekend. Here a well-worn path winds through a wooded valley and climbs to a rocky bluff with views of the Meramec River. The 93-acre park was once owned by the Lemp family, best known for the brewery they ran in the early twentieth century. In the last 100 years it was used as a breeding facility by the Saint Louis Zoo and was also a riverside resort, much like the one at Castlewood State Park farther down the Meramec River southwest of here.

The hike starts on a paved trail at the kiosk next to the parking lot. Cross the wide, new bridge and veer to the right to walk along the eastern sides of the two paved loops, crossing another bridge on the second loop. In 0.2 mile, climb up the hill to the right, where the pavement ends and Bluff Creek Trail

Forget adventure races. Kids can turn any hike into an obstacle course.

starts. Continue to climb for a short distance, and then dip into a wooded valley with an intermittent stream. After 0.4 mile, the trail does a quick left-right jog as it veers sharply uphill. Take a look back at the valley you just traversed; ask kids if they notice a difference between the trees closer to the creek and those on the hillside you're now climbing.

This section is steep but scenic. It shows off the variety of shrubby and taller flora that can grow in such a small area. The topography here makes for a mix of hardwoods along the ridges and other species in the valley. Upland forest species include white oak, red oak, post oak, shagbark hickory, sugar maple, dogwood, redbud, and pawpaw. Species in the bottomland areas include elm, box elder, silver maple, American sycamore, and white oak.

At the top of the hill, mile 0.6, the Meramec River and the valley beyond come into view. Keep watch on small children, as the drop-off just beyond the trail is steep. Be mindful as well of signs that warn hikers to keep off glades, where rangers are working to restore native plants. Past the views, the trail turns south and begins its descent along the bluff past the glades, which are protected by low fences. In spring and fall, you might also see volunteers helping to remove invasive honeysuckle shrubs (see "A Pretty Plague" sidebar).

The trail descends steeply here, with rocks acting as stair steps. Take it slow and remember to stop and enjoy the varying views. At mile 0.9, after heading south and downhill, turn left. (Optionally, you can take a side trail to the right to explore the rocky shore of the Meramec.) In just 100 feet, the Bluff Creek Trail joins the paved trail. Follow the paved trail to the right, crossing the first bridge again, and continue back to the parking lot.

A PRETTY PLAGUE

During your early spring hikes you might notice some shrubs that leaf out long before trees and other plants. In the fall, you'll notice the same plants form bunches of red berries and keep their leaves longer than their fellow forest dwellers. What you're noticing is bush honeysuckle, a nonnative species that many of the parks and preserves in the area are struggling to eradicate.

The invasive shrubs are difficult to remove, and they crowd out natives. Because they are the first to leaf out, they block native plants from getting sun. In the fall, birds love to munch their seeds and spread them far and wide. All this causes problems in two ways: honeysuckle plants steal nutrients in the form of sunlight and soil from the native plants, *and* they don't provide as much nutrition to animals as the indigenous plants.

How can you help? Most importantly, don't plant bush honeysuckle in your own garden! (There is a native honeysuckle vine that works well in local gardens; ask at a garden center or do some research on the Missouri Botanical Garden website.) The invasive variety started getting a foothold in the region about 150 years ago, when people planted it in their gardens for decoration and erosion control. If you already have some honeysuckle on your property, look to the Missouri Botanical Garden for advice on identifying it—and if it is the bush variety, removing it.

The Missouri Department of Conservation and local parks departments frequently hold honeysuckle removal events in the spring and fall. Some of these events are appropriate for kids, and provide a great lesson in giving back to the community. Watch the information kiosks at trailheads for times and dates. Rangers sometimes use controlled burns to reduce the honeysuckle in an area (see "Fire as Friend" sidebar in hike 51).

26 POWDER VALLEY CONSERVATION NATURE CENTER

BEFORE YOU GO
MAP On park website and at visitor center
CONTACT Missouri Department of Conservation
GPS 38.5560° N -90.4285° W
NOTES Dogs prohibited; trails paved and accessible for strollers; bathrooms and water at nature center

ABOUT THE HIKE
SEASON Year-round
DIFFICULTY Easy—moderate
LENGTH 1.2 miles loop
HIGH POINT 645 feet
ELEVATION GAIN 300 feet

GETTING THERE

From Interstate 44 at Kirkwood, take exit 277 for Kirkwood Road and turn left (north). Drive 0.5 mile to Big Bend Road and turn left (west). In 0.25 mile, turn left (south) on Geyer Road. Drive 0.7 mile, and turn right onto Cragwold Road. Follow Cragwold Road for 0.8 mile, and turn right on the Powder Valley driveway. Follow this for about a third of a mile to its end at the nature center, where there is ample parking.

ON THE TRAIL

Powder Valley Conservation Nature Center is a great place to ease into hiking and exploring nature. It has a series of very short paths, so you can stay on the trail for as much or as little time as your kids can handle.

The nature center is an attraction in itself and features a large number of museum-quality exhibits. It's popular with preschool-age kids as well as elementary schoolers on field trips, and admission is free. Listen to the noises a black bear makes, while standing in the shadow of a stuffed *Ursus americanus.* Watch live turtles and snakes. Stage a puppet show. Let the kids loose here, and they will find new things to explore for as long as you let them.

Once you're ready to hike, head south from the parking lot (go left if you're facing the nature center) and look for the Hickory Ridge Trail sign. The trail is

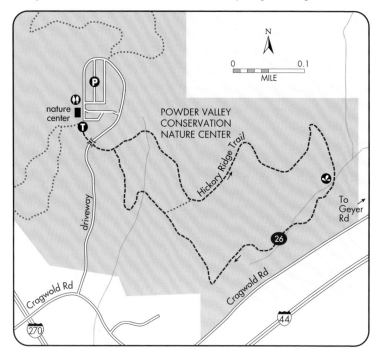

Soaking up a quiet moment by the creek

paved, but some steps at the bridges make it inaccessible for wheelchairs. There are some steep sections that will be challenging for strollers, but pushing little ones in strollers for the whole trail is definitely doable.

In the first tenth of a mile the trail crosses the driveway into the preserve over a lovely bridge. From here, head into the forest, and when you reach the loop junction, turn left. Keep heading down the hill, and at mile 0.3 pass the junction for the short loop. (If you need to return to the trailhead, turn right, and then right again at next junction.)

Continue deeper into the valley, making a number of creek crossings. Several of them have bridges, which kids always seem to enjoy for a break in the norm, as they hike along. Any one of these crossings is a good place for kids to explore the water. Kids can put leaves in on the upstream side of the walkway and see them come out of the pipe downstream.

The trail continues through the valley and then starts to head uphill at mile 0.8. The hickory and oak forest here is dense and a good place to watch for wildlife, including barred owls. At mile 1, pass the other junction for the short-cut; stay to the left to continue uphill to the final junction at mile 1.1; turn left to retrace your steps to the parking lot.

27 LAUMEIER SCULPTURE PARK

BEFORE YOU GO
MAP On park website and at kiosks near parking lot
CONTACT Laumeier Sculpture Park
GPS 38.549888° N, -90.414281° W
NOTES Some sections are wheelchair accessible and most are accessible for strollers; bathrooms and water in Adam Aronson Fine Arts Center when open

ABOUT THE HIKE
SEASON Year-round
DIFFICULTY Easy
LENGTH 1.25 miles loop
HIGH POINT 612 feet
ELEVATION GAIN 60 feet

GETTING THERE
From Interstate 44 in Kirkwood, take exit 277 (Lindbergh Road and Kirkwood Road), and head south on Lindbergh Road. Drive 0.2 mile, and turn right on Watson Road. Drive 0.5 mile, and turn left onto South Geyer Road to enter the park. Drive south for about 0.1 mile, and then the road curves to the left. Turn right at the T intersection after another 0.1 mile, and go another 0.1 mile to the parking area.

Interacting with art: Face of the Earth #3 at Laumeier Sculpture Park

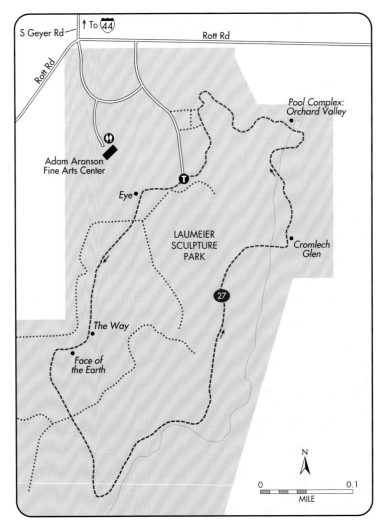

From Interstate 270 in Kirkwood, take exit 5A (State Route 366E and Watson Road) and turn right onto South Geyer Road. Drive 0.1 mile and enter the park. Drive south for about 0.1 mile, and then the road curves to the left. Turn right at the T intersection after another 0.1 mile, and go another 0.1 mile to the parking area.

MetroBus 48 stops at Lindbergh and Rott roads, about half a mile from the park.

ON THE TRAIL

Laumeier (rhymes with "cow hire") Sculpture Park is a unique and special place in the heart of St. Louis County. World-renowned artists display their work here on a grand scale, and the best part is that kids can get up close and personal with the art; in many cases it's okay to touch, climb on, crawl through, and bang on the art (but make sure to watch for and abide by any signs to the contrary).

The park opened in 1976, when the land was donated to the county parks department. A year later it became a nonprofit arts center and today is an outdoor museum on 105 acres. Your journey through Laumeier will start at the center of the park and then head south past some of the park's most impressive installations, then shift into the woods of the eastern part of the park before turning north and then curving back to the park entrance. *Note:* Maps printed by Laumeier are oriented with south at the top; all maps in this book are oriented with north at top.

From the lower parking lot, head uphill to the Museum Lawn and immediately take in the giant eyeball sculpture simply titled *Eye*, about three feet in circumference and one of the iconic works in Laumeier's collection. From there, turn south toward another iconic sculpture at 0.2 mile, *The Way*, sixty-five feet high and made of salvaged steel oil tanks painted red. Continuing down to the right through the South Lawn, kids love to explore *Face of the Earth #3*, a huge face recessed into the ground, where they can dangle their feet into the smiling "mouth."

Continue across the South Lawn to the education shelters, where classes and summer camps are centered. Take the branch of the Art Hike Trail that heads straight (southeast) into the woods here. Follow the trail to a junction with a side trail at mile 0.6, and turn left to walk along the creek. The trail includes two creek crossings that can make the trail damp after rains, and in 0.2 mile the trail goes past a spring house: a stone and wood structure built over a spring as a sort of air-conditioned oasis.

A few minutes past that at mile 0.8 is *Cromlech Glen*, a huge earthen amphitheater. It's a fascinating space for kids and adults alike. Explorers can climb on top of the bowl, run around inside, and even roll down the steep but short grassy slope. A short distance farther on the trail, at mile 0.9, is a throwback to the land's status 100 years ago as a family estate. Called *Pool Complex: Orchard Valley*, it features a two-story wooden structure of stairs and platforms at the edge of a vast empty pool. Many kids could easily spend a half hour exploring this one-acre site.

Next along the trail is a series of installations focused on dogs: there's a leash attached to a zip line so pooches can run for a short distance at their own pace and a series of dog houses shaped like buildings in a tiny town (kids love to crawl into these, too). Just past this, the trail crosses another unnamed creek and leads back uphill to the parking lot.

Opposite: *Exploring at Pere Marquette State Park, hike 28*

EAST OF ST. LOUIS

28 PERE MARQUETTE STATE PARK

BEFORE YOU GO

MAP At visitor center or at www.greatriverroad.com
CONTACT Illinois Department of Natural Resources
GPS 38.972853° N, -90.543313° W
NOTES Inaccessible for strollers and wheelchairs; bug spray is a must in spring and summer; bathrooms and water at visitor center

ABOUT THE HIKE

SEASON Year-round
DIFFICULTY Difficult
LENGTH 2 miles loop
HIGH POINT 825 feet
ELEVATION GAIN 570 feet

GETTING THERE

From Interstate 270 in north St. Louis County, take exit 31B to US Highway 367 north and continue for 4 miles. Continue north on US 67 and across the Clark Bridge to Alton, Illinois. Continue on US 67 west through downtown Alton, and then turn left to go north onto Illinois State Route 100. Continue on SR 100, also known as the Great River Road, 20 miles north to Scenic Drive, the entrance to the park. Turn right into the park, then turn left immediately and park at the visitor center.

ON THE TRAIL

Pere Marquette is one of Illinois's most beloved state parks, and has been a favorite destination for generations, with its campgrounds, cabins, and lodge. In winter, the park's proximity to the river makes it a prime location for viewing bald eagles. The educational displays at the visitor center provide an exceptional

Columbine

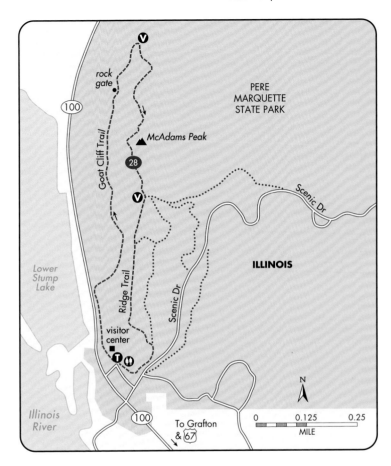

chance for kids to learn about native plants and animals. It even has a live "eagle cam" view of a bald eagle nest within the park and a life-size replica of a nest big enough for a child to stand in! The park is well worth the one-hour drive from St. Louis any time of year for a day of exploring the trails and enjoying the views. The town of Grafton, just south of the park, has a lot of good options for refueling after the hike.

This trail takes you high above the broad Illinois River valley, near the confluence of the Illinois and Mississippi rivers. It leads you up the hillside, past cave openings hidden by trees, thick forest, and astounding boulder piles.

Start from the parking lot in front of the visitor center. The Goat Cliff Trail, which is blazed in yellow, starts close to the road; start your hike northward. In less than a quarter of a mile, the trail heads uphill and away from the road. At

HISTORY LESSON: CIVILIAN CONSERVATION CORPS

When the Great Depression was raging in the 1930s, the federal government hit upon a way to employ young men and improve the network of parks that was growing across the country: the Civilian Conservation Corps, or CCC. As part of the New Deal, young, unemployed men worked in the parks building lodges, roads, trails, and shelters. The evidence of this program can be found all over our region.

Washington State Park (hikes 68 and 69) has some of the finest examples of buildings from this era. Company 1743, a segregated company of African American workers, were inspired by the Native American petroglyphs featured here and named their barracks "Camp Thunderbird." They built the stone dining lodge that still serves as the park's store and carved a thunderbird symbol into the stone chimney. They also built roads, laid the stone for the 1000 Steps Trail, and built fourteen buildings, including the octagonal lookout shelter on the 1000 Steps Trail.

Cuivre River State Park (hikes 41 and 42) started as a recreation demonstration area where the CCC and Work Projects Administration worked together to build roads, bridges, camps, and a picnic shelter.

At Meramec State Park (hikes 74, 75, and 76), "Three Cs" built a number of buildings, including many that still stand today and are on the National Register of Historic Places, including the shelter on the Lodge Trail and the Observation Tower.

Babler State Park (hikes 9, 10, and 11) was established in the 1930s. Two CCC camps were established in the park to build trails and structures.

On the Illinois side, the famous lodge at Pere Marquette State Park (hike 28), on the National Register of Historic Places since 1985, was built by CCC workers, as was the large shelter and viewing platform on McAdams Peak. Many of the buildings at Giant City State Park (hikes 39 and 40), as well as its historic lodge, were built by CCC workers. In 2006, the people who now run the lodge paid for a statue dedicated to the young workers of the '30s, and some of the men who had laid the stone attended the dedication ceremony.

a third of a mile, come upon the first of several boulder piles that will be hard for adventurous little hikers to resist climbing. But be careful, as the pile is on the west side of the trail and so is precariously placed just above the steep hill, with the road and the river far down on the other side. At 0.5 mile, encounter more boulders and rocky cliffs, some of which provide dramatic backdrop for the types of hardy wildflowers that thrive in the cracks and crevices between rocks. Here the trail also offers a short respite of downhill hiking.

Heading back uphill again, at 0.7 mile the trail passes under a gate of sorts: a rock wall that tilts over the trail opposite another boulder pile and cliff. Take a minute to admire this fascinating formation. Continue uphill past a few more piles of rocks and cliffs until just under 1 mile, where the rocks narrow the trail to less than two feet across. In a tenth of a mile there's an overlook that makes this hike a worthwhile one to try in winter; the view is not so dramatic in summer, when the lush forest isolates the viewer in a cocoon of green. Past the overlook, the trail takes a sharp right—watch for the yellow blazes painted on trees. Between the trees to the left one can catch glimpses of a valley in the interior of the park. At mile 1.3, the trail goes moderately uphill for a tenth of a mile. On the left side of the trail, look for an old maple with some interesting patterns in its bark. Is there a face? The shape of an owl? Maybe a galloping horse?

At 1.6 miles there's a short, steep uphill to the junction of several trails. Turn right to see a shelter with a viewing platform that marks McAdams Peak, 372 feet above the Illinois River. This is also where the Goat Cliff Trail ends. Take some time to enjoy the view, which includes birds flying below where you're standing on the high peak. Nearby plaques describe how the McAdams family influenced this area and how the Civilian Conservation Corps (see "History Lesson: Civilian Conservation Corps" sidebar) made its mark on this and other Illinois state parks.

Back at the junction, look for the blue blazes in the shape of arrows that signify the Ridge Trail, the trail heading southwest. The track goes steeply downhill through thick brush. The atmosphere is jungle-like and the trail is narrow. Enjoy the feeling of being alone in the world, of secluded isolation—but be sure to check for ticks once you're back at the parking lot, after brushing up against a lot of foliage along the way. The trail terminates just behind the visitor center.

A combination of natural and manmade stairs invites hikers to explore.

29 TWO RIVERS NATIONAL WILDLIFE REFUGE

BEFORE YOU GO
MAP On park website
CONTACT US Fish and Wildlife Service
GPS 38.968660° N, -90.543035° W
NOTES Accessible for some strollers; area closed mid-Oct. until Dec. to protect migratory birds (check website); bathrooms and water seasonally at trailhead

ABOUT THE HIKE
SEASON Year-round
DIFFICULTY Easy
LENGTH 3 miles roundtrip
HIGH POINT 510 feet
ELEVATION GAIN 280 feet

GETTING THERE
From Interstate 270 in north St. Louis County, take exit 31B to US Highway 367 north. Drive 4 miles. Continue north on US 67 and across the Clark Bridge to Alton, Illinois. Continue on US 67 west through downtown Alton, and then turn left to go north onto Illinois State Route 100, also known as the Great River Road. Drive 20 miles north to Scenic Drive. Turn left across the road from Pere Marquette State Park, and immediately left again, going 0.2 mile to the parking area.

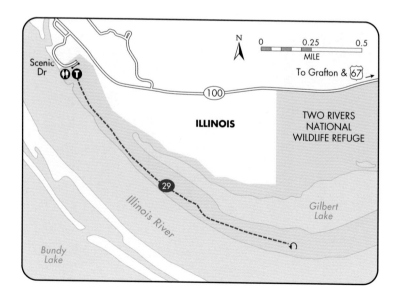

The river floodplain is fertile ground for animal tracks.

ON THE TRAIL

This is one of the best spots for wildlife viewing in the St. Louis area. On the banks of the Illinois River, you'll see your fill of birds of many varieties. In the woods around the trail, deer, raccoon, opossum, and even river otters call the area home year-round. If you're here in winter or early spring, stop by the Pere Marquette State Park visitor center across the road. If there are any bald eagle nests along the trail, the ranger there should be able to tell you where to look.

The trail here is easy, wide, and level, so it's a nice alternative to the steep grades at Pere Marquette. It's a good place for little kids to test their budding hiking skills, or for caregivers to push them in a jogging stroller.

This trail is located on one small sliver of the 9225-acre Two Rivers National Wildlife Refuge. Most of the refuge is between the Mississippi and Illinois rivers and borders the confluence, making the area a magnet for nearly

300 bird species. The combination of wetlands, open water, forests, and prairies makes for several different kinds of habitats and harbors a smorgasbord of food for the birds overwintering and passing through.

This hike starts at the northwest end of the Gilbert Lake Division of the wildlife refuge. From the parking lot, walk southeast toward the water and look for the wide gate and trailhead sign. The path makes its way between the Illinois River and Gilbert Lake, a shallow, marshy body of water that harbors many species of fish, amphibians, and bugs, so make sure to bring bug spray if you're here in spring or summer. Along this first stretch of trail are some of the trees that harbor bald eagle nests in the winter, plus the huge sycamores and hickories common to the region.

Starting around mile 0.6, watch to the left (north) to spot wildlife in the brush, darting in and out of the area near Gilbert Lake. Enjoy the walk along the path between the stands of huge trees. But keep one eye on the path, too. This bottomland soil is perfect for absorbing imprints from the myriad animals that pass through. Consult your guide to wildlife tracks to try to figure out what's been passing through recently.

At mile 1.5, a vehicle turnaround to the left of the path marks the spot to turn around to keep this hike to 3 miles.

BALD EAGLE VIEWING

The confluence of two of the nation's most significant waterways—the Mississippi and Missouri rivers—provides our region with the opportunity to view one of the most remarkable birds and our nation's symbol, the bald eagle.

Bald eagles are one of the country's great environmental success stories: they numbered in the hundreds of thousands when they became the national symbol in the 1700s, but dwindled to as few as 500 nesting pairs in the mid-twentieth century due to habitat loss and overuse of pesticides. They've since rebounded and now there are estimated to be about 70,000 bald eagles in North America.

Each winter the birds congregate at the confluence, where geology creates open waters that make for ideal fishing conditions for the majestic birds. Local naturalists and environmental groups gather at Columbia Bottom Conservation Area (hike 3) and the Old Chain of Rocks Bridge and set up scopes to allow better viewing of the birds. You can watch them rest in the trees on either side of the Mississippi or ride the ice floes as they watch for prey. Volunteers also provide warming tents and docent talks by experts from the Wild Bird Sanctuary in Valley Park.

Check with Great Rivers Greenway or the Missouri Department of Conservation for details on these events, which usually happen the first or second week of January.

The higher elevations at Pere Marquette State Park (hike 28) can also provide good places for eagle spotting.

A dusting of snow transforms the landscape

30 HORSESHOE LAKE STATE PARK

BEFORE YOU GO
   MAP On park website and at park office
   CONTACT Illinois Department of Natural Resources
   GPS 38.695097° N, -90.074413° W
   NOTES Accessible for jogging strollers; limited shade (hot in summer); bathrooms
      at trailhead

ABOUT THE HIKE
   SEASON Fall, winter, spring
   DIFFICULTY Easy
   LENGTH 3 miles loop
   HIGH POINT 445 feet
   ELEVATION GAIN 130 feet

GETTING THERE

From St. Louis, take Interstate 64 (known locally as "40") east to Illinois, and continue on I-55 north for 3 miles. Take exit 6 for State Route 111 toward Wood River and turn left (north) onto SR 111. In 3 miles, turn left (east) on Horseshoe Park, then follow the road 0.7 mile to the parking lot.

ON THE TRAIL

Horseshoe Lake is popular with birders and fishing enthusiasts, but it also has miles of trails where walkers and hikers can take a sun-kissed stroll. Walkers Island is a great location for spotting all kinds of fowl, plus deer, frogs, and tadpoles. The lake was created when levees were built along the Mississippi River to prevent flooding in the area, where farmers were trying to get established. But its history goes much farther into the past than that: on the north shore

LIGHTS OUT: BUDGET PROBLEMS

Horseshoe Lake was closed briefly in the spring of 2016 because the state was unable to pay the park's electric bill. A private donor paid the bill, allowing the park to reopen. And it has remained open as of this book's publication.

of the lake is evidence of the native culture that created the famous Cahokia Mounds site a few miles south of here (hike 31). This is a much smaller site—a suburb of Cahokia, so to speak—but important to archaeologists nonetheless.

From the parking lot, head south along the tree line to where the trail is carved out of the forest between the open field and the lake. Birds such as cardinals dart across the trail, and ducks swim along the edge of the island, just past the bushes to the left of the trail. Shortly after the half-mile mark, take a bridge over a seasonal stream, and at 1 mile the trail leads to a campground, which includes a bathroom, picnic tables, and playground.

A quarter mile past the campground, the trail enters a stand of mature trees, mostly sycamore. The trail continues through some slightly higher grasses and then through a gate to a dirt road that's more typical of the trail surface at Horseshoe Lake. At mile 1.8, jog to the right and cross a swampy area—don't worry, the trail surface is elevated slightly on mounded earth to keep feet and stroller wheels dry. This area is a good spot to look for frogs.

At mile 2.2, go around another gate, and hike along the tree line between forest and field. These fields on Walkers Island are ever-changing—some are managed by park naturalists to simulate the prairie that was once the dominant landscape in this area, so you may see them filled with shoulder-high grasses or decimated by controlled burns. Other fields are used by farmers who have temporary agricultural leases, growing beans and other crops. As you hike next to this field, the parking lot comes into view. At mile 2.7, turn right at a trail junction for a straight shot back to the parking lot.

31 CAHOKIA MOUNDS STATE HISTORIC SITE

BEFORE YOU GO
> **MAP** On agency website and at interpretive center
> **CONTACT** Illinois Historic Preservation Agency
> **GPS** 38.653530° N, -90.059660° W
> **NOTES** Accessible for most strollers; limited shade (hot in summer)

ABOUT THE HIKE
> **SEASON** Fall, winter, spring
> **DIFFICULTY** Easy
> **LENGTH** 3 miles loop
> **HIGH POINT** 480 feet
> **ELEVATION GAIN** 100 feet

GETTING THERE

From St. Louis, take Interstate 55 east and cross into Illinois. In 5.7 miles after entering Illinois, take exit 6 for State Route 111. Turn right onto SR 111, and then take an immediate left on Collinsville Road. Drive 2 miles, and turn right onto Ramey Street. Drive 0.2 mile to the interpretive center and museum parking lot.

ON THE TRAIL

Cahokia Mounds is well known among archaeologists as the site of remnants of the most sophisticated prehistoric civilization north of Mexico. In AD 1100, as many as 20,000 people lived on about 4000 acres here—a population larger than that of London at the time. Today you can explore the site of the Mississippian tribe's cultural and architectural achievements at this UNESCO-recognized World Heritage Site.

The land around Cahokia was first set aside in the early 1900s, when the State of Illinois started gradually acquiring parts of the park. The entire historic site is now 2200 acres in size.

Trails lead hikers to dozens of the mounds built by hand with millions of cubic tons of earth. You'll also experience re-creations of Woodhenges—circles of cedar posts placed to act as calendars. This walk will take you past some of the most important features of the historic site without overtaxing little legs.

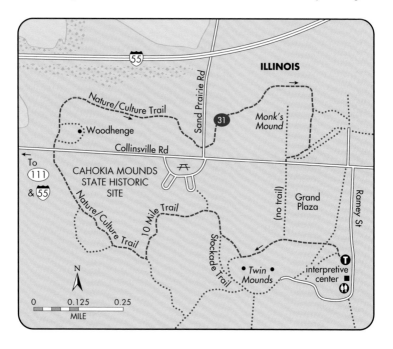

Walking toward Monk's Mound

Start your walk at the interpretive center, heading west on the 10 Mile Trail, signed in red. Many trails near the interpretive center are paved, and the rest of the trails are easy for jogging strollers. As you stroll past the Grand Plaza on your right and the Twin Mounds on your left, spot part of the stockade, a 2-mile long defensive wall made of upright logs. The trail then jogs northwest (right) at a junction at mile 0.4 and then north (right) at a junction at mile 0.5. Make left turns at mile 0.6 and 0.7, staying on the 10 Mile Trail as you pass the picnic area and cross Stockade Wall Trail. Turn right onto the Nature/Culture Trail, signed in green, at mile 0.8. Head north, taking two more right turns at miles 0.9 and 1.1. At mile 1.2, use caution when crossing Collinsville Road.

Just north of the road, check out the most complete re-creation of a Woodhenge at Cahokia. An interpretive sign shows how the Mississippians used these groupings of pillars to determine when solstices and equinoxes would take place.

Next the trail heads east for nearly a mile (bisected by a crossing of Sand Prairie Road at mile 1.8) through open fields, small stands of trees, and some smaller mounds, as you make your way toward the most impressive of the historic site's features: Monk's Mound, constructed to elevate the chief's home above the rest of the city. It rises to 100 feet, and was constructed by people who carried earth in baskets on their backs, 22 million cubic feet worth. Today, explorers can climb to the top via a series of steps at mile 2.5 of this hike. The view from the top of the mound includes downtown St. Louis and the Gateway Arch. After the climb, walk back across Collinsville Road (again being cautious of traffic) to the interpretive center, which has a number of detailed exhibits where adventurers of all ages can learn more about the original inhabitants of this land.

Note: It's best to avoid this hike in the summer, as there is very little shade. During cold or wet weather it becomes an excellent choice, though, because it's very flat and there are no slippery rocks.

32 ELDON HAZLET STATE RECREATION AREA: CHEROKEE TRAIL

BEFORE YOU GO
MAP On park website and at headquarters
CONTACT Illinois Department of Natural Resources
GPS 38.668076° N, -89.311815° W
NOTES Path to cemetery is wheelchair accessible; trails closed part of fall and winter (check website); pit toilets at trailhead

ABOUT THE HIKE
SEASON Year-round
DIFFICULTY Easy
LENGTH 3 miles loop
HIGH POINT 511 feet
ELEVATION GAIN 80 feet

GETTING THERE
From St. Louis, take Interstate 64 (known locally as "40") east into Illinois. Take exit 19B to US Highway 50 east, and follow the signs for US 50 for 28 miles. Turn left (north) onto State Route 127, and in 3 miles turn right (east) on Hazlet Park Road. In 0.9 mile turn left to stay on Hazlet Park Road. Drive 1.5 miles to the park entrance. Veer right (south) and turn left immediately to stay on Hazlet Park Road. Drive 0.5 mile and turn left and immediately right to continue on Hazlet Park Road. Drive 0.4 mile to the trailhead at the end of the road.

The cemetery on Carlyle Lake was established by the area's first European settlers.

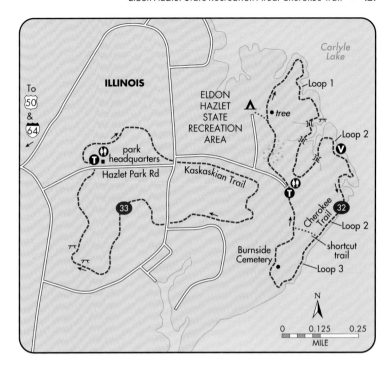

ON THE TRAIL

Eldon Hazlet State Recreation Area is on the west shore of huge Carlyle Lake, the largest manmade lake in Illinois. Two miles wide and ten miles long, it is popular with boaters, and its shores feature campgrounds and cabins. The park offers 9 miles of trails, from the deep forests to the waterfront to prairies.

The Cherokee Trail comprises three loops that total 3 miles. To start with Loop 1, first head north from the parking lot, just past the outhouses. The trail here is a wide, mowed grassy track between two stands of trees for 0.2 mile. Turn left almost immediately at a junction to start on Loop 1. A sign here points the way for Loops 2 and 3 also, but it may be in disrepair and therefore difficult to see.

Along the loop, notice several posts with numbers on them from an old tree identification program. Unfortunately, many of the posts are missing, and some of the trees they called out have fallen since the markers were erected. Park staff hope to find volunteers to revive the program and create new interpretive brochures.

After 0.25 mile, the trail heads past a swamp, where observers can spot frogs hopping in and around the water. You may feel like you're in Florida's

Everglades here, but there's no need to worry about encountering any alligators on this trail.

Just past the swamp at mile 0.35 is a junction where the trail to a youth campground heads to the left; turn right to keep on the Loop 1 trail. Watch for the remnants of a large tree. The burls, almost as wide as the trunk itself, make it look like the tree was enveloped by lava from an ancient volcano.

At 0.6 mile, catch your first view of the lake. The lake truly appears huge here. A bench provides a good spot to take in the view, or venture a little farther down the trail to an area that's good for picking your way down the trailside and splashing in the stream that empties into the lake.

Continue on the trail, crossing three streams with footbridges. The trail gets more faint through this, the most wild section of the Cherokee Trail loops. The forest is dense, with downed trees across the trail in several spots. Have a map handy and, if possible, a GPS tracking app on your smartphone.

At mile 1.1, return to the junction of Loop 1 and Loop 2. Turn left to continue your journey through the forest on Loop 2. Cross more creeks and enjoy views of the lake as you stay relatively near the shore. At mile 1.6, there's another lovely lake overlook. Pass a shortcut trail on the right, and continue on Loop 3.

At mile 2.1 is the Burnside Cemetery, a family plot for some of the earliest Anglo settlers of this land. Ask your kids to think back to what it must have been like to live in the mid-1800s. How did the pioneers cook food? Light their houses at night? Travel to visit other farms?

From the cemetery, take the paved path to walk a third of a mile back to the parking lot.

33 ELDON HAZLET STATE RECREATION AREA: KASKASKIAN TRAIL

BEFORE YOU GO
MAP On park website and at park headquarters
CONTACT Illinois Department of Natural Resources
GPS 38.668789° N, -89.325039° W
NOTES Accessible for strollers; bathrooms and water in park headquarters (open sporadically); trails closed part of fall and winter (check website)

ABOUT THE HIKE
SEASON Fall, winter, spring
DIFFICULTY Easy
LENGTH 2.5 miles loop
HIGH POINT 540 feet
ELEVATION GAIN 250 feet

GETTING THERE
From St. Louis, take Interstate 64 (known locally as "40") east into Illinois. Take exit 19B to US Highway 50 east, and follow the signs for US 50 for 28 miles. Turn left (north) onto State Route 127, and in 3 miles turn right (east)

Winter reveals trees' true shapes.

on Hazlet Park Road. In 0.9 mile turn left to stay on Hazlet Park Road. Drive 1.5 miles to the park entrance. Veer right (south) and turn left immediately to stay on Hazlet Park Road. Turn left into the park headquarters parking lot.

ON THE TRAIL

Eldon Hazlet State Recreation Area is best known for the summertime fun of its campgrounds on the shores of huge Carlyle Lake, but it also has miles of trails exploring forests and prairies. The Kaskaskian Trail explores the center of the park and is almost completely flat, so it's great for beginners.

Despite the level elevation profile of this hike, there's a lot of scenic variety, and little kids will love having plenty to look at while not working too hard. There are also opportunities to bail out by taking a park road back to the parking lot if anyone completely melts down.

Start the hike from the parking lot at the park headquarters, and head northwest through a field and into the woods. There are a number of unmarked side trails of various sizes, used by hunters during managed hunts, but it is easy to stay on the main path. For the first half mile the path wanders through the forest, exploring stands of evergreen, oak, and sycamore. Note also that there is a great deal of nonnative, invasive honeysuckle (see "A Pretty Plague" sidebar in hike 25), as in many Illinois and Missouri parks.

At mile 0.6, cross the park road and continue east. Look for the brown hiking icon sign. The trail continues its winding way through the forest as it heads east toward the lake. At 1 mile, turn right at a sign that indicates a group camping site to the left. Just a tenth of a mile later, watch for the arrow signs that direct you to stay to the right as you turn back west. The trail dips in and out of the shade for a stretch around mile 1.2; then walk over a short bridge over a shallow wash.

The trail crosses the road near cottages at mile 1.4. A quarter mile later, watch for a stand of evergreen trees that covers the ground in needles over a short stretch of trail. Ask your kids if they can feel how much softer the trail is underfoot when it's covered with the leaves. At mile 1.7, find the first of two benches in this final mile of the trail. At 2 miles, turn right at another signed junction. At 2.4 miles, reach the field across from the parking lot. Follow the mowed trail (avoiding the spiky grasses in the field) to return to the parking lot.

34 STEMLER CAVE WOODS NATURE PRESERVE

BEFORE YOU GO
MAP On park website and at trailhead
CONTACT Illinois Department of Natural Resources
GPS 38.465967° N, -90.154468° W
NOTES No camping; dogs prohibited; trails very muddy and slippery the day after a hard rain

ABOUT THE HIKE
SEASON Fall, winter, spring
DIFFICULTY Easy to moderate
LENGTH 2.3 miles loop
HIGH POINT 720 feet
ELEVATION GAIN 380 feet

Resting trailside at Stemler Cave Woods

GETTING THERE

From Interstate 255 in south St. Louis County, drive southeast across the Mississippi River into Illinois. Take exit 6 to State Route 3 south. Drive 1 mile and turn left (southeast) onto North Main Street. Drive 1.5 miles and turn left (north) onto East Cherry Street. Drive 0.5 mile and turn left (north) onto Bluffside Road. Drive 2 miles and turn right (east) onto Stemler Road. Drive 1 mile and turn right into the parking lot.

ON THE TRAIL

Stemler Cave Woods is only half an hour from St. Louis, but it feels like it's out in the middle of nowhere. The nature preserve is only 200 acres, but its old-growth forest, prairies, and sinkholes make it a fascinating and easy trek through the woods.

This land, set aside in the 1980s, is named for the family of German immigrants that lived on it for generations before donating it to the state. Today it is owned and managed by the Illinois Department of Natural Resources, but it's cared for in large part by Friends of Stemler Cave Woods, one of a number of conservation groups that have emerged to help maintain natural areas in the face of the state's budget woes. Its trails are wide and relatively level, and eleven interpretive signs give plenty of opportunity to keep up kids' interest as they walk.

From the small parking lot, walk past the kiosk and turn left. The first sign you see describes the karst geology that defines most of the southwest Illinois

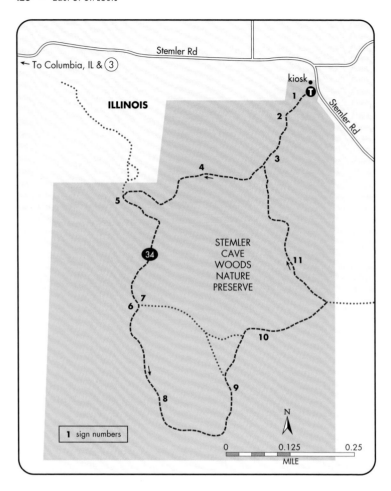

and southeast Missouri hikes in this book. In a karst landscape, the underlying rock is soft, producing a lot of caves and sinkholes.

At 0.2 mile, read the second interpretive sign, about sinkholes. Shortly after that, the third sign emphasizes protection of our water sources, which are particularly susceptible to contamination in karst areas. Ask kids what they think some sources of water pollution might be.

At mile 0.4, turn right at the junction, to take the trail counterclockwise. Here the trail becomes even more wide and level. Sign 4, at mile 0.6, describes the variety of animal species present in Stemler Cave itself, which is closed to the public.

Watch for sign 5 at mile 0.8, which also marks a junction with a longer trail. Take a left to stay on the interpretive trail. Sign 6 is also at a junction, where you turn right. (Here you could take a left to cut southeast for a shorter 1.5-mile hike.) Do check out the sign, and take a few minutes to explore the amphibian pond just 30 feet or so down the shortcut trail.

At mile 1.3, sign 8 talks about the wildlife you might see along the trail. A tenth of a mile later, the trail takes a hard left, and then does so again in another tenth of a mile. Turn right at the junction at mile 1.6, and right again at mile 1.7, to stay on the main loop. Watch for the hard left around mile 2, moving northeast toward home.

Sign 11 is just off the trail at mile 2.1, in front of a sinkhole pond that, for now, is filled with water. The trail returns to the first junction at mile 2.2, so take a right to return to the parking lot.

35 SALT LICK POINT LAND AND WATER RESERVE

BEFORE YOU GO
MAP On park website and at trailhead
CONTACT Village of Valmeyer
GPS 38.303538° N, -90.309098° W
NOTES Obey signs that prohibit climbing in caves or mine shafts and on bluffs; trails inaccessible for wheelchairs and strollers

ABOUT THE HIKE
SEASON Fall, winter, spring
DIFFICULTY Moderate to difficult
LENGTH 3 miles loop
HIGH POINT 805 feet
ELEVATION GAIN 650 feet

RAISING VALMEYER

Just a few minutes' drive from Salt Lick Point is a historic oddity: the old town of Valmeyer, and 2 miles up the hill, the new Valmeyer. In the great flood of 1993, 90 percent of the buildings in Valmeyer were destroyed. Instead of rebuilding in the path of future floods, the town decided to move up 400 feet in elevation.

From Salt Lick Point, drive south on Bluff Road to Main Street and turn right. Notice that a few buildings were rebuilt, but mostly there are streets with no houses lining them. Then turn around and head east on State Route 156 about two miles. Turn left on Meyer Avenue to drive through new Valmeyer. There's a gas station and a small restaurant in the twenty-year-old town. It's fascinating to see the old and new towns and contemplate the decision to move the whole town out of harm's way.

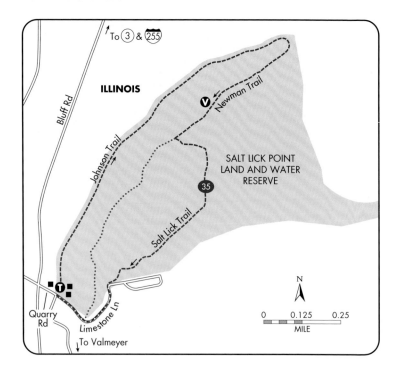

GETTING THERE

From Interstate 255 in south St. Louis County, drive southeast across the Mississippi River into Illinois, and take exit 6 to State Route 3 south. Drive 0.3 mile and turn right on Palmer Road. In 0.2 mile, it turns into Bluff Road. Continue 13.5 miles and turn left onto Quarry Road, then immediately left into the parking lot at the trailhead.

ON THE TRAIL

Mine shafts, bluff views, and secluded forests make this hike a unique combination of sights and sounds. Interpretive signs along the way help kids and adults alike learn more about this corner of Illinois.

The hike starts near a cluster of old buildings remaining from when the land was quarried. Head northeast on the Johnson Trail, walking through the forest on the dirt service road. After a tenth of a mile, look up to the right to spot big rectangular holes in the cliffs—the openings of old mine shafts. Watch for wooden trail signs on the trees that show mileage and an abbreviation for the trail, like JT .3.

At mile 0.3, encounter huge boulders that dropped off the cliff as the limestone wore away. Ask kids if they can guess how long the boulders have been there. At 0.5 mile, point out some of the handiwork of the volunteers that maintain this preserve: handwritten signs identifying the wildflowers that this area is known for. Continue on the wide path through the forest, with fallow fields visible to the left through the trees. At mile 0.9, on the right the bluffs are closer to the trail, rising dramatically from the forest.

At mile 1.2, turn right at the TRAIL sign and then right again, following the signs for the Newman Trail to Salt Lick Point. The trail heads straight up the hill from the bottomland and is very steep, but only for a few hundred feet. After it levels out, meander through the forest, the bluffs at your right, a gorge with a seasonal creek running through it on the left. At mile 1.5, the trail steepens again until around mile 1.6, where you turn right on a very short side trail to a vista point at Bandits Glade. Take this vista trail, making sure everyone is obeying the signs that advise staying back from the cliff. After returning from this side trail, hike another third of a mile to the junction where the Newman Trail meets the Salt Lick Trail. Turn left on the Salt Lick Trail, and take a gentle downhill through the forest on a wide, pleasant path. (Turning right leads you on a slightly shorter but steeper path back to the parking lot.) Another signed

Salt Lick Point has glades, forests, and scenic views.

glade appears, with an explanation of the term: a treeless area with soils that are drier than the surrounding land, allowing some rock to be exposed.

The trail gets steep again at 2.5 miles, so watch your step, especially when it's muddy. At mile 2.6, peek around the barbed wire fence into an old mine shaft; through the shaft, you can hear trucks rumbling down the road on the other side of the hill. At 2.7 miles the Salt Lick Trail ends, so continue along Limestone Lane to get back to the parking lot. Look to the right to view a couple of old shafts where you can see straight through the hill.

36 FULTS HILL PRAIRIE NATURE PRESERVE

BEFORE YOU GO
MAP On park website
CONTACT Illinois Department of Natural Resources
GPS 38.155865° N, -90.189744° W
NOTES No camping; inaccessible for wheelchairs and strollers; no bathrooms or water

ABOUT THE HIKE
SEASON Fall, winter, spring
DIFFICULTY Moderate
LENGTH 1.5 miles loop
HIGH POINT 760 feet
ELEVATION GAIN 390 feet

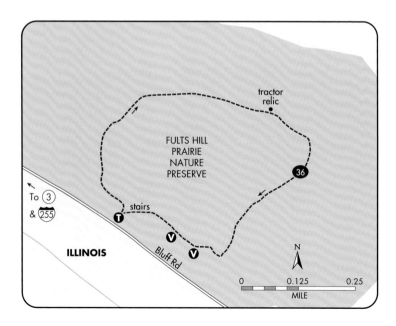

A tractor abandoned decades ago has become part of the landscape.

GETTING THERE

From Interstate 255 in south St. Louis County, drive southeast across the Mississippi River into Illinois, and take exit 6 to State Route 3 south. Drive 0.3 mile, and turn right on Palmer Road, which turns into Bluff Road in 0.2 mile. Follow signs to stay on Bluff Road for 41 miles. Watch for the preserve sign on the left and turn into the parking lot.

ON THE TRAIL

Fults Hill Prairie Nature Preserve is a tiny preserve—only about 500 acres—but it packs a punch, with broad views of the Mississippi River Valley. It provides one of the best examples in the area of the upland prairies that dominated Illinois before widespread agriculture. In 1986, it was recognized federally by the US Department of the Interior as a National Natural Landmark.

From the small parking area, let the kids make the first decision: head to the left to start the hike with a steep hill, or go right for stairs—a lot of stairs.

This hike as described here starts by heading up the hill to the left. In this direction, the trail begins with a steady, steep uphill climb through thick mixed forest, then into a grassy glade, then back into forest and back into grass again. After a quarter mile, the trail levels out and becomes a pleasant walk through the forest. At 0.65 mile, watch the forest to your left. See if the kids can spy an old relic of a tractor, complete with a hook for pulling it by horse. It's not going anywhere anymore, though, since several trees have grown through and around it, consuming sections of the metal wheel parts.

After another half mile, at mile 1.1, the trail heads downhill. Keep little ones close, as there is a steep drop-off. The next tenth of a mile offers a few overlooks. Carefully step out onto the rocks and check out the views of the nearby bluffs and the hills on the Missouri side of the valley.

At 1.4 miles, have everyone count the stairs that lead back to the parking lot.

37 PINEY CREEK RAVINE STATE NATURAL AREA

BEFORE YOU GO
MAP At the trailhead
CONTACT Illinois Department of Natural Resources
GPS 37.890474° N, -89.638230° W
NOTES Inaccessible for strollers and wheelchairs; rocky trails can be dangerous when icy; no bathrooms or water

ABOUT THE HIKE
SEASON Spring, summer, fall
DIFFICULTY Difficult
LENGTH 2 miles loop
HIGH POINT 580 feet
ELEVATION GAIN 190 feet

GETTING THERE
From Interstate 255 in south St. Louis County, drive southeast into Illinois, and take exit 6 to State Route 3 south. Drive 25 miles, and continue east on SR 154. Drive 19 miles, and turn right at SR 4. Drive 6 miles, and turn left (east) onto SR 150. Drive 2.5 miles, and turn right on Sparta Street, which turns into Rockcastle Road in 0.5 mile. Drive 3.7 miles, and turn right onto Wine Hill Road, then immediately left onto County Road 5. Drive 2.4 miles, and turn left onto County Farm Road, which becomes Murphysboro Road. Drive 1.7 miles, and turn right onto Piney Creek Road, which is gravel. Drive just over 1.5 miles, and turn left into the gravel parking lot with the sign for the natural area.

ON THE TRAIL
This hidden-away preserve is best known for a wall of prehistoric rock art that constitutes the largest such grouping in Illinois. But there's much more to this

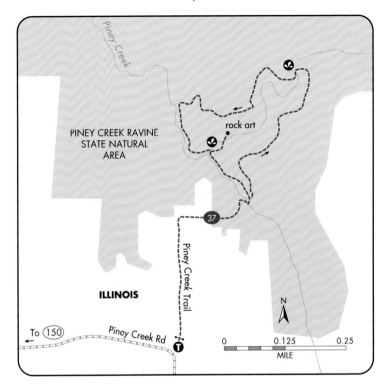

hike than that: spectacular rock formations, diverse natural environments, waterfalls, and pools for splashing on a hot summer day.

Start by walking from the parking lot around the gate onto a wide path between two pastures. You're likely to hear cows mooing on this quarter-mile straight and level path to the boundary of the preserve.

Head downhill to your first crossing of Piney Creek. Watch for the bright green posts that mark the trail, especially helpful at creek crossings and when the woods get thick above the ravine.

Just up the hill from the stream crossing, at 0.4 mile, is the start of the loop. Head to the right and walk the loop counterclockwise to see amazing rock formations created by the creek before you get to the human-created rock art.

The trail traverses the top of the ravine for nearly half a mile through forest that contains a mix of deciduous trees and native pine, which are rarely found in Illinois. Then the trail descends into the ravine for another creek crossing at mile 0.8. Take some extra time here to enjoy this remarkable spot, where dramatic rock formations and pools have been created by the bends in the creek.

This rock art is thought to be between 500 and 1500 years old.

The creek makes a sharp bend to your right here, and the trail heads uphill and to the left. Make your way about half a mile through thick forest before descending again and skirting the bottom of some cliffs. Take care if you get close to the cliffs; the wind creates deep piles of leaves here, and you may think you're stepping on solid ground when your foot is actually about to sink into two feet of dried leaves!

Around mile 1.25, watch for the side trail to the rock art, on the left. Signs guide you a short way through the woods to the cliffs, where a large interpretive sign explains what some of the etchings and paintings signify. Historians believe that some describe religious visions, or convey information about events and land claims. Some are drawings, and others are carvings pounded into the rock using chisels and other tools.

European settlers discovered these beautiful and fascinating creations in the 1870s, and this became a popular place for outings. Unfortunately, many decided to add their own drawings to the walls, damaging some the centuries-old native work. Be sure to note that it is now illegal to deface the cliff and images, which are believed to be 500 to 1500 years old.

After you've taken in the ancient art, retrace your steps to the main trail. Once you are back on the Piney Creek Trail, completing the loop, you'll need to cross the creek again, which might mean getting your feet wet, since the stream is wider and deeper here. Use caution, take your time, and enjoy the scenery. Less than a quarter mile later, you'll leave the loop behind and head back to the preserve boundary and the parking lot.

Note: There's likely to be a fair amount of mud in some parts of the hike, and the creek at one of the crossings can be up to your ankles, so be prepared with a change of clothes and dry shoes waiting in the car.

38 SHAWNEE NATIONAL FOREST: LITTLE GRAND CANYON TRAIL

BEFORE YOU GO
MAP On park website and at trailhead
CONTACT US Forest Service
GPS 37.680515° N, -89.394919° W
NOTES Bathrooms and water at trailhead; not recommended for parents carrying children in packs; rocks are slippery when frozen and parts of trail are underwater after heavy rain

ABOUT THE HIKE
SEASON Year-round
DIFFICULTY Difficult
LENGTH 3.2 miles loop
HIGH POINT 750 feet
ELEVATION GAIN 750 feet

GETTING THERE
From State Route 149 in Murphysboro, Illinois, turn left on South 20th Street. Drive 1.7 miles, and then continue onto Town Creek Road for 0.7 mile. Turn left (south) onto Hickory Ridge Road and drive 6 miles, following signs to stay on this road. Turn right onto Little Grand Canyon Road and drive 0.2 mile to the parking lot.

ON THE TRAIL
This dramatic hike, known as the Little Grand Canyon Trail, takes you down one canyon slot, across a river bottom, and up another slot—it's hard to say which canyon is more grand. This National Natural Landmark was carved by erosion out of the sandstone Shawnee Hills near the Big Muddy River, which is part of the Mississippi River floodplain.

This hike involves a lot of scrambling on slippery rocks, so don't try it with children who have to be carried in packs. And check the forecast before you go—icy temperatures will make the rocks too slippery, and heavy rains will make the river bottom between the canyons impassable. One final caveat: dogs with short legs may need help getting up certain sections of the trail, especially the areas with steeper steps.

Little Grand Canyon lives up to its name.

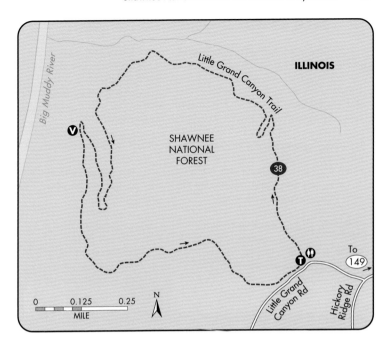

Take the trail downhill from the parking lot (farthest from the bathrooms), and walk on a gravelly path for about half a mile. The trail is blazed with white diamonds and is mostly well marked. At the half-mile mark, the trail turns sharply left to head straight down the canyon slot. Keep an eye out for the steps carved out of the rocks by the Civilian Conservation Corps in the 1930s; they're a big help, but there will also be times when you will just have to hop down or even slide a bit. Be sure to turn around often to take in the view up the canyon. The rock formations are breathtaking, and the moss that colors parts of the walls green provides a striking and beautiful contrast.

After the 300-foot climb down the slot, the trail turns sharply left and then right, following the cliffs along a creek that flows into the Big Muddy River. Here is easier footing, as well as constant views of the remarkable 100-foot-tall cliffs. At about one mile, the trail crosses a small creek and the path can be a bit hard to find. Take a minute to orient yourself, and watch for the existing blazes. Stay close to the cliffs and watch for the gaps in the trees to follow the trail, especially where streamlets cross the trail.

At 1.4 miles, the trail veers left (south) and in between two sets of cliffs, soon climbing again into the second slot. Some sections are very steep, so younger kids might need a boost. This section, too, lives up to the "Grand Canyon" moniker. Stop often to catch your breath and take in the view.

GREAT GETAWAY: SHAWNEE NATIONAL FOREST

The Shawnee National Forest comprises two swaths of land in Southern Illinois, arguably housing some of the most spectacular hiking in the region; trail names like Garden of the Gods and Little Grand Canyon don't disappoint. Giant City State Park may be the most beautiful and fun state park in the region. It has miles of trails, fun climbing walls, and some of the most spectacular rock formations around.

Lodging: Carbondale, the biggest town around and home of Southern Illinois University, is your base of operations. You can find dozens of hotels at all price points, as well as grocery stores and restaurants. There are many vacation homes all over the forest area, for rent via the internet: try searching for "vacation rentals."

Camping: Giant City State Park, just twenty minutes south of Carbondale, has a spacious campground with 85 sites for cars and trailers and a smaller site for walk-ins. Shawnee National Forest has seven campgrounds scattered throughout its 286,000 acres. There are several private campgrounds as well. Lake Glendale is centrally located and has about 60 campsites.

Activities: There is a wide variety of fun things to do in the area.

Dungeons and Dragons Park, Carbondale: Officially known as Jeremy Rochman Memorial Park, it was created by a local businessman after the tragic death of his teen son. Jeremy loved playing Dungeons and Dragons, so his father created a playground with life-size dragons and wizards and a huge castle play structure complete with hidden passageways.

Swimming: Lake Glendale Recreation Area has a huge lake with a cordoned-off swimming area for kids of all ages. Bring a canoe or paddleboard for extra fun.

For history buffs: The Pope County Courthouse in the town of Golconda was known for holding runaway slaves who'd been caught along the Underground Railroad. Other sites deep in the forest harbor terrain that runaways could conceal themselves in.

At mile 2, the trail emerges from the canyon at an overlook of the river valley. From here it traverses the bluff high above the canyon and the river, with great views all along the path, especially in winter. Turn eastward for the final mile, a level, relaxing stroll through the forest all the way back to the parking lot.

39 GIANT CITY STATE PARK: GIANT CITY NATURE TRAIL

BEFORE YOU GO

MAP On park website and at park office on Giant City Road
CONTACT Illinois Department of Natural Resources
GPS 37.595606° N, -89.188734° W
NOTES Inaccessible for wheelchairs and strollers

ABOUT THE HIKE

SEASON Year-round
DIFFICULTY Easy to moderate
LENGTH 1.2 miles loop
HIGH POINT 750 feet
ELEVATION GAIN 250 feet

The "streets" on Giant City Nature Trail look like they were carved by humans.

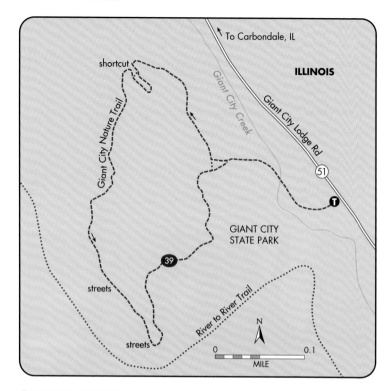

GETTING THERE

From Carbondale, Illinois, head east on East Walnut Street to South Giant City Road, and turn right (south). Drive 9.7 miles (passing the main entrance to Giant City State Park at 9.4 miles), and turn right onto South Church Road. Drive 0.3 mile, and turn left on Stonefort Road. Drive 0.3 mile, then take the first left onto Giant City Lodge Road (Route 51). Drive 0.2 mile and turn right into the parking lot for the trailhead.

ON THE TRAIL

This nature trail shows off the main attraction at this park, the namesake Giant City streets, formed by millennia of earthquakes and erosion. It meanders among huge boulders, scenic forests, and the unique features of the "streets."

The formations on this trail are known as Makanda sandstone. Blocks of the stone larger than houses slid down the hill over the centuries after being undercut by Giant City Creek. The blocks settled close to each other, creating city "streets" that look as if they were carved out by man. The trail itself is short, but allow at least an hour to see and explore the cliffs, boulders, and rock formations.

Start your hike by heading up a steep but short hill to the main loop at 0.1 mile, walking across the shallow creek. Follow the arrows to the right, immediately noticing a lot of boulders and rock piles to climb and explore. All throughout this trail there are routes for scrambling to suit the smallest walkers and ones to challenge big kids. At mile 0.3, watch for a shortcut trail to the right that makes for a quick scramble of just 50 feet or so over a rugged outcrop, meeting up again just a hundred feet or so along the main trail.

Continue along the trail, passing dramatic cliffs that loom over the trail to the left. At mile 0.6, enter the "streets." You'll see graffiti from past visitors across the decades; remind kids that it's now considered unacceptable to carve your name or messages into these natural monuments. Allow everyone plenty of time to scramble and explore. You'll find yourself and your kids scrambling and climbing and oohing and aahing in wonder at these incredible natural structures.

Next the trail heads uphill, continuing to wind around more spots for climbing and scrambling. At mile 0.9, it crosses a spur to the River to River Trail, a 160-mile trail stretching from the Ohio to the Mississippi rivers, hitting some of the most special sites in Illinois. Then it reaches the top of the hill and crosses a service road before heading down the hill. At mile 1.1 take the trail to the right to get back to the parking lot.

Across the street from the Giant City Nature Trail parking lot is a short trail that leads to Devil's Standtable. This oft-photographed geologic oddity was created by the vagaries of erosion and the relative hardness of the various kinds of rocks being eroded across the layers of land. Just cross the street and look for the trail signs, heading right to see it for yourself.

40 GIANT CITY STATE PARK: TRILLIUM TRAIL

BEFORE YOU GO
MAP On park website and at park office on Giant City Road
CONTACT Illinois Department of Natural Resources
GPS 37.624834° N, -89.201953° W
NOTES Inaccessible for wheelchairs and strollers; bring a flashlight for peeking into caves and slots

ABOUT THE HIKE
SEASON Year-round
DIFFICULTY Moderate to difficult
LENGTH 2 miles loop
HIGH POINT 650 feet
ELEVATION GAIN 300 feet

GETTING THERE
From Carbondale, Illinois, head south on Illinois Avenue and turn left on Pleasant Hill Road. Drive 0.5 mile, and turn right (south) on Springer Ridge

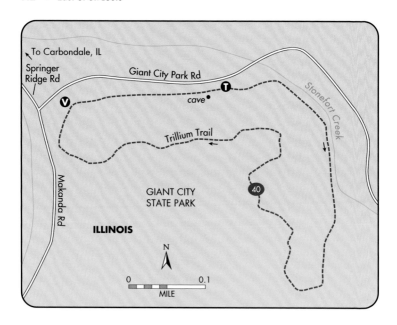

Road. Drive 5.6 miles, turn left (east) onto Giant City Park Road, and in 0.2 mile turn right into the parking lot.

ON THE TRAIL

The Trillium Trail is less crowded than the Giant City Nature Trail, but might be even more scenic. The sandstone cliffs that line the trail are awe-inspiring; the first time I hiked this trail, I lost count of how many times people in our group looked around and cried out, "This is amazing!"

This trail is in the Fern Rocks Nature Preserve, a part of the state park set aside because of its exceptional natural features, including the soaring sandstone bluffs and the plant life, including two endangered varieties of wildflower.

Geologists estimate that the bluffs are about 250 million years old. Watch for reddish-brown lines and waves in the rock; these are caused by iron in the water.

To start the clockwise hike, head uphill into a lush forest. Ferns decorate the cliffs to your right, sometimes growing right out of the rock. Dozens of species of plants are able to take root on these damp north-facing cliffs with just a small amount of organic matter. The cliffs visible just off the trail are an amazing way to start the hike, but they are just a taste of what's to come.

The trail curves southeast and south along Stonefort Creek, with more cliffs along the right. At 0.2 mile, close to the creek, you'll find some of the most vibrant wildflower diversity of just about any hike around. This moist

The Trillium Trail is a bouldering dream come true.

and moderately sunny breeding ground makes a colorful show if you're lucky enough to be here in the spring.

As you continue on the trail, watch for more places to climb and scramble. The pointy knobs and smooth divots in the sandstone make for natural climbing holds, though rope climbing is not allowed in this particular location (visit park headquarters for information on where climbing is allowed). There are a lot of low rocks for younger scramblers, too.

At mile 0.8, the trail starts to climb. Some stone steps have been set into the hillside, thanks to the efforts of the Civilian Conservation Corps (see "History Lesson: Civilian Conservation Corps" sidebar in hike 28). The climb finishes with wooden steps built against the hillside. Next, the trail journeys through the forest atop the sandstone bluff for about a half mile, with views of the bluffs across the road and of other parts of the park. At mile 1.5, the trail descends. The cliffs and rock formations continue to delight along this section; watch for a great cave just before you get back to the parking lot.

Opposite: *Chatting with friends is one of the best parts of a group hike.*

41 CUIVRE RIVER STATE PARK: LAKESIDE TRAIL

BEFORE YOU GO
MAP On park website
CONTACT Missouri State Parks Department
GPS 39.031626° N, -90.918263° W
NOTES Bathrooms and water seasonally at trailhead and dock parking lot; fishing allowed in the lake (stocked with bass and catfish)

ABOUT THE HIKE
SEASON Fall, winter, spring
DIFFICULTY Moderate
LENGTH 3.5 miles loop
HIGH POINT 580 feet
ELEVATION GAIN 120 feet

GETTING THERE
From Interstate 70 west of St. Louis, take exit 210 for US Highway 61 north. Drive 12 miles and turn right (east) on State Route 47. Drive 3 miles and turn left (north) on SR 147. Drive 1 mile and turn right (north) on Walker Road. Drive 2 miles and turn left (west) on Overlook Drive. Drive 0.2 mile and turn right (northwest) onto Midway Drive. Drive 0.5 mile and turn left into the beach parking lot.

Preschoolers often have bursts of energy on the trail—and sometimes they beg to be carried a few minutes later.

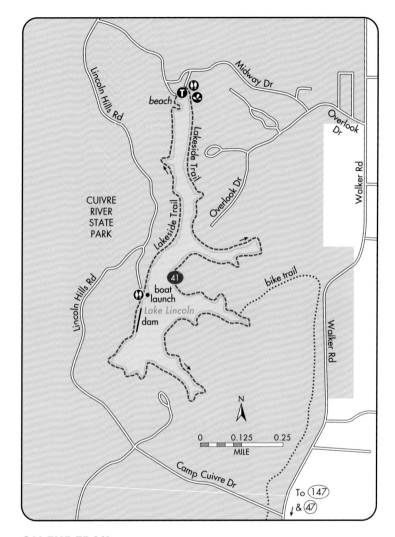

ON THE TRAIL

Cuivre River State Park offers a remarkable wilderness and recreation experience across 6400 acres just an hour from St. Louis. Camping, backpacking, fishing, and boating are available in addition to day hiking. The Lakeside Trail skirts 55-acre Lake Lincoln's entire shore, offering views of the lake, of course, plus verdant valleys and forests. Beavers are busy here, with many of the lakeside trees showing evidence of their handiwork. Watch the water: if you're lucky you'll see one swimming in the lake.

This trail has little shade, but if you brave it in the summer, you can cool off at the end with a dip in the lake, since the parking lot is next to the beach.

From the trailhead go southeast to take the green-blazed Lakeside Trail loop clockwise. Along this first stretch of trail, you can see stairs leading up the hill to the campground. This section along the lake's longest finger is mostly in sun as it hugs tightly to the shore. After 0.75 mile, the trail jogs east along the next finger of the reservoir. Although it also follows the water's edge here, this valley is fairly narrow and so provides some shade.

Cuivre River State Park is considered by many to be a taste of the Ozarks in central Missouri. Whereas most of this area north of Interstate 70 is relatively flat, the Cuivre River parkland has some of the natural features that southern Missouri is famous for, like bluffs, springs, and sinkholes. Lake Lincoln is man-made, but start watching around mile 1 for attributes that look more like the trails south of here, such as rocky outcrops.

At mile 1.1 the trail circles back to the main part of the lake. Your young companions may find that this is a good place for yelling and hearing their echoes across the valley. The trail soon jogs east again, tracing the second finger of the lake.

The trail continues with a similar feel as it winds around the next finger of the lake at mile 2, and then around the southwestern tip. Reach a junction with a bike trail blazed in orange at mile 2.3; follow the green blazes to the right, toward the main part of the lake. As the trail heads back north, it crosses the dam that created the lake at mile 2.8. At the dam the trail jogs west and uses a bridge to cross the spillway. During this part of the trail, you may come across some short but steep drops right next to the trail, so keep a close eye on small children.

After the bridge, go uphill and walk past the boat launch at 2.9 miles. As you traverse the final three-quarters of a mile, the trail can be very narrow, so use caution. You'll soon be able to see the parking lot and beach.

42 CUIVRE RIVER STATE PARK: LONE SPRING TRAIL

BEFORE YOU GO
 MAP On park website and at park office
 CONTACT Missouri State Parks Department
 GPS 39.065736° N, -90.932786° W
 NOTES Inaccessible for strollers and wheelchairs; bathrooms and water at park
  office and other locations

ABOUT THE HIKE
 SEASON Year-round
 DIFFICULTY Moderate to difficult
 LENGTH 3.5 miles loop
 HIGH POINT 700 feet
 ELEVATION GAIN 420 feet

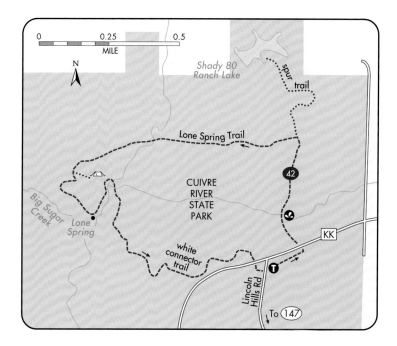

GETTING THERE

From Interstate 70 west of St. Louis, take exit 210 for US Highway 61 north. Drive 12 miles and turn right (east) onto State Route 47. Drive 3 miles and turn left (north) on SR 147, where you'll see a sign. Drive 2 miles and turn right (north) on Lincoln Hills Road (the park office and bathrooms will be on your left as you make this turn). Drive about 6 miles to the small parking area just south of State Highway KK.

ON THE TRAIL

This section of Cuivre River State Park is a favorite among backpackers because of its picturesque campsite and nearby perennial spring. It's also great for day hikers, since it features beautiful scenery, various types of trail and forest, and relatively few difficult sections.

From the parking lot, take the trail east for a few hundred feet on mowed grass through some trees and alongside a meadow. Carefully cross the highway to continue onto the north section of the trail. Lone Spring Trail is blazed in yellow and well signed, with yellow blazes visible wherever you are on the trail.

This portion of the trail is in a designated wild area, which the state defines as a park segment of 1000 acres or more that shows little human impact and provides great opportunity for solitude. As you head north, the traffic noise

Kids of all ages can't seem to resist throwing rocks into streams and ponds.

from the highway fades quickly, and it's obvious as you walk through quiet forests why this area has been given this special designation.

The trail here is peaceful and level. There are few ups and downs in elevation, and the forest is consistently dense. This is a good section to practice tree identification skills. Watch for the fascinating honey locust, which has bark sprinkled with skinny spikes an inch or two long. These are especially interesting in winter when trees are leafless.

(At mile 0.6 is a side-trip spur trail to Shady 80 Ranch Lake, where you can fish and even camp on a sheltered platform. A summer lakeside picnic would be idyllic here. It's a beautiful spot and worth the detour if your group is feeling energetic—the hike to the lake will add 1.1 miles to the trip's total distance.)

Heading west from the head of the spur trail, the trail makes its first of two crossings of a fork of Big Sugar Creek. The crossings are usually dry but can present an opportunity for splashing during wet periods. Watch for toads. The oak forest thins and thickens, making for changing scenery that will keep those with short attention spans from getting bored.

(At mile 1.5 consider adding a short, 0.1-mile visit to the backpackers' camp down the spur trail on your left. It's a few minutes to the campsite, and it's

FIRST CAMPOUT

The backpackers' camp near the spring along the Lone Spring Trail is a perfect spot for a first backpacking trip. You would need to hike only a couple miles each day, and water for filtering is close by at the spring; when you only have to carry enough water for drinking on the trail, your backpack gets significantly lighter. There are benches and a fire pit, and the camp's setting on a ridge makes it feel like a special spot perched above the rest of the park. There are fewer places in the area more lovely for building an evening fire and then waking up in the dawn light.

worth the trip as a rest and snack stop. To consider an overnight stay, see the "First Campout" sidebar.)

Past the spur to the backpackers' camp, hike a downhill section that ends at Lone Spring, mile 1.75. This water source runs most of the year, sometimes drying up in late summer and early fall. If you plan to rely on the spring for water, check with a ranger or call the park office to make sure it's flowing. As with any natural water source, don't drink from the spring without treating the water. If you have a water filtration device, bring it along. Many kids love to help filter water by pumping, squeezing, or sucking, depending on what type of filter you have. The spring is just past the halfway point of this hike, so it's a perfect place to take a break and replenish your water supply. Make the second creek crossing at mile 1.9.

White connector trail #7 intersects Lone Spring Trail at mile 2.5, just before you reach State Highway KK. The connector, less than a quarter mile, lets hikers avoid walking on the highway. Turn left (east) onto the connector trail, which takes you through another dense forest with gentle rolling elevation changes. Use caution when crossing State Highway KK to reach the parking lot.

43 INDIAN CAMP CREEK PARK

BEFORE YOU GO
   MAP On park website
   CONTACT St. Charles County Parks and Recreation Department
   GPS 38.885072° N, -90.939268° W
   NOTES Inaccessible for wheelchairs and strollers; water fountain at trailhead, and bathrooms elsewhere in park

ABOUT THE HIKE
   SEASON Year-round
   DIFFICULTY Moderate
   LENGTH 1.7 miles loop
   HIGH POINT 4600 feet
   ELEVATION GAIN 250 feet

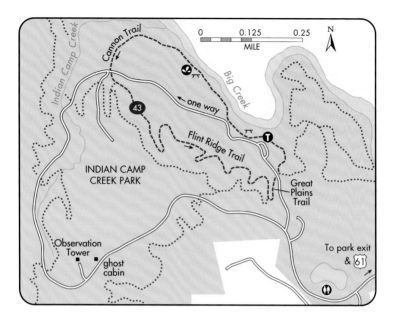

GETTING THERE

From the junction of Interstate 64 (US Highway 61) and I-70 at Wentzville, drive north 0.9 mile on US 61. Turn left (west) on Dietrich Road, drive 1 mile, and turn right onto the main park road. Drive about three-quarters of a mile, passing Indian Camp Creek Park Lake and entering the one-way loop road, and park in the first small lot on the right.

ON THE TRAIL

Indian Camp Creek Park is a great place for hikers of all levels. It has miles of trails with plenty of options for longer or shorter hikes. It's also St. Charles County's largest park, at 603 acres, and stands as a testament to how fortunate the people of the county are to have such a wealth of accessible parkland.

This trek samples a few trails with varying levels of difficulty. It has nice smooth sections but some places where beginning hikers can practice and build confidence.

Heading west from the parking lot, turn left at the water fountain to enter a dense forest on the Cannon Trail. The trail follows the river. Just past mile 0.3 a bench awaits, marking a good location for scooting down to the river to splash. This section trail is flat and level and makes a great adventure for the newest walkers.

At mile 0.5 the trail emerges from the forest. In spring and summer this field is thick with Queen Anne's lace, brown-eyed Susan, and other wildflowers. The trail crosses the road at mile 0.6, and you enter a forest with older oaks and

Evergreens provide color on winter hikes at Indian Camp Creek Park.

other deciduous trees. Almost immediately after this, turn left (southeast) at a trail junction onto the Flint Ridge Trail. This section takes you through dense forest that offers a taste of trekking through the old-growth forests that parks advocates have worked so hard to preserve throughout St. Charles County.

At mile 1.4 turn left onto the Great Plains Trail. At mile 1.5 cross the road again, and turn left to return to the Cannon Trail. From here it's less than a fifth of a mile through the forest to get back to the parking lot.

On your drive out of the park along the one-way loop road, treat yourselves to a stop at the Observation Tower on the left, an old grain silo that you can climb to get a broad view of the surrounding countryside. In the same area of the park, discover a "ghost" of an original homestead cabin; the re-creation features metal beams outlining the corners and roof of the cabin, and a stone "chimney" to show what a homesteader's cabin might have looked like in the 1800s.

44 QUAIL RIDGE COUNTY PARK

BEFORE YOU GO
MAP On park website
CONTACT St. Charles County Parks and Recreation Department
GPS 38.801085° N, -90.834351° W
NOTES Sections are accessible; composting toilet at trailhead and elsewhere in park

ABOUT THE HIKE
SEASON Year-round
DIFFICULTY Easy to moderate
LENGTH 2.1 miles loop
HIGH POINT 650 feet
ELEVATION GAIN 250 feet

GETTING THERE

From Interstate 64 in Wentzville, take exit 1C for Prospect Road. Take the third exit of the traffic circle to head west on Prospect Rd. Drive 0.3 mile and turn right on Interstate Drive. Drive 1 mile to the park entrance. Turn left into the park on Quail Ridge Parkway and immediately turn left onto Bluestem Way. Drive 0.3 mile, turning left to stay on Bluestem. Follow the signs for the disc golf course. Turn left onto the short drive that leads to the large parking area for the disc golf course.

ON THE TRAIL

Quail Ridge County Park is one of several parks in St. Charles County that are beautifully maintained and have plenty of amenities. Quail Ridge has playgrounds, picnic areas, a disc golf course, a fishing pond, a popular dog park, and, of all things, the Horseshoe Pitchers Hall of Fame.

Of course, it also has trails. There are rugged trails in thick forests, wide mowed paths in prairies, and paved walkways at the edges of stands of trees. Whatever outdoor experience you're looking for, it's available here.

This hike explores several aspects of the park. The trailhead shares a parking lot with the disc golf course. The trail begins when you head southeast from the edge of the parking lot into the trees. Soon arrive at a small clearing that has some of the disc golf holes. Watch carefully for the sign that points north to Stealey Way downhill to the left; it's easy to miss. The path is narrow and the forest dense, giving a sense of being transported from the suburban streets and parking lots to a remote woodland. The trail dips into a

"Mush, Daddy! Mush! Mush!"

picturesque wash that connects with the stream to the east at mile 0.2, where the shade is thick and cooling in the summer and after rain there can be enough water to splash in.

During the first third of a mile, three short trails jut off Stealey Way in close succession: Bluebird, Dove, and Cardinal. (Hiking one or more of these in any combination would be perfect for beginners, since the distances are short and it's easy to change the length as energy wanes during the hike.) As you hike past them on Stealey Way, you first come to the junction for the Bluebird Trail, with the Dove Trail appearing less than a tenth of a mile afterward. (The Cardinal Trail juts off from the Dove Trail.) After these junctions, the trail ascends through a pretty flowering dogwood grove. The trail has some more ups and downs before crossing a wide, dry creek bed. Watch for the signpost that points left for Stealey Way at mile 0.4, where the trail takes a sharp turn to the west. Here the path becomes wide and mowed, sandwiched between forest and prairie (it's parallel with Peruque Creek for a bit but the creek is not visible from the trail). With the trees to the south, it's delightfully shaded, making it a great choice for a morning hike on a hot summer day.

At the 0.8-mile mark of the hike, turn right at the junction with the Finch Trail. In just under a tenth of a mile, follow the trail to the right, then left. The track is a bit narrower and brushy for a bit. At mile 1.3 the Finch Trail forks again, with both choices ending up in the same place in a quarter of a mile. (The path to the left is just a skosh shorter.) At mile 1.5 the trail ends at the paved path. Turn right and then right again to arrive at a playground, bathroom, and benches, a great place for a midhike snack. After this, the paved trail winds its way between a series of pavilions through the mowed grass and the forest, ending back at the parking lot.

45 FRANK, EMMA ELIZABETH, AND EDNA REIFSNIDER STATE FOREST

BEFORE YOU GO
> **MAP** On park website and at trailhead
> **CONTACT** Missouri Department of Conservation
> **GPS** 39.065724° N, -90.932713° W
> **NOTES** Inaccessible for strollers and wheelchairs; road and trail may be impassable after heavy rain; privy in state forest about a mile past trailhead

ABOUT THE HIKE
> **SEASON** Spring, summer, fall
> **DIFFICULTY** Difficult
> **LENGTH** 1.5 miles loop
> **HIGH POINT** 780 feet
> **ELEVATION GAIN** 270 feet

GETTING THERE
From Interstate 70 just west of Wright City, take exit 199 for Wildcat Drive. Turn left to cross the freeway, then turn right onto Veterans Memorial Parkway.

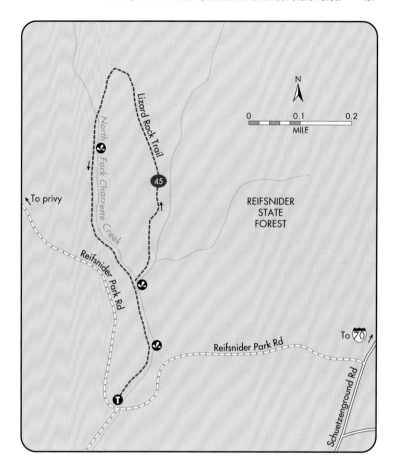

Drive 2 miles, and turn left on Strack Church Road. Drive 1 mile, and turn right onto West State Highway M. Drive 1 mile, and turn left onto Schuetzenground Road. Drive 2.75 miles, and turn right onto Reifsnider Park Road. Drive 0.4 mile on the gravel road to the parking area on the left, just after the road crosses the North Fork Charrette Creek.

ON THE TRAIL
Lizard Rock Trail is short but packs a punch, offering something a little different from the trails usually found in St. Louis and St. Charles counties. The trail is heavily forested; its main feature is the North Fork Charrette Creek that, for part of the hike, is one and the same with the trail.

Reifsnider State Forest feels rugged and remote.

From the parking area, head north to cross Reifsnider Park Road and walk close to, but not on, the creek. For the first quarter mile, the trail passes through a thick forest of oak, buckeye, dogwood, and pine. Cliffs are within view on both sides, giving the sense of walking through a portal; let the kids' imaginations run with the feeling. Where are we going? Could this be a magic portal?

Then, after that first quarter mile, the trail merges with the creek. Let your feet get wet as you splash along, or use the rocks and stones to play "hot lava." A series of flat stones make a platform out into the creek across from a side canyon. Look for the trail to continue into the woods, just 20 feet or so past the side canyon. It's easy to miss—this area has fewer blazes and trail markers than most parks and trails in Missouri, so take it slow.

At mile 0.5, the trail jogs sharply to the right and across the creek. (The path heading straight, which you'll return on, continues along the creek.) There are two steep but short climbs up to the ridge above the creek. In this section, the trail is much less distinct than it was before the creek crossing, and much less traveled. But it is worthwhile for its wildflowers and the variety of trees. The canopy provides a lovely experience on a hot day. Just keep your eyes open, and you should have no trouble following the trail. At 0.8 mile, watch for where the trail jogs left, turning nearly 180 degrees. Here there is, in fact, a helpful sign marking the way. This is where the trail heads sharply downhill, and wood beams in the path turn it into a series of gentle steps.

Just past mile 1, the trail meanders through a forest near the creek. The path is the most faint in this area. It's easy to lose the trail, but keep heading south, with the creek close by on your right, and you soon come out onto the creek bed.

The trail and creek bed converge again for about a third of a mile. Take your time and enjoy the rocks, pools, and running water of broad North Fork Charrette Creek. Then the trail heads to the right up onto the forest floor again. From here, retrace your steps back to the parking lot.

46 BROEMMELSIEK PARK

BEFORE YOU GO
MAP On park website and at visitor center
CONTACT St. Charles County Parks and Recreation Department
GPS 38.716325° N, -90.804052° W
NOTES Inaccessible for strollers and wheelchairs; bathrooms and water at visitor center and picnic shelters along trail

ABOUT THE HIKE
SEASON Fall, winter, spring
DIFFICULTY Easy to moderate
LENGTH 4 miles loop
HIGH POINT 750 feet
ELEVATION GAIN 660 feet

GETTING THERE
From Interstate 64 in O'Fallon, take exit 6 (State Highway DD and Winghaven Boulevard). Drive southwest 4.4 miles on State Highway DD, and turn right on

---

FUN SIDE TRIP: AG GARDEN

At the northern end of Broemmelsiek Park is the Agricultural Education Garden, where volunteers grow crops that were historically cultivated in St. Charles County. The garden features a scarecrow, a windmill, and several hulking pieces of ancient farm equipment, along with historical photos and signs explaining how each one worked. There are also two large and fun playgrounds, plus a great area for splashing, about a quarter mile south of Schwede Road from the Ag Garden.

Crossing a creek is like running a fun obstacle course.

Broemmelsiek Drive into the park entrance with the large sign. Drive 0.1 mile and turn right into the visitor center parking lot. Park in front of the visitor center.

ON THE TRAIL

Broemmelsiek County Park has something for everyone: equestrian trails, fishing ponds, an off-leash dog park, and even a sky viewing area, where on clear Friday nights astronomy enthusiasts help novices learn about the stars. It's yet another example of the tremendous quality and quantity of properties in the St. Charles County parks system.

This hike is a good one for moderately experienced hikers who want to try a somewhat longer trail than they're used to, since the terrain is easy and there are a number of places where it's convenient to shorten the trail if someone gets too tired. It's also a fun trail that provides a lot of visual variety as it dips in and out of the forest and prairie without a huge amount of elevation ups and downs.

From the visitor center parking lot, go downhill to the north about 20 feet through a lawn to the trail. At mile 0.1, carefully cross the park entrance road. In a third of a mile the trail meets up with one of the creeks that flows into Betty's Lake (unless there's been a very heavy rain recently, it shouldn't be necessary to get wet). The trail is mostly level for the first half mile as you follow

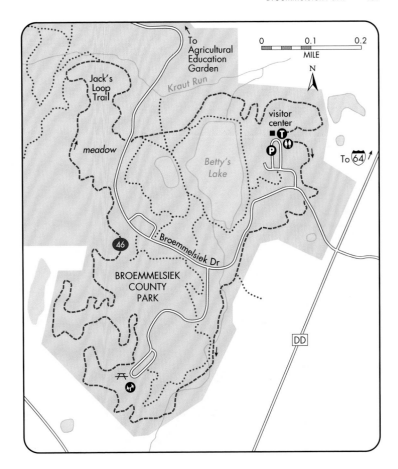

along the creek. At mile 0.7, leave the creek as the trail starts to head gently uphill.

At mile 1.1 the trail passes the hilltop group picnic site and playground—a nice diversion (and a good spot to shortcut back down the road if the hike needs to be cut down to 1.8 miles). By mile 1.3 enter a forest of mostly oaks and hickories but also a few pines. Over the next half mile, the trail skirts the edge of the forest, then enters again, dipping in and out and providing a nice variety of scenes. You'll experience the first of many long switchbacks as the trail maintains a gentle grade, moving up and down through the forest.

At mile 1.7 a pond comes into view outside the park property. At mile 2.2 cross another narrow stream, and leave the forest shade for a short distance. You emerge close to the park road at mile 2.3, then jog left and enter a broad meadow, a really lovely spot with a meandering path through high grasses and views of the surrounding forest. Park rangers have spent extra time on this particular section of the park, using controlled burns to restore the native grasses and flowers (see "Fire as Friend" sidebar in hike 51).

The trail enters dense forest at mile 2.9; you come to a signed junction shortly after this point. Turn right (east) to follow signs for Jack's Loop Trail. Carefully cross the park road at mile 3. The trail continues its pleasant meander between open fields and dense forest without any significant uphill or downhill challenges as you make your way east. At mile 3.6 the trail jogs south, giving you less than a half mile of forest stroll back to the parking lot.

47 AUGUST A. BUSCH MEMORIAL CONSERVATION AREA

BEFORE YOU GO
MAP On park website and at visitor center
CONTACT Missouri Department of Conservation
GPS 38.705035° N, -90.740330° W
NOTES Fallen Oak Trail accessible for strollers; one step on either side of the bridge, so inaccessible for some wheelchairs; bathrooms and water at visitor center

ABOUT THE HIKE
SEASON Year-round
DIFFICULTY Easy
LENGTH 0.75 mile loop
HIGH POINT 670 feet
ELEVATION GAIN 180 feet

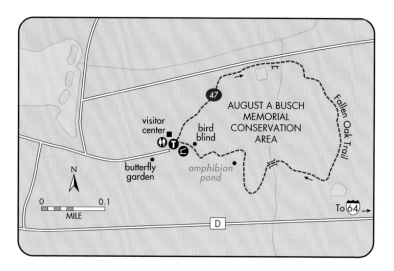

Boating and birdwatching are fun possibilities at August A. Busch Memorial Conservation Area.

GETTING THERE

From Interstate 64 in St. Charles, take exit 9 at State Route 94, and turn left (southwest) onto SR 94. Drive 1 mile, and turn right (west) onto State Highway D. Drive 2 miles to the park entrance. Turn right into the park where you see signs on the right and left, and turn right again to go to the visitor center parking lot.

ON THE TRAIL

August A. Busch Memorial Conservation Area is a vast tract of nearly 7000 acres that has been a haven for anglers and other outdoors people for decades. It includes dozens of fishing lakes of varied sizes, bike trails, and a visitor center with exhibits about the local waterways, including live turtles. The short trail presented here, combined with the easy adventures described in the "Fun Side Trip: Auto Touring" sidebar, provides a lovely overview of this beloved space. And it would be easy to make an entire play day for preschoolers and older kids by incorporating the visitor center, nearby butterfly garden, and several of the other short trails.

The area also has an interesting history: during World War II, it was used to store explosives. About 100 bunkers were carved into the hillsides, some of which are still visible from the road.

For this trail, start at the visitor center. Ask a ranger for a copy of the interpretive trail pamphlet, and then head east to the paved Fallen Oak Trail, which

FUN SIDE TRIP: AUTO TOURING

If your group is still feeling energetic after hiking in the conservation area, take the auto tour counterclockwise around it (this takes about twenty minutes). This self-guided drive passes some of the most scenic meadows and lakes in the park. The map at nature.mdc.mo.gov provides details of the auto tour. Just past Lake 33, look for the sign for the Woodland Trail on the right, a quarter-mile unpaved loop in the forest. Off to the left after you start is a small pond delightfully crowded with frogs. Whether the kids decide to hike the quick loop or not, they'll love to watch the frogs hop in and out of the water.

starts at the edge of the parking lot, near the picnic shelter. Head into the thick woods and locate the display board describing the blight of bush honeysuckle (see "A Pretty Plague" sidebar in hike 25). Read it with your kids and then look around you to find the shrubs; this is especially easy before and after other shrubs leaf out, and in early fall when the bright red berries are visible. Once you know what to look for, you'll see honeysuckle everywhere.

Take the trail to the left. At mile 0.1 pass an unsigned path to the right. For this hike, stay straight and make your way through dense forest. Mile 0.25 is marked by a bench, and a small pond is sometimes visible to the right, depending on how wet it's been; then the trail goes slightly uphill. Here you start to see plaques describing the different species of trees, including persimmon, oak, and hickory.

A bridge takes you over the creek at mile 0.5. Check the interpretive brochure here to learn about features of the landscape, like mud in the seasonal creek that can be a good place to spot animal tracks. At mile 0.6 take the side trail on the left to an amphibian pond; then retrace your steps back to the main trail. A bit farther along, stop at a bird blind. Kids love peeking through the holes to see if there are any birds feasting at the feeders. Just past the bird blind, take a left at the fork to return to the visitor center.

48 WELDON SPRING CONSERVATION AREA ("LEWIS AND CLARK TRAIL")

BEFORE YOU GO

 MAP On park website

 CONTACT Missouri Department of Conservation

 GPS 38.691353° N, -90.724542° W

 NOTES Inaccessible for wheelchairs and strollers; no bathrooms or water at trailhead

ABOUT THE HIKE

 SEASON Year-round

 DIFFICULTY Moderate to difficult

 LENGTH 5 miles loop

 HIGH POINT 725 feet

 ELEVATION GAIN 860 feet

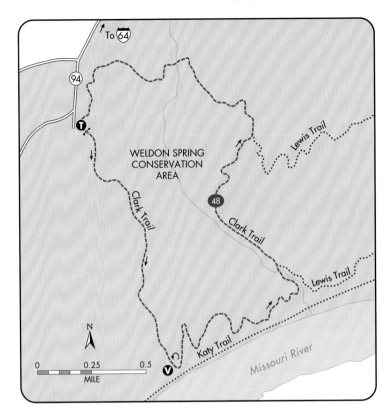

GETTING THERE

From Interstate 64 in St. Charles, take exit 9 at State Route 94 and turn left (southwest) on SR 94. Drive 4 miles. About a mile past Francis Howell High School, turn left into the parking lot.

ON THE TRAIL

This is one of the more popular trails in the region, and for good reason. It showcases a variety of the region's native ecosystems, with beautiful views of the Missouri River. Though it might be a bit long for some littler ones, it doesn't have any big hills or very technical stretches. This hike is referred to locally as the "Lewis and Clark Trail," instead of Weldon Spring, the name of the conservation area.

Start from the parking lot by stepping over the gate that blocks cars from the wide path. The Clark Trail heads southeast through a dense forest of mixed deciduous trees. The trail here is wide and mostly easy for little legs. Watch for large sycamore trees, plus smaller oaks and ash trees.

A dog who can hike at least five miles at a time is a fun companion for hiking kids.

At about one mile, hikers start to see views of the river. Once you get to the river vista at 1.3 miles, there are number of spots along the bluffs that afford remarkable views. Keep a close eye on the more adventuresome young explorers, as there are some steep drop-offs. Some rock formations are close to the trail and yet far enough from the cliff to allow for some fun rock scrambling. Take some time to explore this area and take in the view. (If you're not sure your group will make it the full 5 miles, this is a good spot to turn around to make the hike just 2.7 miles.)

From here, the trail takes a zigzagging path along the bluff top, providing more views across the river valley. Far below, next to the river, is the Katy Trail, one of the area's best-known bike paths (see "Paved Trails and Bike Paths" sidebar). Across the river is the Howell Island Conservation Area (hike 8).

Weldon Spring trails are named after explorers Lewis and Clark because this region is where they first encountered Native Americans, shortly after departing St. Louis on their exploration of US territories. Ask your children to imagine what it might have been like to venture into this unknown land, tasked by the president to document everything they saw and map a route to the Pacific coast.

Around mile 2.6 the trail jogs left at an intersection as it heads northwest along a creek; the trail's intersections with the creek are not big enough to require a bridge. At 2.7 miles, the Clark Trail intersects with the Lewis Trail, which heads southeast from here. (Adding the Lewis Trail to your journey would make your hike 8.5 miles.) Continue straight to stay on the Clark Trail heading north. This section of the hike hugs the unnamed creek that creates the valley that the Clark Trail encircles; it then flows into the Missouri River.

The trail veers to the east at mile 3.1, meeting up with the other end of the Lewis Trail at mile 3.5. Angle left to go north and continue on the Clark loop. The trail crosses the trickle of a creek again at mile 4.2, and continues through the mixed deciduous forest. Keep an eye out for wildflowers in the spring and colorful mushrooms year-round.

At mile 4.6 the trail gets close to the road, returning to the parking lot after a relatively flat final half mile.

PAVED TRAILS AND BIKE PATHS

Sometimes a narrow, rugged trail is a bit too much of a challenge for small kids, especially if one parent is trying to wrangle multiple kids for an outing. That's when a nice, wide trail can be ideal: parents or older siblings can push a stroller or pull a wagon, and kids can propel themselves on tricycles, big wheels, bikes, or scooters. The trails listed here are all many miles long, but can be made into a nice out-and-back stroller walk or jog starting from just about anywhere. When your kids are older, or if you manage to get some adult time, consider one of these trails for a bike ride of nearly any length, even including some overnights.

Grant's Trail, www.stlouisco.com, is a popular option for walkers, joggers, and cyclists. It stretches 8 miles, from its north end near Interstate 44 to its south terminus at Interstate 55 and Union Road. There are several trailheads in the middle of the trail and on the ends where cyclists and walkers can park. The trail's two biggest attractions are Grant's Farm (www.grantsfarm.com), a theme-park-style destination with zoo animals and a tram ride, and the historic home of President Ulysses S. Grant (www.nps.gov/ulsg). The trail goes past restaurants and convenience stores on Watson Road. There are many dining and shopping options in downtown Kirkwood, just a mile from the north end of the trail.

River des Peres Greenway, www.greatriversgreenway.org, is managed by Great Rivers Greenway, a regional district funded by sales tax that runs trails and parks across the region. River des Peres connects the Shrewsbury MetroLink station and Carondolet Park in the city of St. Louis. It's popular with commuters as well as recreation-seekers.

Katy Trail, www.bikekatytrail.com, is perhaps the best-known bike path in the region. It's not paved, but its packed surface is fine for most road bikes and strollers. At 237 miles, it's the longest rails-to-trails project in the country, stretching almost from St. Louis to Kansas City. Its eastern end is near St. Charles, where there are several parking areas that make for a good jumping-off point to explore the trail.

49 MATSON HILL PARK

BEFORE YOU GO
MAP On park website and at trailhead
CONTACT St. Charles County Parks and Recreation Department
GPS 38.623868° N, -90.815049° W
NOTES Inaccessible for wheelchairs and strollers; popular with mountain bikers, so be alert and corral children when they pass; porta-potty at trailhead

ABOUT THE HIKE
SEASON Year-round
DIFFICULTY Moderate to difficult
LENGTH 3 miles loop
HIGH POINT 670 feet
ELEVATION GAIN 260 feet

The myriad verdant shades of green are almost otherworldly in Missouri summers.

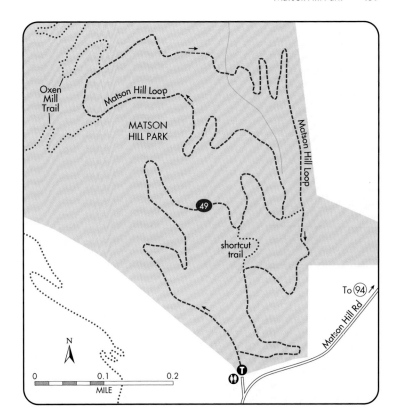

GETTING THERE

From Interstate 64 in St. Charles, take exit 9 for State Route 94 south. Drive 9.5 miles, and turn right on Howell Road (just past Defiance). Drive 1 mile, and turn left on Matson Hill Road. Drive 1.25 miles, and turn right to park at the trailhead.

ON THE TRAIL

Matson Hill Park is hidden way back in the part of St. Charles County that's known for wineries and the Daniel Boone historic site. It feels remote, and that's the idea—the parks department wants this set-aside space to resemble the setting the way it was when Boone moved here in 1800. Boone was known for settling Kentucky, having lived in Virginia after the Revolutionary War. But his family was also instrumental in settling this area of Missouri, even before Lewis and Clark's explorations west made it more well known.

You may not see much of the game that was plentiful more than 200 years ago and that Boone loved to hunt, but you will feel the wild, rugged nature

Mushrooms can add almost as much color and visual variety as spring wildflowers.

of these hills much the way Boone would have. As you hike, encourage kids to imagine what it might have been like to explore these woods before water came out of pipes, cell phones guided you to the trail, and food came wrapped in plastic from the store.

Head out from the parking lot past the information board, and turn left at the junction to start the loop going clockwise. Immediately find yourself in thick forest. Just about all parts of this trail are mostly level, but with just enough rocks and roots thrown in to make things a little challenging for short legs. After a third of a mile the grade angles down a bit, the trail continues to be deeply shaded and woodsy. A couple of gentle switchbacks make the downhill easy. Watch for a wide variety of trees, like pawpaws, sycamore, and hickory, plus a massive maple at a bend in the trail around mile 0.75. At 0.9 mile is a junction that was unsigned as of my last trip here. Turn left to stay on the 3-mile Matson Hill Loop.

The trail is level and flat for a bit, then has a few stream crossings, which are mostly dry unless there's been a recent heavy rain. At mile 1.75 and a tenth of a mile later, pass junctions for the Oxen Mill Trail. In both places, continue to the right to stay on the Matson Hill Loop. At mile 2.1, the trail crosses another stream branch and becomes somewhat rockier. Take your time hiking up the switchbacks that follow. At mile 2.5, pass the junction for the cutoff from the beginning of the loop. From here it's just more than a half mile to the parking lot.

Note: The nearby Daniel Boone Home has daily tours. Check www .danielboonehome.com for information and history about the Boone family homestead here in the Femme Osage Valley.

50 KLONDIKE PARK

BEFORE YOU GO
MAP On park website and at trailhead
CONTACT St. Charles County Parks and Recreation Department
GPS 38.582106° N, -90.832472° W
NOTES Inaccessible for wheelchairs and strollers; bathrooms at trailhead open intermittently

ABOUT THE HIKE
SEASON Year-round
DIFFICULTY Moderate to difficult
LENGTH 1.5 miles loop
HIGH POINT 720 feet
ELEVATION GAIN 550 feet

GETTING THERE
From Interstate 64 in St. Charles, take exit 9 for State Route 94 south. Drive 13.5 miles, and turn left onto the signed park road for Klondike Park. Drive 0.2 mile uphill and bear left to the conference center parking lot.

ON THE TRAIL
Klondike Park is a remarkable spot on the bluff above the Missouri River in St. Charles County. Part of its 250 acres was once a silica sand quarry, but now it has miles of hiking trails, spectacular views of the river, and camping and cabins. This trail starts out very steep but has a quick payoff when it reaches a stunning overlook high above the Missouri. It's a short but very beautiful hike with a variety of sights and terrains.

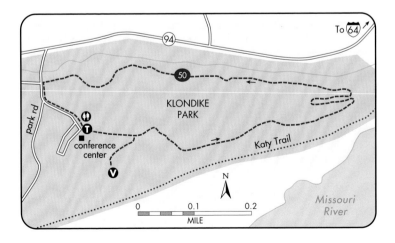

Views from Klondike Park across the Missouri River are especially dramatic when fall colors are on display.

Start your hike by going straight uphill to the east from the conference center parking lot on the paved trail. In less than a tenth of a mile, turn right to get to the overlook. Check out the view, but also keep an eye on the younger hikers; there are tempting boulders that, if climbed, will get them dangerously close to the edge of the cliff.

Backtrack to the junction, where there's a sign that describes several Native American tribes and their interactions with the Lewis and Clark party, which started from St. Louis in 1804. This area was one of the first places where the famous explorers first encountered the indigenous inhabitants as they made their way west. Encourage kids to imagine what it must have been like for the members of Lewis and Clark's party, the first white people to see this land. And then ask them to think of what it must have been like for those on the other side of those meetings, seeing these strange newcomers for the first time.

Turn right and head uphill (less steeply this time) and into the forest on a rocky trail. At mile 0.2 the trail veers left along the fence above the river. Heed the signs that prohibit throwing things over the fence, since hikers and bikers on the Katy Trail are just below. The trail continues along the bluff for a third of a mile. Continue to check out the view across the fence of the Missouri River and the lands across the river. Soon the trail starts to descend gradually along two steep switchbacks, transforming from the high-bluff views to a dense forest of sycamores, ash, and maples. Watch along the first switchback at mile 0.7

for kids who might go straight toward some rocks that look good for climbing, and make sure they turn left to stay on the trail. Shortly after that, hike past some areas where it's tempting to take shortcuts down the switchbacks. Explain to kiddos that it's not only dangerous for them, but it's bad for the health of the forest to create shortcuts down the hill because it encourages erosion and damages trees and undergrowth.

At mile 0.9 the trail is done descending and meanders through thick forest, crisscrossing washes with bridges. In some areas, you can spot the creek off to the right through the trees. Watch for exciting displays of a variety of mushrooms in the shadier, damper areas. At mile 1.4 reach the road and turn left (south); the final tenth of a mile is on the shoulder of the park road. The only traffic is from the park users, but keep children close by when you are near the side of the road nonetheless.

51 ENGELMANN WOODS NATURAL AREA

BEFORE YOU GO
MAP On park website and at trailhead
CONTACT Missouri Department of Conservation
GPS 38.562148° N, -90.774122° W
NOTES Dogs prohibited; inaccessible for strollers and wheelchairs; no bathrooms or water at trailhead

ABOUT THE HIKE
SEASON Year-round
DIFFICULTY Moderate
LENGTH 2 miles loop
HIGH POINT 820 feet
ELEVATION GAIN 450 feet

GETTING THERE
From Interstate 64 in Chesterfield, take exit 19B for State Route 340 south. Drive 4.7 miles to SR 100 west and turn right. Drive 5.8 miles to State Highway T (St. Albans Road), and turn right (west). Drive 6 miles, make a sharp right (northwest) onto Adda Road, and immediately turn right into the parking lot.

From I-44 in Eureka, take exit 264 for SR 109 north. Drive 6 miles, and then turn left (west) onto SR 100. Drive 2 miles, and turn right (west) onto State Highway T (St. Albans Road). Drive 6 miles, make a sharp right (northwest) onto Adda Road, and immediately turn right into the parking lot.

ON THE TRAIL
Engelmann Woods Natural Area doesn't have a fancy visitor center or dramatic views, but it does provide a respite from the paved parking lots and busy roads of the west St. Louis suburbs. It's a bit of a hidden gem tucked away amidst the ranches and estates of Franklin County.

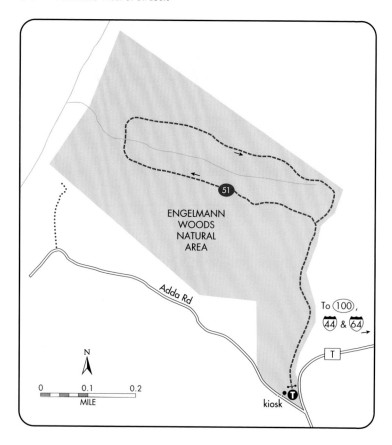

The area also showcases some of the largest trees in the area, with giants up to three feet in diameter and nearly 200 years old. Engelmann Woods was donated to the Missouri Botanical Garden in 1942 and purchased by the Missouri Department of Conservation in the 1980s. It was named for George Engelmann, a German-born botanist who extensively cataloged plants throughout North America in the 1830s and was a key adviser to Henry Shaw, founder of the Missouri Botanical Garden.

When starting your hike here, note that the trailhead layout is a bit deceptive: the signs, map, and kiosk are off to the left, and there's a remnant of a trail, but the real path is to the right, along a dirt access road, behind a metal gate. Step around the gate to head down the road. After 0.4 mile reach the loop that

Opposite: Teach map-reading skills early, but wait until they're older before allowing kids to make directional decisions.

FIRE AS FRIEND

Parks around the region and across the country use controlled burns to keep forests and prairies healthy. This practice started centuries ago, when native peoples realized that occasional low-intensity fires could encourage the growth of plants they wanted to cultivate. They also found that fires would discourage reproduction of plants that would crowd out the beneficial flora. Rangers use fire in this way at rural locations like Shaw Nature Reserve (hikes 59 and 60) and Young Conservation Area (hike 61), and even at urban Forest Park (hikes 1 and 2).

At Young Conservation Area, fires help the growth of oak and walnut, which are great sources of food and shelter for wildlife. Maple and ash trees, on the other hand, create too much shade and inhibit the growth of beneficial plants and trees on the forest floor. Fire has also been used in recent years at nearby LaBarque Creek Conservation Area (hike 63). Watch for signs explaining the use of fire in different sections of these conservation areas.

In Forest Park, fire is an effective and efficient way of clearing invasive species without using destructive methods like spraying or mowing. Fire also breaks down dead or dying plants into nutrients that the living plants can use much sooner than if they were allowed to decompose without fire. This makes for warmer and more nutrient-rich soil in which the native seeds sprout and grow in the spring.

takes you down into the valley. Hike the loop clockwise, heading down the hill to the left.

The trail is mostly easy to follow, but in some sections the path blends into the surrounding forest, especially in fall and winter when leaves cover the ground. Watch for the familiar brown signs with a hiker symbol, as well as more natural-looking signs made of wood with two bootprints, to indicate that you're on the right track. The loop descends into a creek bottom through old-growth forests that have been protected for longer than most in the region. Outdated management practices, including fire suppression, have changed the nature of the forest so that more shade-tolerant sugar maples have grown in place of oaks. The MDC is setting controlled burns to change the tide back toward more natural growth patterns (see "Fire as Friend" sidebar).

At 0.9 mile the trail crosses the creek (which can mean wet feet during rainy periods) and passes through the ravine for a bit before heading back up the hill. The ravine that makes up the middle section of this hike is often damp, so tell the kids to keep a sharp eye for salamanders. But also use caution heading up the steep hill, since footing can be slippery. Continue to wend up the hill, where you're likely to observe a spectacular array of colors—from wildflowers in the spring and from changing leaves in the fall. The trail crosses some steep washes in this section as it heads uphill to the bluff. Here, at 1.6 miles, retrace your steps along the dirt road that takes you back to the parking lot.

52 LONG RIDGE CONSERVATION AREA

BEFORE YOU GO

MAP On park website and at trailhead
CONTACT Missouri Department of Conservation
GPS 38.279197° N, -91.165182° W
NOTES Accessible for all-terrain strollers; popular with hunters in late fall and winter—check MDC website for details; no bathrooms or water at trailhead

ABOUT THE HIKE

SEASON Fall, winter, spring
DIFFICULTY Moderate
LENGTH 3.75 miles loop
HIGH POINT 920 feet
ELEVATION GAIN 530 feet

GETTING THERE

From Interstate 44 in Sullivan, take exit 230 to State Highway JJ and turn right. Drive 1.7 miles on State Highway JJ, turn left on Acid Mine Road, and make an immediate right on Luechtefeld Road. Drive 0.5 mile, and turn left to stay

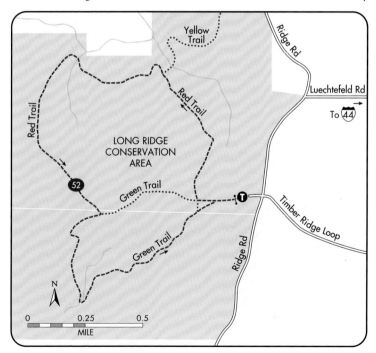

on Luechtefeld. Drive 0.9 mile, and turn left onto Ridge Road. In 0.5 mile, turn right at the second trailhead, which has a large parking lot.

ON THE TRAIL

This hike is a great choice for those who would rather push a stroller than carry a baby or small child on their back. All the trails are wide service roads, so if you have a sturdy jogging stroller with big tires, push away for miles. The Long Ridge Conservation Area gets a lot of attention from park rangers, because it's going through a restoration process. You'll notice a number of areas where bulldozers have plowed off-trail and into the forest. Because the trails are wide here, they get a lot of sun, so it's best to pick a different place to hike on hot summer days. The trails are also open to equestrians, so look out for horses and their evidence along the trail.

Start out heading west from the parking lot through the gate to the Green Trail. Stay to the right past the first junction, and at 0.2 mile turn right to get on the Red Trail. The trails in this conservation area are exceptionally well marked, and there's even an information board with a map tacked to it at each trail junction. Take a moment at this junction to appreciate the exceptionally tall deciduous trees.

The trail in this section turns from gravel to dirt, then heads gradually downhill for about a half mile. At 0.85 mile reach the bottom of this hill and come to a lovely meadow decorated with Queen Anne's lace. Going forward, start heading uphill and into denser forest. At the junction with the Yellow Trail just past the meadow, turn left to stay on the Red Trail. The track continues through a charming forest of oak, pine, and maples, crossing a narrow creek at mile 1.

The junction with the Green Trail at mile 2.25 provides a good spot to decide if you want your hike to be trimmed shorter. (Turning left gets you to the parking lot in about half a mile, for a 2.7-mile hike.) Turn right onto the Green

This valley at Long Ridge Conservation Area is beautiful and remote.

GREAT GETAWAY: LAKE OF THE OZARKS

Lake of the Ozarks is one of Missouri's most popular tourist attractions. It was created in 1931 by damming the Osage River to generate hydropower, but it quickly became a mecca for outdoor recreation. It's about equidistant from both St. Louis and Kansas City, so it gets millions of visitors a year.

Lodging: There are dozens of hotels, from high-end resorts to basic motor lodges. You can also find cabins, condos, and vacation homes for rent.

Camping: Lake of the Ozarks State Park has more than 150 campsites. There are many RV parks and campgrounds near the lake and each of the state parks.

Attractions: Many native Missourians fondly remember childhood vacations spent playing mini golf, driving go-karts, and splashing at waterparks around Lake of the Ozarks. Boating and jet skiing are also popular. Just about any outdoor adventure you can imagine is available around Lake of the Ozarks.

Trail for this hike, and in a half mile you descend into a small but picturesque valley. The electric greens that are typical of humid Missouri forests deepen as you get closer to a seasonal creek at mile 2, and the spring wildflowers multiply. At mile 2.8 the trail ascends, and at mile 3.6 turn right at the Green Trail junction to head back to the parking lot.

53 LAKE OF THE OZARKS STATE PARK

BEFORE YOU GO
MAP On park website and at trailhead
CONTACT Missouri State Parks Department
GPS 38.115230° N, -92.562692° W
NOTES Bathrooms near trailhead

ABOUT THE HIKE
SEASON Year-round
DIFFICULTY Moderate
LENGTH 3.2 miles loop
HIGH POINT 915 feet
ELEVATION GAIN 650 feet

GETTING THERE
From Osage Beach, take Osage Beach Parkway southeast until it turns into State Route 134 and SR 42. Drive 2 miles, and then follow the signs to turn right (south) to stay on SR 134. Drive 1 mile, passing the visitor center and arriving at the trail information center. The trailhead is behind the bathroom.

ON THE TRAIL

This is a true wilderness experience just minutes from the tourist attractions of Osage Beach and "the Lake." The Woodland Trail goes through the 1275-acre Patterson Hollow Wild Area; wild areas in state parks are special sections set aside because of their pristine nature and to minimize future human impact. Experienced hikers can even pack in tents and sleeping bags and stay overnight in the backpacking camp. Caregivers shepherding those with tinier feet can use a connector trail to shorten the hike to 1.75 miles.

The Woodland Trail loop is marked with blue blazes that are visible all along the trail. The connector trail is blazed in white.

The trail starts out heading north and then west on a gentle downhill slope, rolling up and down. About a quarter mile from the trailhead, stay to the right to follow the trail counterclockwise. The trail meanders through a forest of mostly oaks before crossing a seasonal creek (often dry) at 0.4 mile. At 0.6 mile the main trail meets the connector trail (hikers can turn left and follow the white blazes for the 1.75-mile hike).

The trail continues to roll through a mixed forest until mile 1.1, where it hugs another seasonal creek. Watch for a spring feeding a trickle into the creek around mile 1.6, and then two pairs of eight-foot metal posts; ask what each hiker thinks these were for. Another 0.2 mile down the trail, a sign points to the backpacking camp, which sits just 100 feet or so off the trail. Some logs placed around a fire ring there provide a nice spot for a rest and a snack. If you stop there, ask your kids if they think it would be fun to carry tents and sleeping bags here and spend the night. You might be surprised at the answer!

The remaining 1.4 miles back to the trailhead are on a more level, less rocky track, though it goes uphill for a portion. If you do plan a future overnight here,

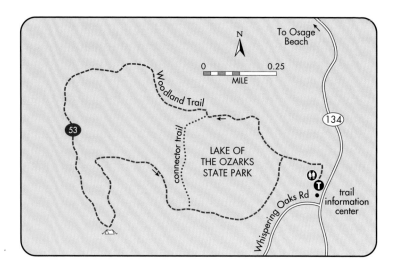

Lake of the Ozarks State Park offers respite from the hustle and bustle of the lake area tourist attractions.

it might be better for beginning backpackers to use this portion of the loop to travel out and back instead of carrying heavy loads over the entire loop.

At mile 3, turn right (east) at the loop junction to retrace your steps to the trailhead.

54 HA HA TONKA STATE PARK

BEFORE YOU GO
  MAP On park website
  CONTACT Missouri State Parks Department
  GPS 37.973989° N, -92.770332° W
  NOTES No camping; bathrooms near castle

ABOUT THE HIKE
  SEASON Year-round
  DIFFICULTY Moderate
  LENGTH 3 miles loop
  HIGH POINT 905 feet
  ELEVATION GAIN 740 feet

GETTING THERE

From Osage Beach, take US Highway 54 south through Camdenton, and turn right (south) on State Highway D. Drive 2.4 miles to the park entrance. Continue 2.6 miles, passing the turnoff to Ha Ha Tonka Castle, to reach the post office. Turn right to park across the street from the post office. The trailhead is at the north side of the parking lot.

ON THE TRAIL

This hike hits many of the most famous sites of this remarkable park, including a spring, quarry, and twentieth-century castle. Starting the hike on the south

GEOLOGY

Missouri can be roughly divided into north-south halves by the Missouri River, approximately where the glaciers of the last ice age stopped before their retreat, leaving a different type of soil and rock in the south. The caves and springs that are so emblematic of Missouri are the result of chemical reactions in the limestone and dolomite bedrock.

One of Missouri's nicknames is the Cave State. To date, more than 6300 caves have been discovered in the state, thanks to the karst geology of the region, which consists of soluble rocks like limestone and gypsum. The longest cave in the state is 28.2 miles (Crevice Cave in Perry County), and the deepest is 383 feet. Cave exploration is a growing hobby in Missouri, with a number of clubs organized around caving.

The other defining feature of Missouri geology is springs. Missouri has some of the biggest in the world. Eleven of the springs in Missouri discharge more than 50 million gallons of water a day—each. The biggest, Big Spring in Carter County, has an average output of 276 million gallons a day. The world's largest, Wakulla Springs in Florida, puts out only slightly more than that on average.

The hills southwest of St. Louis are what remain of the oldest mountain range on the continent. The St. Francois range of the Ozark Mountains was formed more than one billion years ago. As a result of its age, the range is now a series of low rolling hills rather than the jagged peaks that are common in the western part of North America. These hills were formed by volcanic calderas, geologic masses that were up to fifteen miles in diameter, emitting lava from multiple vents in small eruptions. These eruptions created rhyolite, a type of rock that is visible in many of the hikes in the southwest portion of the wider St. Louis region, such as Elephant Rocks and Johnson's Shut-Ins. Deposits of other rocks and minerals have been used for commercial purposes, and have helped give towns such as Iron Mountain and Graniteville their names.

Southern Illinois, home to several gorgeous hikes in this book, offers geology similar to that of southern Missouri.

The haunting ruins of Ha Ha Tonka Castle

side of the pool provides great views of Ha Ha Tonka Castle and avoids the crowds vying for space in the castle parking lots.

Head down the steps carved into the trail and turn right to start on the Spring Trail. You're immediately treated to views of Ha Ha Tonka Castle and a water tower to the north across a narrow finger of Lake of the Ozarks.

During the first quarter mile of the trail, notice side trails on the right to a spring and a natural bridge. Continue straight at 0.2 mile to switch to the Dell Rim Trail. (At mile 0.4 you might want to try a short side trail to the water tower on the right, an eighty-foot structure that provided water via a gravity-fed system to the mansion. Just past the water tower are the remnants of the carriage house.)

When you reach the castle at mile 0.7, take time to walk around it, peering in at the crumbled walls and the remnants of joists that held up the floors. The castle was the dream of Kansas City businessman Robert Snyder. He bought about 5000 acres in the area to create a country estate and began construction in 1905. Tragedy struck the following year, when Snyder was killed in one of the state's first fatal automobile crashes. His sons completed construction, and eventually the European-style mansion became a hotel. In 1942, the castle and stable were decimated by fire. Today visitors can view its stone remnants.

Before you move on, check out the overlook just west of the castle, which takes in the sinkhole, the spring, and parts of Lake of the Ozarks.

When you're ready, find the trailhead for the Quarry Trail on the north side of the castle, near the mule cart. Go left to hike this trail clockwise. (If your group is tired, you can skip this loop, but it explores a beautiful forest and has

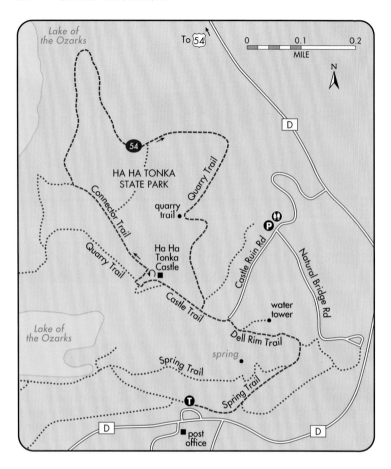

some excellent views.) The Quarry Trail loop traverses an area primarily comprising dense forest that provides shade in the summer and colorful leaves in fall. In some spots, the forest thins enough to afford a view of the lake.

Toward the end of the loop, the trail passes through the area quarried by the workers building the castle. Areas of rock that were carved away are still visible.

The loop trail arrives back at the paved trail between the castle and its carriage house at mile 2.2. Retrace your steps past the castle parking lot, water tower, and spring to return to the post office parking lot.

Opposite: Pickle Springs (hike 73) has even more dramatic views in winter.

SOUTH OF
ST. LOUIS

55 CLIFF CAVE COUNTY PARK

BEFORE YOU GO
MAP On park website
CONTACT St. Louis County Parks and Recreation Department
GPS 38.459307° N, -90.290418° W
NOTES Inaccessible for strollers and wheelchairs; start may be hard to cross after
   heavy rain; bathrooms at pavilion past trailhead and railroad tracks

ABOUT THE HIKE
SEASON Year-round
DIFFICULTY Moderate to difficult
LENGTH 2.5 miles loop, 2.7 miles with roundtrip
   to Cliff Cave
HIGH POINT 520 feet
ELEVATION GAIN 280 feet

GETTING THERE
From Interstate 255 in St. Louis, take exit 2 for Telegraph Road and turn right
(south). Drive 1.5 miles, and turn left onto Cliff Cave Road. Drive 1.5 miles,
and turn right into the gravel parking area just before the railroad tracks.

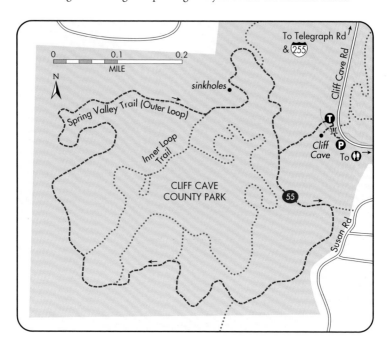

A view from near the entrance to Cliff Cave

ON THE TRAIL

Like most Missouri caves, the one at Cliff Cave County Park is closed to visitors to protect the threatened native bat populations. But there's still plenty to see at this park that borders the Mississippi River. This hike starts out with a short spur to visit the cave, then returns for another short walk to the start of the Outer Loop Trail.

There are plenty of legends about Cliff Cave. It's said to have been a hideout for horse thieves, a meeting place for Confederate sympathizers, and even a tavern for the earliest European explorers. Native Americans likely used the cave for its consistent temperature of 57 degrees. Its proximity to fishing in the Mississippi River and fresh spring water would have also attracted people to the cave.

Starting from the parking lot, head back in the direction you drove, and walk across a short footbridge over a drainage ditch to the trailhead. For the spur portion of this hike, make a hard left and go straight into the valley with your back to the road. Locate a trail that's unmarked but not difficult to follow, leading to the cave the park is named for. Walk about a tenth of a mile down the pretty ravine to the towering entrance, which is blocked by a metal grate made of thick beams. Peek in to read the sign explaining that the bats that live here are on the endangered species list. They are very sensitive to disturbances, thus the ban on human intrusion (see "Protecting Bats" sidebar in hike 74). It also calls this the second-longest cave in St. Louis County, at 4723 feet. Intrepid adventurers might enjoy climbing up the side of the cliff to get a view from the ridge atop the cave.

Returning to the footbridge by the road, you're already at mile 0.2 of this hike. Look for signs for the Spring Valley Trail, denoted with a red diamond icon. The trail quickly crosses another tiny waterway before snaking up a steep, rocky stretch. Take your time here, offering words of encouragement to anyone who might be flagging, as this steep portion is less than a quarter mile and is the only difficult section of the trail. At the top of the hill, mile 0.4, the loop portion of the trail begins. (For additional adventure, explore the trails weaving through the inner part of the park.)

The Outer Loop Trail is mostly level and walkable for kids of all ages. It winds through oak and hickory forest and reveals examples of a significant local geologic feature: sinkholes. The plateau that the loop trail traverses features a few ponds that show where the bedrock, made of limestone and dolomite, has eroded to create these sinkholes, which have filled with water. Take the loop clockwise, going left at the top of the steep trail, and follow the Outer Loop signs. When you come to a side path that heads into the neighborhood that surrounds the park at mile 0.5, veer right to stay on the main trail. You see a few more of these side paths as you make your way through this dense forest and marvel at how far away it feels, even when you're quite close to civilization.

Proceed through the forest, noting the ravines and washes in the forest as you hike. The final mile of the loop features a number of water-filled sinkholes where people sometimes spot snapping turtles. Spend some time observing quietly at these ponds, and see what wildlife each person manages to spot.

At mile 2, reach the junction with a connector trail that leads to other park trails that can take hikers closer to the Mississippi. Stay straight to keep on the Outer Loop Trail. At mile 2.4, head down the hill to retrace your steps to the trailhead.

56 BEE TREE COUNTY PARK

BEFORE YOU GO
MAP On park website
CONTACT St. Louis County Parks and Recreation Department
GPS 38.408818° N, -90.331886° W
NOTES Porta-potty at trailhead; water fountains seasonally throughout park

ABOUT THE HIKE
SEASON Fall, winter, spring
DIFFICULTY Easy to moderate
LENGTH 1.7 miles loop
HIGH POINT 465 feet
ELEVATION GAIN 190 feet

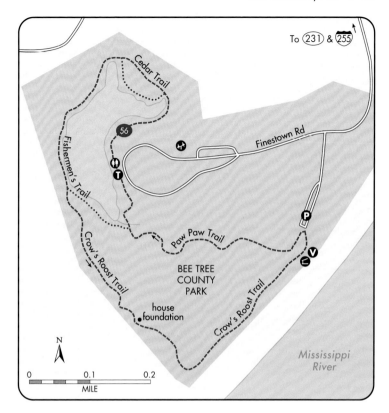

To (231) & (255)

Cedar Trail

56

Fishermen's Trail

Finestown Rd

T

P

V

Paw Paw Trail

Crow's Roost Trail

BEE TREE
COUNTY
PARK

Crow's Roost Trail

house
foundation

N

Mississippi
River

0   0.1   0.2
MILE

GETTING THERE

From Interstate 255 in south St. Louis County, take exit 2 for Telegraph Road and turn right (south). Drive 4 miles, and turn left (south) onto Becker Road. Drive 1.5 miles, and turn left onto Finestown Road. Drive 0.5 mile to the park entrance, and then continue 0.3 mile, passing the playground and driving down the hill to the lake, where you can park along the road.

ON THE TRAIL

Bee Tree County Park is another gem of a county park—it's close to a lot of residents and has a broad set of amenities, including some wonderful trails. On a short hike at Bee Tree you can experience an incredible variety of environments, plus a broad view of the Mississippi River. The land that is now Bee Tree Park was owned by a telephone company magnate in the 1920s and purchased in 1969 by a group who donated it to the parks department.

Start your hike with a lovely walk around the tiny lake; Fishermen's Trail, which circles the lake, is less than a mile long. It's paved for about 100 feet and

Big brother and little sister explore nature together.

then becomes a wide gravel path, navigable for nearly all strollers and some wheelchairs.

From the parking area along the road, turn right (north) to take the Fishermen's Trail. Gaggles of geese are almost always around for kids to observe along the way. At 0.2 mile go straight at a junction to take the Cedar Trail into the forest. This is a pretty side trail up a gentle hill through a stand of trees. It's only 0.1 mile, so at mile 0.3 stay straight again to rejoin the Fishermen's Trail. Continue to hug the lake and watch for fish jumping; the lake is stocked by the Missouri Department of Conservation, so you're likely to see anglers catch and release from the dock.

As you approach the south end of the lake, turn right at the junction at mile 0.6 to take the Crow's Roost Trail uphill. The trail is gradual at first and then gets steep for a bit before leveling out again. Watch for the foundation of an old house on the left at mile 0.8.

Once you reach the 1-mile mark of this hike and turn left, the river starts showing itself, especially when the leaves are off the trees. For the next quarter mile, walk along a high bluff above the river. There are several gaps in the trees where hikers could walk to the edge of the bluff for a better view, so keep little ones on the main trail. At 1.2 miles a large shelter provides a broad vista over miles of the Mississippi River and large swaths of the bottomlands across the state line. Keep an eye out for eagles and other large birds soaring over the bluffs and down to the water.

The Crow's Roost Trail ends at the shelter. (If you're pushing a stroller, take the road from the parking lot here back down to the lake.) Look for the Paw Paw Trail, where the woods meet the field opposite the overlook. Head downhill on this trail through pretty woods on a track that's narrower and rockier than the previous trails. At mile 1.6 the lake comes back into view; the trail parallels a drainage ditch and then crosses the creek bed. A fallen tree has damaged a boardwalk here, so watch for mud as you cross the wash. From here it's just a few steps back on the Fishermen's Trail to the road and the parking area.

57 STRAWBERRY CREEK NATURE AREA

BEFORE YOU GO
   MAP On park website
   CONTACT City of Arnold
   GPS 38.415269° N, -90.364885° W
   NOTES Porta-potty at trailhead; low-hanging branches uncomfortable for someone
     carrying a child in a high-riding backpack

ABOUT THE HIKE
   SEASON Spring, summer, fall
   DIFFICULTY Moderate
   LENGTH 2.25 miles loop
   HIGH POINT 550 feet
   ELEVATION GAIN 350 feet

Strawberry Creek Nature Area is a walk on the wild side.

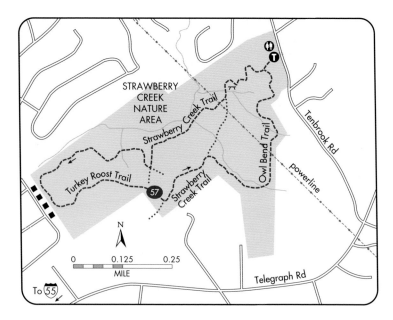

GETTING THERE

From Interstate 55 in Arnold, take exit 190 for Richardson Road and turn left (southeast). Drive 0.75 mile, and turn right (south) on Jeffco Boulevard. Drive 0.4 mile, and turn left (east) on Telegraph Road. Drive 1 mile, and turn left (northwest) on Tenbrook Road. Drive 0.5 mile, and turn left into the parking lot.

ON THE TRAIL

If you like an adventure, this one's for you. Strawberry Creek Nature Area is wild and rugged, with foliage hanging low over the trail in many places, and grasses and other plants swishing about your ankles and even knees as you walk. The trail markings can sometimes be hard to find, but since the park is tiny—just 120 acres—it would be hard to get truly lost; still, a map and compass are a good idea. There are a lot of trail options, so it's easy to create a loop of nearly any size to accommodate your group's energy level.

For this hike, start on the gravel path from the parking lot, turning right in about 50 yards to join the Strawberry Creek Trail loop, blazed in red. Here the trail is relatively wide. At a quarter mile watch for a bench that overlooks a stream, and then get ready to head into the thickest forest. A fat trunk on the path forces you to decide whether crawling under or clambering over is best. At mile 0.3, pass through the powerline right-of-way, where the grass is mowed.

After that, the forest doesn't get any thinner, and grasses brush your calves as you walk through. At mile 0.5, turn right to leave the Strawberry Creek

Trail and take the Turkey Roost Trail farther into the preserve. After mile 0.75, enter deep shade and meet a stream crossing where everyone's feet may get a bit wet.

Around the 1-mile mark, turn left, and then hike up and away from the houses at the western border of the preserve. After a steep but short incline, come to a mowed field that borders another property. Be a good neighbor and respect private property; the trail hugs the forest along the open field, and then dives back into the forest at a visible gap in the trees.

At mile 1.4 turn left onto the Strawberry Creek Trail for less than a quarter mile. Then at mile 1.6 go right (east) to shift to the Owl Bend Trail. Soon get to a challenging creek crossing, where hikers use logs and rocks to step across, hopefully without getting wet. At the T intersection at mile 1.7, turn left (north) to stay on the Owl Bend Trail (the path is clear, though unsigned). At mile 2 pass under the powerlines again. From here it's less than a third of a mile to the right-hand turn at the loop junction to go back to the parking lot.

58 MASTODON STATE HISTORIC SITE

BEFORE YOU GO
    MAP On park website and at trailhead
    CONTACT Missouri State Parks Department
    GPS 38.379518° N, -90.384583° W
    NOTES Trails inaccessible for wheelchairs and strollers; bathrooms at museum

ABOUT THE HIKE
    SEASON Year-round
    DIFFICULTY Moderate
    LENGTH 2.3 miles loop
    HIGH POINT 710 feet
    ELEVATION GAIN 390 feet

GETTING THERE

From Interstate 55 in Imperial, take exit 186 for Imperial Main Street, turn right, and then make an immediate right on Outer Road. Drive 0.75 mile to Museum Drive, and turn left. Drive 0.3 mile, making right turns until you reach the museum parking lot.

ON THE TRAIL

Archaeologists have been visiting the area that is now Mastodon State Historic Site since the early 1800s, when bones of prehistoric mastodons were first discovered here, just half an hour south of St. Louis. Today hikers can walk through a forest full of varied landscapes that include honey locust, maple, dogwood, oak, and cedar, plus dramatic bluffs and views to go with your history lesson.

Either before or after your hike, the museum provides about thirty minutes of fun and education (there is an entry fee). It features models, mastodon

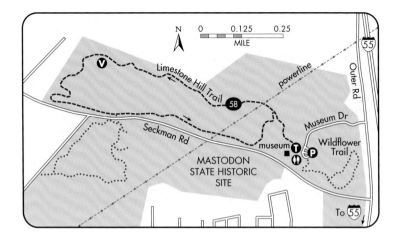

skeleton replicas, and other displays on the geologic and human history of the area, including the Clovis native culture that thrived here 10,000 years ago.

From the museum parking lot, hike northwest on a connector trail. The forest composition transitions to more evergreens as the trail dips and rises approaching the junction with the Limestone Hill Trail loop at mile 0.2. Turn right to hike the loop counterclockwise, heading uphill through the forest. In a bit, cross an open area that's been cleared of trees for powerlines. Then at mile 0.3 you begin to see even more evergreens, providing some nice variety for those hiking in winter. The trail starts to go steadily uphill at 0.4 mile, becoming steep at times. After about a tenth of a mile, the trail becomes closer to level but continues uphill. Take your time, as the trail is rocky.

The trail loops to the west and continues uphill, topping out at about 0.75 mile with views of Seckman Valley.

The next quarter mile heads downhill over some rough terrain. The trail descends some natural stair steps that can be especially slippery when wet. At mile 1 veer right in a thick forest, and at mile 1.1 jog left. Here the trail levels out as it runs along Seckman Road on the right (south) with the low cliffs on the left.

Continue at a leisurely pace here, enjoying the close-up look at the limestone cliffs. In some sections, exposed tree roots make for interesting patterns just below the rocks. The trail continues to be rocky and slippery in places until mile 1.7, when it veers left (north) into a gorge. Listen for the flow of a creek if it's rained recently. Ascend the hill with the aid of some rocky steps making another natural stairway. This is perhaps the most picturesque section of the hike, with the gorge diving away from the trail, the stream, and moss-covered rocks.

At mile 1.8 reach the loop junction and turn right to head back to the parking lot.

Some kids love carrying their water on their back and drinking from a straw.

Beware of another trail near the museum, the Wildflower Trail, deceptively short at 0.4 mile. It leads to the site of the mastodon bone discovery, or the "bone bed," but no bones are visible. This trail consists mostly of a long series of wooden stairs heading down the hill, without much payoff.

MISSOURIANS LOVE THEIR PARKS

Trails and the outdoors may not be the first things outsiders think of when it comes to Missouri. BBQ, the Arch, and the state's "Show-Me" slogan probably come to mind first, but take a closer look and it's quickly apparent how important parks and trails are to Missourians.

Missouri was named the "Best Trails State" in 2013 by American Trails, a nonprofit organization that works to better the nation's biking and hiking trails. It gives the award every two years to a state that has made big improvements to its paths. Among Missouri's accomplishments is being home to the Katy Trail, the longest developed "rail trail" (a trail made from an unused rail line) in the country.

The state park system has more than 1000 miles of trails and is one of the premier state park systems in the country. Its dedicated funding system of a half-cent sales tax has been approved by voters five times, by at least a two-thirds majority.

59 SHAW NATURE RESERVE: BRUSH CREEK AND WILDFLOWER TRAILS

BEFORE YOU GO
  MAP On park website and at visitor center
  CONTACT Missouri Botanical Garden
  GPS 38.28374° N, -90.49357° W
  NOTES Admission fee; free for kids under twelve and Missouri Botanical Garden members; pets prohibited; some trails accessible for strollers; water fountains and bathrooms at visitor center and Bascom House

ABOUT THE HIKE
  SEASON Fall, winter, spring
  DIFFICULTY Moderate
  LENGTH 2.8 miles roundtrip
  HIGH POINT 680 feet
  ELEVATION GAIN 320 feet

GETTING THERE

From Interstate 44 in Eureka, take exit 253 for US Highway 66 and Gray Summit. Turn left (south) and then immediately right onto West Osage Street. Then immediately turn left into the nature reserve on Pinetum Loop Road. Stop at the visitor center to pay the entry fee, and ask for a map and a guide to the native trees along the Brush Creek Trail. Then get back in your car, follow signs on Pinetum Loop Road to the Bascom House, and park in that lot.

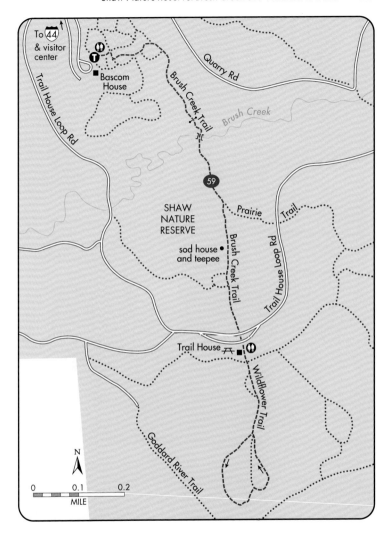

ON THE TRAIL

Families find an amazing array of opportunities for exploring and learning at Shaw Nature Reserve, the wilder cousin of the Missouri Botanical Garden. This hike takes explorers from the wildflower demonstration garden, across some easy, wide paths, and then into the more rugged territory of the preserve near the Meramec River.

Kids can have all kinds of adventures at Shaw's Nature Explore Classroom.

From the parking lot near the Bascom House, head east about 50 feet and downhill through the Wildflower Garden. This area features a maze of winding paths and treasures to discover, like ponds that are home to turtles and cozy nooks with benches. Plan on spending at least fifteen minutes here before starting the hike in earnest. Continue down the hill to the east until you reach the wide path of the Brush Creek Trail at mile 0.3. Turn right onto the trail, blazed with posts that have blue-painted tops.

The trail heads south, crossing Brush Creek at mile 0.6. Hikers can choose how to cross: to the right is a series of stepping stones, and on the left is a picturesque bridge. Continue uphill through the forest, passing the intersection of the Prairie Trail at mile 0.7. At 0.85 mile, discover a clearing with a large teepee and sod house. The teepee is a skeleton of what Native Americans lived in, without the canvas, but the right size to give an idea of how they looked on

MISSOURI BOTANICAL GARDEN

Shaw Nature Reserve is owned and run by the Missouri Botanical Garden, which is recognized as one of the premier botanic gardens in the country. The garden itself, near Tower Grove Park in the city of St. Louis, is home to a vast collection of plants and gardens, including the indoor Climatron which houses tropical plants. The children's garden is a wonderful diversion during summer—and it has fountains where kids can splash and cool off. Inside the Climatron is a kids' area with opportunities for free play with toys, a bug habitat at kids'-eye level, crafts, and educational activities.

the plains. The little sod house is part of a forty-year effort in sections of Shaw to simulate the prairie habitat that once covered a third of Missouri. Volunteers researched building methods, helped collect the materials, and worked with staff to build the "soddie" in 2004 in order to give visitors an idea of what life was like for humans in the early years of European settlement on the prairie.

At 1.1 miles, arrive at the Trail House, which has a covered picnic area, drinking fountains, and bathrooms. Down the steps from the Trail House, follow signs for the Wildflower Trail. This area is more rugged than the trails closer to the visitor center and the Bascom House, but it offers a close-up look at fascinating cliffs and views of the Meramec River area. When everyone is ready, loop back around to the Trail House, retracing your steps back to the Bascom House and Wildflower Garden.

60 SHAW NATURE RESERVE: PRAIRIE AND WOLF RUN TRAILS

BEFORE YOU GO
  MAP On park website and at visitor center
  CONTACT Missouri Botanical Garden
  GPS 38.476024° N, -90.826134° W
  NOTES Admission fee; free for kids under twelve and Missouri Botanical Garden members; pets prohibited; all trails accessible for rugged strollers (gravel or grass); water fountains and bathrooms at visitor center and Bascom House

ABOUT THE HIKE
  SEASON Fall, winter, spring
  DIFFICULTY Easy to moderate
  LENGTH 3 miles loop
  HIGH POINT 690 feet
  ELEVATION GAIN 470 feet

GETTING THERE
From Interstate 44 in Eureka, take exit 253 for US Highway 66 and Gray Summit. Turn left (south) and then immediately right onto West Osage Street. Then

immediately turn left into the nature reserve on Pinetum Loop Road. Stop at the visitor center to pay the entry fee, and ask for a map and guide to the native trees along the Brush Creek Trail. Then get back in your car, follow signs on Pinetum Loop Road to the Bascom House, and park in that lot.

ON THE TRAIL

Shaw Nature Reserve is a huge tract full of trails crisscrossing prairies, forests, and gardens. There's even a unique playground made from natural materials. As with the affiliated Missouri Botanical Garden in the city of St. Louis, there is something of interest for nature lovers of all ages here.

From the parking lot near the Bascom House, head downhill through the Wildflower Garden. Don't worry about getting lost; just keep heading downhill through the tangle of trails, enjoying the labeled flowers and trees. As you descend, find a couple of ponds and benches, and a boardwalk across a swampy area that kids are likely to want to explore.

Reach the bottom of the Wildflower Garden at mile 0.3. Turn right and head south on the Brush Creek Trail, which is blazed with posts that have

These stepping-stones are one of hikers' favorite features at Shaw Nature Reserve.

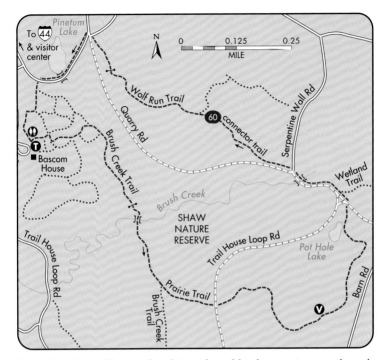

blue-painted tops. The gravel path is wide and level as you journey through the forest.

At mile 0.5 the trail goes through a fence designed to keep deer out of the demonstration gardens near the Bascom House and the visitor center. A tenth of a mile later it crosses Brush Creek, and here you have two options: walk over the bridge or pick your way across the creek on the stepping stones. Continue through the forest; at mile 0.7 turn left (east) onto the Prairie Trail. The path changes from gravel to mowed grass. This trail, not surprisingly, primarily traverses the large prairie situated at the center of the park. Signs describe the types of plants that make up this ecosystem and the preserve's efforts to maintain the prairie here.

At mile 0.9 there's a small stand of trees just before the path crosses Trail House Loop Road, which is gravel; stay straight on the grassy path. The trail continues through the prairies, with views of the surrounding forest that are especially pretty in the fall. The trail goes slightly uphill at mile 1.1, and at 1.2 miles a viewing platform gives an overview of the prairie. Some manmade structures are visible in the distance, but it's easy to imagine the early settlers seeing the land for the first time in this state.

Next to the platform is a trail junction where you turn left (northeast) to stay on the Prairie Trail. At a clearing with a large tree in the middle, mile 1.5,

BACKPACKING

When your kids are ready to take outdoor adventures to the next level, consider taking an overnight trip into the wilderness with just what you can carry on your backs. Wilderness camping is quite different from car camping, and in a lot of ways it's more fun. When you're camping with a big tent and a big gas stove and lounge chairs, it's easy to fill up the entire minivan (plus a rooftop box!) with an overwhelming amount of gear. But when you're backpacking, there's a liberating feeling to narrowing down your packing to the bare essentials, because every ounce counts, even if you're only carrying it a mile or two. And in a big campground with a lot of RVs, trailers, big groups of people, and blaring stereos, it's easy to again feel overwhelmed, and not by the wonders of nature. When you head out for an overnight hike, you'll see some other day hikers, but you're not likely to run into anyone else who plans to sleep out under the stars.

Spending a night in the woods, even if it's just a mile from the car, is a special experience. You're in a pristine forest with your family and friends, maybe in a field surrounded by trees, or under a lovely canopy of tightly packed branches. The kids are eagerly gathering wood and kindling for an evening fire while the adults relax and unpack.

One of the many fantastic features of Missouri state parks is the number of places set aside for backpacking. Most state parks in Missouri allow campers to set up for the night anywhere, but there are also designated sites in parks around the state. These usually have a fire ring already constructed, with some rocks or logs circled around for relaxing while your food cooks on the fire. It reduces the amount of work required to set up a campsite, while minimizing the overall impact on the forest by camping where others have camped before. The campsites are also usually near water—a key consideration when backpacking, since carrying all the water you'll need even for one night can add an intolerable number of pounds to your pack.

The gear needed for an overnight trip can be easy and inexpensive to get. All the local outdoor gear shops have used-gear sales throughout the year, and army supply stores offer gear at low prices. Check newspaper classified sections and online sale sites for other sources of used gear. Searching online for overnight backpacking gear lists will give you a good idea of what you'll need.

Online videos and guides will help you figure out the best way to filter water and protect your food from animals. Make sure you call the park office before you go, to see if there are any issues with the spot where you plan to camp.

turn left. In another tenth of a mile pass Pot Hole Lake right near the end of Prairie Trail at the gravel Quarry Road. Turn left (west) onto Quarry Road and continue past the shuttle bus stop. This road is closed to all but service vehicles on Fridays, Saturdays, and Sundays. Cross Brush Creek over a wide bridge at mile 1.8 and bear left to stay on Quarry Road.

Very shortly after that, at mile 1.9, keep a sharp eye for an unsigned connector trail on your right, and turn down that trail. It's fairly obvious, but since it's unsigned you could miss it. Don't worry if you do; just continue on the road until you reach the next junction, with the Wolf Run Trail, and turn left. When you're on the connector trail, find yourself in a beautiful, dense wood filled with oak, hickory, and pine. Join the Wolf Run Trail at mile 2.3 by going straight. (A right turn would take you on a longer journey around the northern portion of the Wolf Run Trail, and eventually back to the road to the parking lot.) The trail straddles the forest and prairie, making a striking and beautiful contrast with the grasses and the tall, dark evergreen trees.

At mile 2.4 pass through another deer gate and continue through the woods. The trail crosses a gravel road at mile 2.6 and ends where you turn left onto the paved road. Skirt the south end of Pinetum Lake. Turn left just past the bridge over the lake's spillway, and head up the gravel trail. Turn right to head up the hill through the Wildflower Garden and then to the Bascom House and the parking lot.

61 YOUNG CONSERVATION AREA

BEFORE YOU GO
MAP On park website
CONTACT Missouri Department of Conservation
GPS 38.447478° N, -90.663162° W
NOTES Not wheelchair accessible; no bathrooms or water

ABOUT THE HIKE
SEASON Spring, fall
DIFFICULTY Moderate
LENGTH 3 miles loop
HIGH POINT 560 feet
ELEVATION GAIN 150 feet

GETTING THERE
From Interstate 44 in Eureka, take exit 264 for State Route 109 and turn left (south). Drive 2 miles to State Highway FF, and turn right. In 2.8 miles, turn left into the north parking area for Young Conservation Area.

ON THE TRAIL
The Taconic Loop Trail guides you across picturesque LaBarque Creek and into the dense forests of the northern edge of the Ozark region. This is one of many picturesque hikes in the area just a few miles south of Eureka. This particular conservation area is known for birdwatching and for its fishing pond just a third of a mile from the trailhead.

From the parking lot, walk northwest on the trail, a wide mowed area along the edge of the road. Bear right at mile 0.2 to head toward the creek. A concrete footbridge takes you across the creek and into the forest. Shortly after, turn left at a signed junction for a short walk to a pond where kids can try to catch frogs.

After you leave the pond and return to the main trail at mile 0.5, the path turns into a rocky dirt track. Watch for a sign that describes the Timber Stand Improvement program, which involves removing struggling and nonnative trees to improve overall forest health. At 1 mile, the loop portion of this trail begins; take a left to hike the loop clockwise and enjoy some time at the creek before heading uphill through a pine forest. At mile 1.1, the creek crossing offers plenty of opportunity for splashing, hunting after frogs and tadpoles, and more splashing. A beautiful spot with clear water, it's shaded for additional hot-weather enjoyment. Just a tenth of a mile past the creek is the junction for the much longer LaBarque Hills Trail. Make a sharp right (northwest) to stay on the Taconic Loop Trail.

During this portion of the loop the trail heads slightly uphill and into a pine forest. Pause now and then through this section and take a deep breath, enjoying that unmistakable scent of the evergreen trees. Watch for evidence of forest fires and ask your kids if they can think of any reasons why fires might be good for the forest (see "Fire as Friend" sidebar in hike 51).

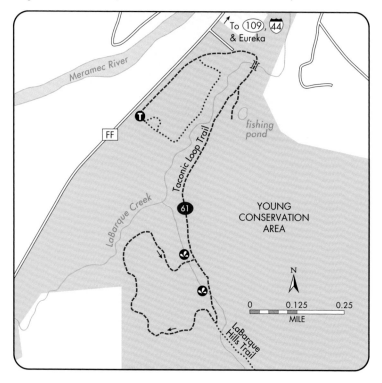

Walking toward the forest at Young Conservation Area

At 1.7 miles, look for a sign describing ongoing ecological restoration in the area. Here you can ask your kids to brainstorm about ways scientists can help and hurt wilderness areas like this one. In this region, maples and ash are less desirable, so forestry experts remove those. This lets the oaks thrive; the oaks are the main source of food and shelter for wildlife.

At mile 2.1 return to the fun creek crossing, and then turn left to retrace your steps back to the parking lot.

62 MYRON AND SONYA GLASSBERG FAMILY CONSERVATION AREA

BEFORE YOU GO
 MAP On park website and at trailhead
 CONTACT Missouri Department of Conservation
 GPS 38.435763° N, -90.675569° W
 NOTES Short section paved and stroller accessible; no bathrooms or water

ABOUT THE HIKE
 SEASON Fall, winter
 DIFFICULTY Moderate to difficult
 LENGTH 3.1 miles loop
 HIGH POINT 650 feet
 ELEVATION GAIN 220 feet

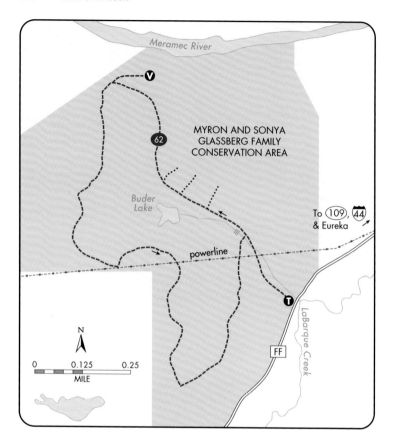

GETTING THERE

From Interstate 44 in Eureka, take exit 264 for State Route 109 and turn left (south). Drive 2 miles, and turn right (west) onto State Highway FF. Drive 4 miles to the Glassberg parking lot on the right. (Just before you arrive you'll see the parking area for Young Conservation Area on the left.)

ON THE TRAIL

Myron and Sonya Glassberg Family Conservation Area just opened in 2012, making it one of the newest conservation areas in the region. It's important because of its role in helping preserve the LaBarque Creek Watershed, an ecosystem that is unusually pristine despite its close proximity to a major metropolitan area. The watershed is 13 square miles, with more than half being publicly owned and 85 percent remaining forested without development. The relatively recent donation of this preserve, along with nearby Young and La-Barque Creek conservation areas, makes this a special place.

At 429 acres, Glassberg is not huge, but it offers hikers a different experience from nearby trails, with its Meramec River overlook, three-acre fishing lake, meadows, and variety of forest types.

From the parking lot, head northwest on the footpath, greeted on your left by an impressive stone monument to the Glassberg family, who donated the land that made this trail possible. The trail is wide and level for the first three-quarters of a mile; it's even paved in a few sections, although the asphalt is quite degraded.

Go to the right at the loop junction at 0.2 mile to head deep into lush forest. On the left, spot some rocky outcrops and low cliffs, and another tenth of a mile up the path come to a small waterfall feeding the stream on the right. At mile 0.7 a few side trails appear on the right, but keep going straight; watch for brown signs tacked to trees that say TRAIL. You can also see Buder Lake, a small body of water created by a dam, on the left. Continue heading uphill through the verdant forest.

At mile 1.1, a sign points right (east) to an overlook. It's about a tenth of a mile to this pretty spot where you can take in the surrounding forest, farmland, and a sharp bend in the Meramec River. Once you've gotten your fill of the view, retrace your steps and turn right to continue southward on the loop. (In spring and summer, this would be a good turnaround place for a 2.4-mile out-and-back hike, because the western half has sections without shade, making it a less pleasant choice in summer sun, and some sections with high grasses, making it less attractive in spring due to ticks.)

A monarch butterfly at Glassberg Conservation Area

From here the trail levels out for a bit and then heads downhill; it's also much narrower than the wide gravel and asphalt paths of the east half of the loop.

The scenery changes again at mile 2, as the trail skirts the boundary between meadow and forest for about a tenth of a mile. Watch for chest-high wildflowers and, in late summer and early fall, monarch butterflies. Reenter the forest, and at mile 2.6 cross the treeless powerline section. From here the trail heads downhill through more forest composed of oak, hickory, and maple. Next the trail goes through a short treeless section with high grasses where the trail is a bit less obvious, but if you pay attention you should be able to spot it with little difficulty. Watch for signs that guide you to the parking lot, and at mile 2.9 turn right to retrace your steps back past the monument to the trailhead.

63 LABARQUE CREEK CONSERVATION AREA

BEFORE YOU GO
MAP On park website and at trailhead
CONTACT Missouri Department of Conservation
GPS 38.422499° N, -90.698769° W
NOTES Inaccessible for strollers and wheelchairs; no bathrooms or water

ABOUT THE HIKE
SEASON Year-round
DIFFICULTY Difficult
LENGTH 3 miles loop
HIGH POINT 810 feet
ELEVATION GAIN 400 feet

GETTING THERE
From Interstate 44 in Eureka, take exit 264 for State Route 109 and turn left (south). Drive 2 miles, and turn right (west) onto State Highway FF. Drive 4.6 miles, turn left onto State Highway F, and immediately turn right onto Doc Sargent Road. Drive 0.9 mile, and turn left onto Valley Drive. Drive 0.1 mile to the parking lot.

ON THE TRAIL
Summers in St. Louis can mean weeks at a time when it just feels too hot to hike, if you can't manage to hit the trail at the crack of dawn. This hike is the perfect antidote. In just more than a mile of mostly shaded hiking, you can reach a tributary of LaBarque Creek that forms a series of pools perfect for splashing, playing, and catching tadpoles.

The entire 3-mile loop features gorgeous scenery and is only forty-five minutes from downtown St. Louis, or thirty minutes from the West County suburbs. Hikers will find a mix of evergreen and deciduous woodlands, along with a lovely pool and seasonal waterfall.

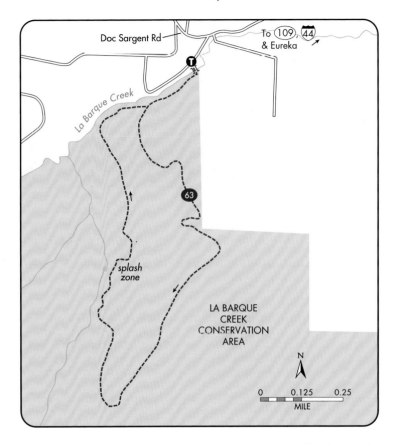

From the parking lot, take the bridge across the creek and head right. The trail follows the creek and then begins to head uphill. At about a third of a mile, the trail splits. The loop is signed clockwise, so head left for this loop. (If your goal is to get to the pool as soon as possible, head right and follow the well-marked trail for 0.7 mile.)

In the clockwise direction, the trail goes mostly uphill, but the grade is gentle. Winter means views of the surrounding hills, while in spring and summer, forests of oak, walnut, and other native trees provide shade. Around mile 1.3 the terrain gets a bit rockier, as boulders dot the landscape. Watch for harmless garter snakes when the weather warms up. At mile 1.6, the trail reaches its southernmost point—as well as its elevation high point—and starts to curve back toward the north.

Just before the marker for mile 2, the trail crosses above the loop's most popular feature—a pool and seasonal waterfall. Look for the spot where a

Scramble downhill from the trail to a pool and some interesting rock formations at LaBarque Creek.

smooth section of the rock cliff forms a slide, and scoot down the cliff of about seven feet to a plateau just above the creek. Some people like to bring a rope to tie around the tree near the slide to make this easier. Be extremely cautious here; send an adult down first to help kids make their way safely. Head to the right (northeast) between the creek and the cliff to where the small seasonal waterfall drops down. This is a great place for wading. Or, you can explore the canyon farther and look for small pools where kids can hunt for tadpoles and small fish.

From here the trail is mostly downhill. At mile 2.2 there's another splash zone, as the trail dips into a small granite bowl with a seasonal stream running through it. This is a gorgeous spot for photos, with the contrast between the trees and the granite in the sunshine.

Once everyone is done splashing, continue on the trail another 0.5 mile to where the loop ends at mile 2.7, and retrace your steps along LaBarque Creek to the parking lot.

64 DON ROBINSON STATE PARK

BEFORE YOU GO

MAP At trailhead
CONTACT Missouri State Parks Department
GPS 38.391995° N, -90.695219° W
NOTES A short portion of Sandstone Canyon Trail is paved and accessible for wheelchairs and strollers; bathrooms and water at trailhead

ABOUT THE HIKE

SEASON Year-round
DIFFICULTY Moderate to difficult
LENGTH 2.6 miles loop
HIGH POINT 810 feet
ELEVATION GAIN 750 feet

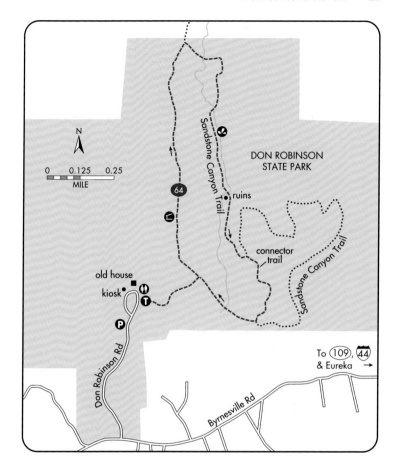

GETTING THERE

From Interstate 44 in Eureka, take exit 264 for State Route 109 and turn left (south). Drive 2 miles, and turn right (west) onto State Highway FF. Drive 4.6 miles, and turn left (south) onto State Highway F. Drive 0.5 mile, and continue onto Lynch Road. Drive 3 miles, and turn right on Byrnesville Road. Drive 2.6 miles, turn right at the sign for the state park, and head up the winding Don Robinson Road to the parking lots.

ON THE TRAIL

St. Louis area hikers got what felt like a late Christmas present in January of 2017: a brand-new state park in the region south of Eureka that's got some of the prettiest landscapes around. Don Robinson State Park opened to crowds of

A winter creekside hike is a special treat at Don Robinson State Park.

hikers and strollers, filling the parking lot even on chilly winter days in its first months open to the public. (At press time the LaBarque Hills Trail was still under construction. Check the park website before you go to make sure the trail you want to hike is open.)

Don Robinson was a businessman who made his fortune selling spot remover. In the 1960s, he fell in love with the area that now bears his name, and he started buying parcels of land. He decided he wanted a property the same acreage as New York City's Central Park, so he stopped buying land when he reached 843 acres. When he died in 2012 at age 84, the land became the property of the Missouri parks system.

This hike starts near the lower parking lot, downhill from the old house and the bathrooms. Look for the red-blazed Sandstone Canyon Trail. The first 0.6 mile of the trail is paved. Head northeast from the parking lot and turn left at the loop junction at mile 0.3. At mile 0.6, the paved section ends at a shelter with benches. From here, a wide path cuts through the forest, offering some lovely views to the west in the winter. At mile 0.8, watch for the red blazes and arrow as the Sandstone Canyon Trail veers right (east). An unnamed trail continues to the north, so watch for the arrows to avoid the unnamed trail and stay on Sandstone Canyon Trail.

From here the trail heads downhill across a series of switchbacks and thick forest for about a fifth of a mile. At 1 mile, the trail enters a glade and veers left. For a short distance the trail is steep and weaves through the forest; watch for the red blazes and arrows.

At mile 1.1 the trail starts to earn its name; you'll encounter the first of many stream crossings in this canyon (which will require some fancy footwork across stones if you don't want to get wet) and see the first of many dramatic sandstone cliffs. The trail undulates through this section, at times rising above the stream that cuts through the canyon, offering dramatic views from a relatively short distance above. Watch for a side trail to the left at mile 1.4, where you can walk out onto an outcropping and take a steep trail (careful, it's almost a slide) to the creek bed for some splashing.

Continue through the canyon, as the beautiful views continue one after another. At mile 1.7 there's a junction where turning left heads down to the creek again (a 300-foot side trip). On the right are the ruins of an old structure. Follow the arrow to go straight and start climbing out of the canyon. Make a few more creek crossings before heading steeply up around mile 1.9. At mile 2, turn right and follow the white arrows to switch to a connector trail (or you can decide to continue straight for a longer 4-mile loop and some more forest views). Turn right when you reach the red-blazed Sandstone Canyon Trail again at mile 2.2, then take a left at the junction at mile 2.4, and retrace your steps on the paved trail to the parking lot.

65 ROBERTSVILLE STATE PARK

BEFORE YOU GO
   MAP On park website and at park office
   CONTACT Missouri State Parks Department
   GPS 38.427859° N, -90.818269° W
   NOTES Inaccessible for strollers and wheelchairs; bathroom at office when open

ABOUT THE HIKE
   SEASON Year-round
   DIFFICULTY Moderate
   LENGTH 2.75 miles loop
   HIGH POINT 624 feet
   ELEVATION GAIN 170 feet

GETTING THERE
From Interstate 44 in Gray's Summit, take exit 253 and turn left, then immediately right onto State Route 100. Drive 0.5 mile, and turn left on Robertsville

Road. Drive 4 miles, and turn left on State Highway O. Drive 0.5 mile, and turn left onto Montgomery Road. Drive 0.8 mile, and turn left onto Main Park Road. Drive 0.8 mile, passing the campground and park office. Park at the trailhead for Lost Hill Trail, on the right just past the trailhead for Spice Bush Trail.

ON THE TRAIL

Robertsville State Park is one of the quieter state parks in the system, acting partly as an overflow campground for nearby popular parks like Meramec State Park. And while the Lost Hill Trail is brand-new, it has quickly become popular among local hiking enthusiasts. It's easy to see why, with the quiet forest tracks and ample opportunity for viewing wildlife.

From the Lost Hill trailhead, walk straight uphill from the road. When the trail reaches the main loop at 0.1 mile, turn right. Taking the loop counterclockwise brings you to a creek closer to the end of the hike, so splash time can be used as an incentive for tired trekkers. The trail stays within sight of the road until 0.25 mile, and then veers left to head deeper into the forest of ash, maple, and oak. Robertsville State Park gets its name from one of the first white

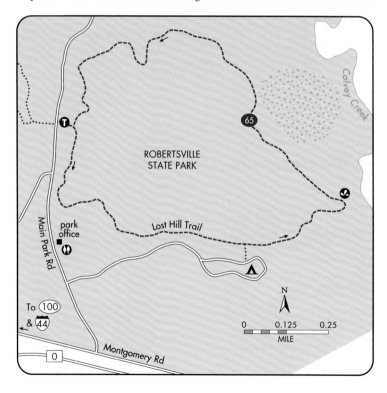

Spotting turtles is always special. This one is a three-toed box turtle.

families to settle in the area. Most of the park was the Robertsville family farm. This area, however, is an example of the hardwood forest that grows on rocky soil not suitable for farming. More open areas near the park entrance and office give an idea of the locations of those original fields.

At 0.6 mile, the trail heads gently downhill and the campground is visible to the right. At 0.75 mile, a forest of dogwoods and plenty of young trees makes for a riot of flowers in the spring. At 1 mile, the main trail intersects with the trail to the campground. Take the left path to stay on the main loop. Watch for a burned-out tree on the right that looks like a work of abstract art more than a tree. The trail continues to gently descend, entering a thick forest and then leveling out around mile 1.3, where the trail also takes a sharp bend to the left. A tenth of a mile later, the slough of Calvey Creek comes into view. During high water this area can be difficult to traverse, but it can also offer a good spot for kids to splash.

The trail makes its way through the floodplain and then a forest of pawpaw trees before rising again into the rocky uphill region. In this last three-quarters of a mile there are a lot of washes, but trail builders have helpfully put logs into them to act as stepping stones. At mile 2.3, the road comes into view again, and there is a downhill then an uphill in the last tenth of a mile before you turn right to head back to the trailhead.

66 VALLEY VIEW GLADES NATURAL AREA

BEFORE YOU GO
MAP On park website and at trailhead
CONTACT Missouri Department of Conservation
GPS 38.255545° N, -90.627288° W
NOTES Inaccessible for wheelchairs and strollers; no bathrooms or water

ABOUT THE HIKE
SEASON Fall, winter, spring
DIFFICULTY Moderate to difficult
LENGTH 3 miles loop
HIGH POINT 680 feet
ELEVATION GAIN 180 feet

GETTING THERE
From Interstate 270 in Sunset Hills, take exit 3 to State Route 30 west, and turn right (southwest). Drive 20 miles, and turn left (east) onto State Highway B. Drive 7 miles, and then watch for the signs for the conservation area. Turn left into the parking lot.

ON THE TRAIL
Valley View Glades Natural Area is a great place to view a somewhat unusual geologic feature: glades. These grassy openings in the forest make for great views, especially here where one of the glades is on a hill, creating a dramatic backdrop to your hike.

The glades in this natural area showcase dramatic views.

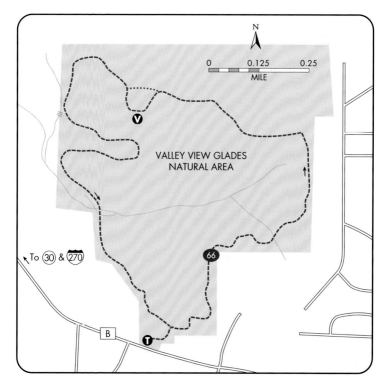

From the parking lot, head downhill, and in less than a tenth of a mile reach the junction for the main loop. Turn right to walk the loop counterclockwise, and glimpse your first view across one of the largest glades in the area. This natural area is unusual in the MDC's holdings, in that it has gone relatively undisturbed by humans. And it's perhaps the place closest to the St. Louis metro area where one can view this type of open, rocky scene. Thanks to the streams that drain the glades, it also has a number of areas with picturesque cliffs and small but pretty waterfalls.

Continue down the trail into a wash, and then head uphill for a bit before leaving the shade of the forest and heading into the first glade at mile 0.2. A third of a mile into the hike, a mixed forest begins, including a number of dead or dying evergreens. This is another aspect of this unusual setting—the thin soil produces smaller, shorter-lived trees than most areas.

For the next half mile, you remain shaded as you wend through forest noticeably less dense than at other nearby conservation areas. Continue through some gentle ups and downs and across washes that feed into the creek, an unnamed tributary of Big River. Cross the creek at a shallow spot at mile 0.6. At 0.9 mile the trail becomes wide and level and takes a sharp left turn to the west as it follows an old road through the type of forest typical of this preserve. At mile 1.2 turn left from the wide, dirt road onto a short 0.15-mile loop trail to see a different view of the first glade, this time from the north.

Back on the main trail, at mile 1.65, enter another glade and walk in the sun for a tenth of a mile. Next the trail enters the trees that surround another creek. At mile 1.7, watch for a small seasonal waterfall to the right of the trail. Next you'll be walking up and down through the forest, crossing the creek twice. The trail and creek are essentially one and the same in stretches starting at mile 2.4, making for a slightly more challenging but very picturesque amble through the shaded forest.

The hike ends with a somewhat difficult climb over rocky and rooty trail. Take your time and enjoy the company of the creek and the views across the glade. Reach the loop junction at mile 2.9, and turn right to return to the parking lot.

67 VICTORIA GLADES CONSERVATION AREA

BEFORE YOU GO
MAP On park website and at trailhead
CONTACT Missouri Department of Conservation
GPS 38.203034° N, -90.542986° W
NOTES Inaccessible for strollers and wheelchairs; no bathrooms or water

ABOUT THE HIKE
SEASON Year-round
DIFFICULTY Moderate
LENGTH 2.3 miles loop
HIGH POINT 740 feet
ELEVATION GAIN 470 feet

GETTING THERE
From Interstate 55, take exit 180 to State Highway Z west. Drive 5.3 miles, and turn right (west) on State Highway A. Drive 4 miles, and turn left (south) onto State Route 21 (Business). Drive 1.3 miles, and turn left onto Main Street. Drive 0.1 mile, and turn right onto Vreeland Road. Drive 0.9 mile; the name changes to Hillsboro Victoria Road. Drive 1.4 miles, and turn right into the signed parking lot.

ON THE TRAIL
A lot of trails in this region showcase the beautiful forests that are near and dear to Missouri hikers, but they sometimes lack a mix of forest and open space that affords big views and changes in scenery. Not so at Victoria Glades. This conservation area provides plenty of verdant deciduous forest, plus pines to offer a different shade of green, and views across the eponymous glades to add some variety. And it's a relatively easy jaunt from South County to this trail just outside the town of Hillsboro.

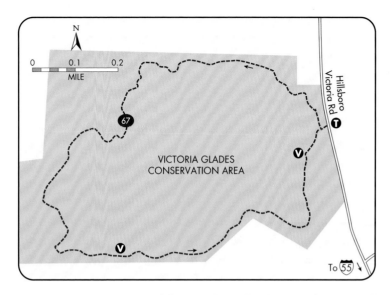

From the parking lot, carefully cross the road and go straight up the hill through the trees to the junction for the loop. Here, decide which part of the trail to see first: if you turn left, you'll enjoy the big views first, heading downhill through shadeless glade. If you turn right you'll enjoy the dense pine-dominated forest. This is the shortleaf pine, Missouri's only native pine. In summer, take the loop clockwise to accomplish the shadeless part of the hike first. It is described counterclockwise here, but either direction is lovely any time of year.

Heading right through the pine forest, soon the trail dips slightly into a creek bed, and then at mile 0.4 goes gradually uphill. A half mile into the hike, walk along a level stretch along the northern edge of the conservation area. At 0.7 mile, a gentle downhill takes you into a grove of mostly oak trees. This southwesterly part of the trail is a tree-lover's delight. Bring a tree identification guide, and see how many you can identify. (The MDC has a free tree ID guidebook and sells another one that helps identify trees in the winter.)

At 1 mile the trail comes to a lovely glade to the right. It's a pretty, open area surrounded by trees; turtles have been spotted by summer midday hikers there. For the next third of a mile the trail parallels several large glades, culminating in an expansive view to the west where the brownish grasses and fall-colored trees are especially spectacular. At mile 1.4 the trail dips into a wash, then heads uphill and veers east away from the glades. In the next quarter mile there are several ups and downs in and out of valleys with creek beds and rocky washes. Some of the rocks can be slippery when wet. Come to a forest with mostly oak at mile 2, then enter a forest that's mostly pine.

Victoria Glades has beautiful forests and glades but doesn't attract crowds of hikers.

The final third of the hike is across the major glade contained in this conservation area. You'll head east, then north across the open field of grass mixed with rocky steps. Watch for the posts throughout this segment that point the way to the correct trail; the tall grasses sometimes make the trail hard to determine.

Just a tenth of a mile before the end of the trail is the biggest view of the day. Take a moment to enjoy the vista, where you can almost see the road you'll soon cross to get back to your car.

68 WASHINGTON STATE PARK: 1000 STEPS TRAIL

BEFORE YOU GO
MAP On park website
CONTACT Missouri State Parks Department
GPS 38.085298° N, -90.684038° W
NOTES Inaccessible for strollers and wheelchairs; bathrooms along trail and seasonally at Thunderbird Lodge

ABOUT THE HIKE
SEASON Fall, winter, spring
DIFFICULTY Moderate to difficult
LENGTH 1.5 miles loop
HIGH POINT 700 feet
ELEVATION GAIN 260 feet

GETTING THERE

From De Soto, take State Route 21 southwest. Drive 9 miles, and turn right (north) onto SR 104 west. Drive 1.2 miles, following signs for the Thunderbird Lodge. Park at the lodge.

ON THE TRAIL

This is a short but strenuous hike in one of the most beautiful state parks in the area. It showcases the big views and early-twentieth-century stone construction of the Civilian Conservation Corps (CCC). You can pair it with the longer Opossum Track Trail (hike 69), which is just as beautiful, and stop on your way in or out of the park to view the park's famous petroglyphs.

The trail starts across the parking lot from the Thunderbird Lodge, which is open seasonally and sells snacks and camping supplies. Head east into the forest with an open field skirting the trees to your left. Across the field is the Big River. After 0.2 mile on the trail, turn right at the 1000 Steps Trail loop junction to head uphill. This is the beginning of the 1000 steps of the trail name. Climb up, up, up the stone steps, pausing occasionally to catch your breath and turn to see the view across the river. You'll also get a view, when you look up, of the remarkable cliffs rising from the top of the hill.

At mile 0.4, take a break at the CCC shelter and take in the view across the river. This is one of the many CCC buildings in the region (see "History Lesson: Civilian Conservation Corps" sidebar in hike 28). Then it's just another few hundred feet uphill to a slight left turn and a short, level walk along

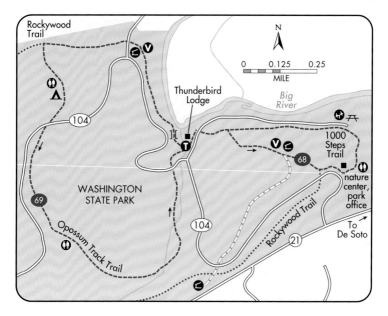

the bluff top. At mile 0.6, stay straight on the yellow-blazed trail (a trip to the right leads to a picnic shelter). Watch for another junction at mile 0.7 with the Rockywood Trail. At mile 0.8 arrive at seasonal bathrooms, along with the park office and nature center. Then veer left again to go down, down, down, watching for slippery rocks. You'll again get to enjoy the broad view across the river, but continue to be aware of your footing.

Reach the bottom of the hill at mile 0.9, where there's a picnic shelter and a playground. Continue west and keep straight as you pass the loop junction at mile 1.2, then retrace your steps the last quarter mile to the parking lot.

A boardwalk protects the carvings at Washington State Park while allowing people to see them up close.

69 WASHINGTON STATE PARK: OPOSSUM TRACK TRAIL

BEFORE YOU GO
   MAP On park website
   CONTACT Missouri State Parks Department
   GPS 38.085298° N, -90.684038° W
   NOTES Inaccessible for strollers and wheelchairs; bathrooms along trail and seasonally at Thunderbird Lodge

ABOUT THE HIKE
   SEASON Year-round
   DIFFICULTY Difficult
   LENGTH 2.5 miles loop
   HIGH POINT 800 feet
   ELEVATION GAIN 550 feet

GETTING THERE

From De Soto, take State Route 21 southwest. Drive 9 miles, and turn right (north) onto SR 104 west. Drive 1.2 miles, following signs for the Thunderbird Lodge. Park at the lodge.

ON THE TRAIL

Washington State Park is perhaps one of the best in the area: you could spend a long weekend exploring its trails, enjoying the campgrounds, and floating the Big River, and still not see everything. And its star feature—petroglyphs accessed by a stroll of less than a tenth of a mile—is unique in the region. (See "Messages from the Past" sidebar.)

This book contains two hikes in the park; Opossum Track Trail is the longer and more scenic of the two. If your group is feeling energetic, consider hiking it along with the 1000 Steps Trail (hike 68) on the same day for a total of 4 miles of vigorous hiking.

The Opossum Track Trail is rugged, with significant elevation change. Bring plenty of water and snacks, and get ready to soak up some scenic beauty as your reward.

Start your hike next to the Thunderbird Lodge. Heading west, cross a small bridge and follow the orange arrows up the steps behind the lodge. In this section two trails merge: the Opossum Track Trail is blazed in blue, while Rockwood Trail is blazed in orange. The climb up the bluff starts right away. The path is steep and rocky but wide. Watch for interesting rock formations along the trail starting around mile 0.2. Keep youngsters close, as steep drop-offs could be dangerous for inattentive hikers. Here too you start to see picturesque views across the Big River valley.

At mile 0.3, stop for a breather at the overlook, marked by a stone shelter built by the Civilian Conservation Corps (CCC) in the 1930s as part of the Depression-era job creation strategies (see "History Lesson" sidebar in hike

There are lots of cliffs to explore at Washington State Park. Keep little ones close.

28). Hiking past the shelter, watch for blazes, which guide you along the rocky path where the trail direction isn't always obvious.

Curve westward and cross the park road at mile 0.4. Then the forest thins a bit, with some small glades visible. The trail is level for a tenth of a mile or so through this lovely forest, then it dips down into a wash, with more rocky steps comprising the trail for a bit. Head uphill for a short distance, and then at mile 0.6 Rockywood Trail heads straight; turn left to follow the blue blazes and stay on the Opossum Track Trail. Here the trail goes uphill again until you reach a campground, which has a seasonal bathroom. At 0.8 mile, head through the camping area and cross SR 104, watching for blue arrows. The trail stays close to the road for about a half mile and reaches the camp pool, playground, and another bathroom at mile 1.4. Curve left; then at mile 1.6 the trail goes very steeply downhill to a gorge, where steep hills rise on either side, making for a close, cozy walk along this creek. In winter the canyon scenery is especially beautiful here.

The terrain rolls along for about a quarter mile and the scenery continues to reward with enchanted views along the creek. Then the trail flattens for an easy final third of a mile to its exit from the forest, across the road from the parking area.

MESSAGES FROM THE PAST

The petroglyphs at the Washington State Park site are believed to have been made by Mississippian Indians around 1000 AD. The site was added to the National Register of Historic Places in 1970. Activities like ball playing and hunting are depicted, as well as the Thunderbird, a powerful symbol for the Indians and the source of the name of the lodge at the park. Today a board-walk allows people to view the petroglyphs up close without damaging them, and signage helps visitors identify the symbols.

70 ST. FRANCOIS STATE PARK

BEFORE YOU GO
   MAP On park website
   CONTACT Missouri State Parks Department
   GPS 37.970213° N, -90.533232° W
   NOTES Check with park office after recent heavy rains since sections near creek can flood; pit toilets, playground, picnic area at trailhead parking area

ABOUT THE HIKE
   SEASON Year-round
   DIFFICULTY Difficult
   LENGTH 2.75 miles loop
   HIGH POINT 845 feet
   ELEVATION GAIN 650 feet

GETTING THERE

From Interstate 55 in Festus, take exit 174B to US Highway 67 south. Drive 19 miles to the well-signed entrance to St. Francois State Park, on your left. Drive 0.4 mile to park at the Mooner's Hollow trailhead.

ON THE TRAIL

Many frequent hikers consider this to be one of the best hikes in the region, for good reason. Some sections have challenging elevation gain, but it's worth the effort to take in the gorgeous valley that houses Coonville Creek and the views from the peaks above. Kids will love the creek crossings, the rocks making the ups and downs more exciting, and the tree roots across the trail providing obstacles to jump over; it's as if nature has provided them with a unique jungle gym. Just remember that you might need to be patient as they explore the challenging trail.

St. Francois State Park is itself a treasure, with a backpacking loop that of-fers distances for both experienced and beginner overnighters. There's also a campground with concrete pads and electric hookups and a trail that offers views across the Big River.

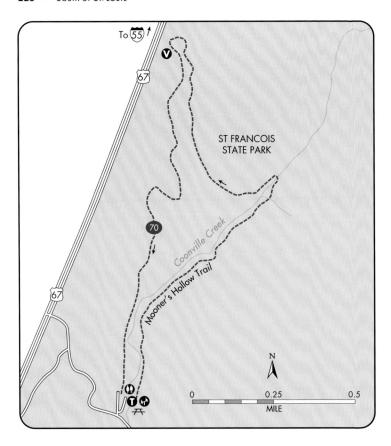

Start your hike by crossing the creek at the trailhead sign for Mooner's Hollow Trail. The trail gets its name from the history of moonshiners using this area to create their signature beverage in the eighteenth and early nineteenth centuries. The cold, clear water springing forth in Coonville Creek and the deep canyons of the area made an ideal environment for their craft.

The first mile of the trail hugs the creek. This makes for view after gorgeous view, with the winding waterway cutting between stands of deciduous and evergreen trees, plus sandstone cliffs. Watch for the blue blazes that make the trail easy to follow. When the trail heads uphill past mile 0.3, keep an eye on little ones as there are some drops. Farther on, around mile 0.5, watch for a pile of rocks and a tiny cave at right. Then the trail once again descends to the creek and back up the hill again over the next half mile.

Descend the creekside hill again and cross a tributary at mile 0.8, and a tenth of a mile later the trail crosses Coonville Creek, then jogs left (southwest).

The trail proceeds uphill at a moderate grade into a stand of Missouri's native evergreen tree, the shortleaf pine. In a quarter mile, a short descent leads to a wash that feeds into Coonville Creek. The trail heads upward again as you walk with that wash to your right.

At mile 1.4 a steep climb takes you to the trail's highest point, providing a beautiful view to the west. From here the trail descends to a level walk through a pretty deciduous forest. Next you'll get an eastward view of a glade around mile 2, with another creek crossing a quarter mile later. For the last quarter mile, the trail again hugs the creek before taking you back to the parking lot.

Mooner's Hollow Trail at St. Francois State Park is a favorite among local hikers.

71 HICKORY CANYONS NATURAL AREA

BEFORE YOU GO

MAP On park website
CONTACT Missouri Department of Conservation
GPS 37.872652° N, -90.302314° W
NOTES No water or bathrooms

ABOUT THE HIKE

SEASON Year-round
DIFFICULTY Moderate to difficult
LENGTH 1.25 miles main loop; 1.75 miles with roundtrip
to waterfall
HIGH POINT 1080 feet
ELEVATION GAIN 500 feet

GETTING THERE

From Interstate 55 north of Ste. Genevieve, take exit 154 for State Highway O, and turn right (southwest). Drive 6 miles. Turn right at State Route 32. Drive 2 miles, and turn right (north) on State Highway C. Drive 3 miles, and turn left (west) on Sprott Road. Drive 1.6 miles to the trailhead parking lot on the left.

ON THE TRAIL

Hickory Canyons Natural Area features two short trails totaling less than 2 miles, but the variety and beauty of the scenery make it worth the trip. Hike Hickory Canyons by itself to get less experienced hikers excited about getting out in the woods, or combine this hike with the better-known Pickle Springs

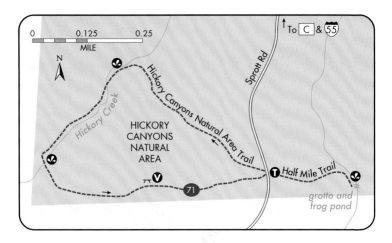

Hickory Canyons has two short trails, one of which ends at this beautiful grotto.

Natural Area (hike 73), about twenty minutes south of Hickory Canyons, to get more miles in for energetic, experienced hikers.

From the parking area, carefully cross the road and walk between the posts labeled HICKORY CANYONS 1 MILE TRAIL. You're immediately plunged into thick forest, with ample shade in summer. Turn right to hike the loop counterclockwise. At 0.1 mile the trail descends gradually into the canyon. On your left, a rocky gap dives away from the trail. Take it slow here and keep your eye on the path. Watch, too, for frogs in the warm months.

The trail itself descends sharply at 0.25 mile. Here you can take in plenty of majestic cliffs, overhangs, and intriguing rock formations. By a third of a mile, at the lowest portion of the trail, kids have a chance to splash in the creek at two crossings, one right after the other. Take time to look left and check out a rock formation that looks like a stack of flat pebbles created by a giant.

After those creek crossings, the trail heads into the forest again and then comes back to hug the creek. The trail crosses Hickory Creek and its tributaries a few more times. At mile 0.7 a sign declares CAUTION: STEEP BLUFFS AHEAD. Indeed, the trail heads away from the creek and steeply uphill until it reaches a "cave" just high enough for kids to squat in. The trail curves left here toward a set of steps and a beautiful area for exploring and enjoying the view over the canyon. Keep little ones close, but older kids can walk along a bluff jutting out between the trail you just climbed and the canyon.

Head up the stairs, where a bench provides a place to rest on the landing. At mile 0.9 check out the view, especially when the trees are leafless.

At 1.25 miles, cross the road and look for the posts that are marked HALF MILE TRAIL. Take this trail, which almost immediately heads sharply down, curving through the forest to some dramatic overhangs, more than high enough for an adult to stand under.

The trail terminates just a quarter mile east of the parking area at a remarkable spot: a pool surrounded by fifty-foot cliffs dripping with ferns. Unless it's been very dry, a series of small waterfalls cascade down the walls. If it's been rainy, get ready for a show. Kids are entranced by the scenery and want to spend as long as you let them splashing in the pool, looking for frogs, and exploring the grotto. Once done, retrace your steps to take the short but steep path back up to the road.

Note: This area is run by the Missouri Department of Conservation, but is owned by the L-A-D Foundation, a group that has been preserving open spaces in southeast Missouri for more than fifty years. Find out more at www.ladfoundation.org.

72 HAWN STATE PARK

BEFORE YOU GO
MAP On park website and at trailhead
CONTACT Missouri State Parks Department
GPS 37.82951664° N, -90.2298534° W
NOTES Inaccessible for strollers and wheelchairs; bathrooms and water at trailhead

ABOUT THE HIKE
SEASON Year-round
DIFFICULTY Difficult
LENGTH 2 miles loop
HIGH POINT 1050 feet
ELEVATION GAIN 430 feet

GETTING THERE
From Interstate 55, take exit 154 for State Highway O, and turn right (southwest). Drive 6 miles, and turn right (west) onto State Route 32. Drive 5.4 miles, and turn left (east) on SR 144. Drive 3 miles, and turn left onto Park Drive. Drive 1.2 miles, following signs for the Whispering Pines trailhead, to the day-use parking area near the playground and picnic shelter.

ON THE TRAIL
This is a spectacular hike any time of the year. It shows off the region's varied and dense forests, streams, shut-ins, and granite formations, plus incredible fall leaf colors and spring wildflowers.

Hawn State Park, covering 1459 acres, has been a state park since 1952. It's considered to be one of the crown jewels of the state park system. You will quickly discover why, on this short but challenging trail.

Start on the Whispering Pines Trail by crossing the bridge over Pickle Creek at the east side of the parking and picnic area. Watch for signs and blazes indicating the trail direction; there are a few eroded areas that look like trails.

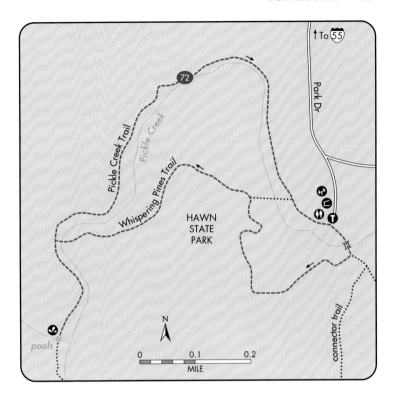

The trail meanders up the hill and turns right to pass a connector trail that leads to a backpacking campsite. This is a great place to keep in mind if you've been wanting to try an overnight backpacking trip. The lovely backpackers' camp is less than a mile from the parking lot, close enough so that, if someone's pack gets too heavy, you can leave some items in the car and come back for them after you set up camp.

As the trail angles around to the southwest after 0.1 mile, following the creek at a distance, enjoy the views, but keep a close watch on small children, as this section gets close to a cliff and there are some tempting ledges. By 0.25 mile, the trail begins heading north in a series of jogs.

After 0.5 mile the trail starts going westward and downhill toward the creek, making for some challenging, rocky sections. More and more lovely views appear through the trees as you move closer to the creek. The forest here features oak and dogwood, and even some stands dominated by short-leaf pine, Missouri's only native pine tree. As you continue down the hill, you begin to understand why this is one of the most scenic and beloved hikes in the region.

The shut-ins at Hawn State Park are an enticing splashing spot.

At 0.8 mile the trail crosses the creek at a wide but shallow spot, where small or timid kids may need some help picking the best boulders to use. Turn left after the crossing (to your right is the start of Pickle Creek Trail), and in a quarter mile find a beautiful cove with shut-ins for splashing, seasonal waterfalls, and boulders for scrambling. Ask the kids if they can spot crayfish swimming around in the pools. If you take some time here to explore, it's likely your kids will ask to come back again and again. Note that there are many opportunities for climbing and bouldering, and kids can climb very high very quickly. Parents who are less comfortable with heights will want to encourage their kids to stick close to the creek.

After enjoying the creek, retrace your steps to the junction of the Pickle Creek and Whispering Pines trails. Instead of turning right to cross the creek and retrace the Whispering Pines Trail, keep going straight to take Pickle Creek Trail along the creek and back to the parking lot. This section sometimes resembles a rock scramble more than a hiking trail, so take your time. Be sure to stop to admire the views of the creek and surrounding cliffs, and encourage others in your group to do so as well.

73 PICKLE SPRINGS NATURAL AREA

BEFORE YOU GO
 MAP Online or at kiosk near parking lot
 CONTACT Missouri Department of Conservation
 GPS 37.799532° N, -90.301232° W
 NOTES Inaccessible for wheelchairs and strollers; no bathrooms or water at trailhead

ABOUT THE HIKE
 SEASON Year-round
 DIFFICULTY Moderate to difficult
 LENGTH 2.2 miles loop
 HIGH POINT 930 feet
 ELEVATION GAIN 440 feet

GETTING THERE

Pickle Springs Natural Area is not easy to find, with few road signs pointing the way, but it's worth the effort. From Interstate 55, take exit 154 for State Highway O and turn right (southwest). Drive 6 miles, and turn right (west) onto State Route 32. Drive 10 miles, and turn left on State Highway AA. Drive 1.5 miles, and turn left on Dorlac Road; the parking lot is on the right in less than a half mile.

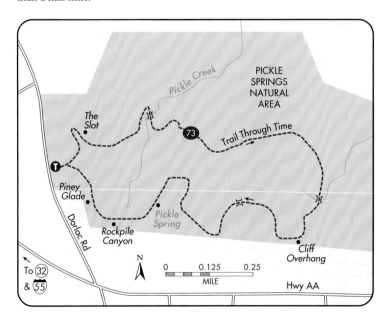

Scrambling over rocks at Pickle Springs Natural Area

ON THE TRAIL

The Trail Through Time loop is one of the most spectacular hikes in the St. Louis region. Incredible rock formations appear all along the hike, as do soaring cliffs and gasp-worthy vistas. It's a great hike any time of year, but it's a special treat when huge icicles form where water flows down the cliffs. To see this spectacle, try to time your hike for when the temperatures aren't too cold but there has been a recent freeze and little to no snow.

From the parking lot, signs point toward the Trail Through Time loop. The trail is well marked with signs indicating the names of the rock formations. A large interpretive sign explains the geology of the region: the area was the beach of an ancient sea that over time became Lamotte Sandstone. Erosion created the cliffs, slots, and hoodoos we see today.

Taking the trail clockwise, everyone in your group will be wowed in the first third of a mile. You soon come upon The Slot after a sharp right turn at mile 0.15. It's a fun scramble down the rocky steps to this dip between two rock walls. This is the first location where you can see icefalls in the winter. At 0.4 mile emerge from The Slot into a fern-dappled forest, the trail already showing off its diversity of landscapes. The trail becomes rooty and rocky again at a half mile and crosses a creek, and at 0.6 mile stairs lead down to more rock formations.

From there, the trail goes up and down, crossing a creek at 1.1 miles. By mile 1.3, reach a spectacular cliff face with overhangs and spaces for older kids to scramble up and into slots above the valley floor. Kids love to run across the creek, check out the "cave" created by the overhanging cliffs, and ogle the ferns and mosses growing in their cool, damp hideaway.

Once your group has explored the area around the cliffs, take a left and hike up and around the cliffs, soon crossing a shallow ravine on a bridge. At mile 1.5 have the kids locate a big, interesting rock that resembles a turtle. From here, follow the arrow sign down to some stairs and then descend a rocky, rooty trail along cliffs. Starting at mile 1.9, you pass Pickle Spring, Rockpile Canyon, and Piney Glade, finishing with some of the hike's most spectacular scenery: more boulders and views of an evergreen forest that is reminiscent of mountain ranges in the western half of the country.

At mile 2.1, a short walk through more forest takes you back to the trailhead.

GREAT GETAWAY: MERAMEC STATE PARK REGION

This is another one of the state's top recreation areas. Thanks to the Meramec River, it has plenty of opportunities for water recreation, as well as hikes with views of bluffs and wildlife. The views even continue underground, as this has a greater number of tourable caves than most regions in the Cave State, as Missouri is known.

Lodging: Meramec State Park has about forty rooms in its motel and cabins. Cabins are also available at Meramec Caverns. There are many hotels all along the Interstate 44 corridor.

Camping: Meramec Cave State Park, Onondaga State Park, and Robertsville State Park each have campgrounds of various sizes and amenity levels. Meramec Caverns also has campsites. There are several small, private campgrounds and RV parks in the surrounding area.

Atttractions: Cave tours are available at Meramec State Park, Onondaga Cave State Park, and Meramec Caverns. Meramec Caverns has zip-lining in addition to the cave tour. For river floats, perhaps one of the most popular summer activities in Missouri, check out Meramec State Park and Meramec Caverns.

Preservation: Much of this area was almost inundated in the name of flood control and irrigation in the 1970s, when the US Army Corps of Engineers started work on a dam to block the Meramec River. The project would have flooded much of Meramec State Park and destroyed other natural treasures. The growing environmental movement empowered grassroots opposition that forced state leaders to reconsider. On August 8, 1978, a nonbinding referendum revealed 2–1 support for leaving the river in its natural state. Funding was removed from the project, and dam construction stopped, marking a major victory for the environmental movement.

74 MERAMEC STATE PARK: NATURAL WONDERS TRAIL

BEFORE YOU GO
MAP On park website and at trailhead
CONTACT Missouri State Parks Department
GPS 38.206251° N, -91.102244° W
NOTES Inaccessible for wheelchairs and strollers; bathrooms and water in visitor center when open

ABOUT THE HIKE
SEASON Year-round
DIFFICULTY Easy to moderate
LENGTH 1.2 miles loop
HIGH POINT 790 feet
ELEVATION GAIN 250 feet

GETTING THERE
From Interstate 44 in Sullivan, take exit 226 to State Highway H and State Route 185, and turn left (south) onto SR 185. Drive 2.5 miles to the park entrance. Turn right onto the park road, and then immediately turn right into the visitor center parking lot.

A winter walk on the Natural Wonders Trail

ON THE TRAIL

With some hikes you have to be patient and hike a mile or two before you hit the big view or the exciting natural feature. Not this one. The Natural Wonders Trail is aptly named, and because it's barely more than a mile in length, it seems there's something new to ooh and aah over every few steps.

This hike starts in the visitor center parking lot. Start up the wooden stairs, walking west into the forest. In about a tenth of a mile turn right to go north and take the loop counterclockwise. Almost immediately find yourself in a forest of unusually tall pine trees. The trail creates a tunnel that feels nearly magical as it cuts through the forest.

At mile 0.2 the trail meets with the Elm Spring Branch creek, which flows into the Meramec River. The trail meanders alongside the stream for a tenth of a mile.

The first of three caves that you walk by is at mile 0.4. This cave is tempting, as the opening is big enough to walk right into. However, most caves in Missouri, including this one, are closed to unguided visitors to protect bats from white nose syndrome (see "Protecting Bats" sidebar). Pull out your flashlight or headlamp to peer in and watch moisture dripping from the ceiling. Next, go across the short bridge along the trail and start a gentle uphill climb. The trail continues through an enchanting forest of pines and deciduous trees.

The second cave comes in to view at 0.6 mile. Take the short side trail of about 50 feet into a shallow valley, guided by signs warning against disturbing the bats. This cave has a much smaller opening that would require spelunkers to get on hands and knees, but be sure to tell kids to stay out.

At mile 1, the third cave is locked tight, but you can get out your flashlight and peek between the bars. You might even get a glimpse of some bats resting on the ceiling.

Before continuing eastward, turn around and take in the view across this small segment of the park, with lovely rolling hills blanketed with trees. As you complete this hike, the forest offers a great place to appreciate the woods surrounding the trail and the care that has been taken over the years to preserve this special spot.

75 MERAMEC STATE PARK: BLUFF VIEW AND RIVER TRAILS

BEFORE YOU GO
MAP On park website and at park office
CONTACT Missouri State Parks Department
GPS 38.217400° N, -91.092053° W
NOTES Inaccessible for wheelchairs and strollers; bathrooms, water, and convenience store (limited hours off season) at trailhead

ABOUT THE HIKE
SEASON Year-round
DIFFICULTY Moderate to difficult
LENGTH 2 miles loop
HIGH POINT 825 feet
ELEVATION GAIN 450 feet

A sturdy trail shelter overlooks the Meramec River at Meramec State Park.

GETTING THERE

From Interstate 44 in Sullivan, take exit 226 to State Highway H and State Route 185, and turn left (south) onto SR 185. Drive 2.5 miles to the park entrance. Turn right onto the park road. Drive 1.3 miles past the visitor center, following signs for the dining lodge. Park in front of the lodge.

ON THE TRAIL

Meramec State Park is a treasure for wilderness lovers. It's just an hour from the city but transports visitors to a different way of life, with rugged trails and campsites, plus a cave that visitors can tour seasonally (call or visit the website to verify the current schedule). Backpackers can sleep along the trail at one of several sites along the 8-mile Wilderness Trail loop. And interpretive exhibits in the visitor center give an excellent overview of the region's geography and the importance of the Meramec River in the region.

The Bluff View Trail is a good choice for those wanting a short but rugged experience, plus frequent changes of scenery. It's a favorite of the park staff.

With your back to the front of the lodge, turn to your left (west) and look for the signed Bluff View trailhead near the road, blazed in blue. Head downhill into the forest, keeping an eye out for poison ivy near the trail. The trees provide some shade but aren't dense, offering views across a low swale where the movements of squirrels and birds are easier to spot than they are in the denser sections of forest. The trail slopes gently down the hill near the road in this section. There are two gaps in the forest where the trail goes under powerlines, at miles 0.2 and 0.3. At mile 0.4, look between the trees to the right for a view across a broader valley that gives some sense of the vastness of this 6900-acre park.

Past the valley view, the forest opens up for a bit and then tightens around the trail again, just before you arrive at the stone trail shelter above the Meramec River at mile 0.5. Pause to take in the view again, watching for groups of large turtles sunning on logs on the opposite bank. In summer you're likely to see flotillas of rafts filled with people on float trips moving down the broad, slow-moving river. The river is the heart of this park and this part of the Ozark region. Its name, Meramec, is believed to have come from the Osage Indian term for "good fish."

From the shelter, head northeast along the bluff and downhill for a bit through a stand of shortleaf pine, Missouri's only native evergreen. Along this stretch are plenty of spots with great views of the river, but keep the young and impetuous close by, as there are many sharp drop-offs. The trail here can be steep and rocky, so take your time, and stop frequently to safely take in the view.

At mile 0.6, the trail levels out near the river and heads again under the powerlines. Then it enters a section with dense foliage and a stream crossing over a footbridge. Just past this, another wash runs over the trail and heads steeply downhill to the river, so watch for wet rocks after rain. There are more spots with great views, and again more drop-offs to be conscious of.

At just under a mile you reach another shelter. Follow the signs and the yellow blazes to turn right toward the jungle-like River Trail. Then, at mile 1.2

the trail comes to a fork; take a left to hike the River Trail clockwise. Here the vegetation is even more dense, and in summer you might feel like you're in the opening scene from *Raiders of the Lost Ark*, where any minute you might stumble upon a golden idol or traitorous guide. Failing that, continue about a quarter mile to return to the trail shelter, turning right to return to the Bluff View Trail. At 1.5 miles another picturesque stream flows across the trail, and after that you'll start to climb again. At 1.8 miles a short side trail intersects near one of the store's outbuildings, but keep to the right to stay on the trail and make your way around the dining area and cabin complex back to the parking lot.

76 MERAMEC CONSERVATION AREA

BEFORE YOU GO
MAP On park website and at trailhead
CONTACT Missouri Department of Conservation
GPS 38.228638° N, -91.075414° W
NOTES Wheelchair accessible; bathrooms and water seasonally at trailhead

ABOUT THE HIKE
SEASON Year-round
DIFFICULTY Easy
LENGTH 1.2 miles loop
HIGH POINT 670 feet
ELEVATION GAIN 200 feet

GETTING THERE
From Interstate 44 in Sullivan, take exit 226 to State Highway H and State Route 185, and turn left (south) onto SR 185. Drive 4.5 miles, past the entrance to Meramec State Park, and turn left (north) into the conservation area entrance. Drive 1.2 miles on the gravel road and park in the large lot.

PROTECTING BATS

White nose syndrome has been devastating bat populations in Missouri since about 2010. The disease manifests as a white fungus on the bat's face, preventing it from breathing. Once it infests the population of one cave, it can kill more than 90 percent of the bats living there. There is no known cure, so the only way to protect the bats is through prevention. This means that most caves are closed to humans, because rangers are afraid the fungus could hitch a ride on boots or gear used in an infected cave and take hold in one that's uninfected.

Some caves on state land are open to the public. These include Onondaga Cave (hike 77) and Fisher Cave at Meramec State Park, which have regularly scheduled tours. One small cave, Indian Cave in Meramec State Park, is open to adventurers who want to explore on their own.

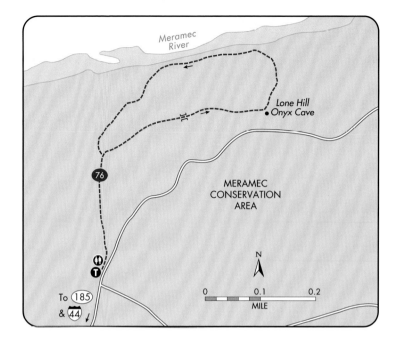

ON THE TRAIL

Meramec Conservation Area provides a special place for those with mobility issues, as well as people who would rather push their children in a stroller than carry them on their back. This trail is almost completely level and, while it's a short stroll, it has no shortage of scenery.

The land for this conservation area, one of the larger in the state at more than 4000 acres, was purchased in the 1920s, around the same time as most of the land for neighboring Meramec State Park.

From the parking lot, head north and then turn left to go northwest. The paved path goes toward the river while two of the longer dirt trails split here to the northeast and east.

At 0.2 mile the trail splits into a loop; veer right to walk the loop counterclockwise. The trail heads directly into a stand of huge pines. Take some time to look up and appreciate their height. Continue along the trail to a forest more typical of this area. At mile 0.4 traverse a long bridge over a wash that allows those on wheels to continue into the forest. Continue another 0.2 mile and reach another well-built structure, a viewing platform for Lone Hill Onyx Cave. As with most Missouri caves, it's closed to prevent the spread of white nose syndrome (see "Protecting Bats" sidebar).

From here the trail heads north and then west along the river. At mile 0.7, discover several areas where you can see the river and across it to parts of

Meramec State Park. At mile 0.9 the trail veers southwest away from the river and heads back toward the loop junction, where you'll retrace your steps to the parking lot. On the drive back, watch for areas on the gravel road where you can pull off and see other parts of the state park across the river. In summer, look for turtles sunning themselves on the branches of partially submerged trees.

77 ONONDAGA CAVE STATE PARK

BEFORE YOU GO
MAP On park website and at visitor center
CONTACT Missouri State Parks Department
GPS 38.056391° N, -91.234257° W
NOTES No permits/passes for hike (see sidebar for information about cave tour); trail inaccessible for strollers and wheelchairs; bathrooms and water at campground and visitor center

ABOUT THE HIKE
SEASON Year-round
DIFFICULTY Moderate to difficult
LENGTH 2.25 miles loop
HIGH POINT 950 feet
ELEVATION GAIN 620 feet

GETTING THERE
From Interstate 44 in Leasburg, take exit 214 to State Highway H, and turn left (south). Drive 6.5 miles to the park entrance and turn right. Drive 1 mile, following signs to the campground and shower house.

ON THE TRAIL
Onondaga Cave State Park is a bit more than an hour from St. Louis, but it's worth the drive along Interstate 44 for the beautiful trail and a tour of a cave that is perhaps Missouri's most scenic (see "Tour the Cave State's Underground Scenery" sidebar). The park has a number of trails near the visitor center and the campground, but Deer Run may be the most scenic.

The hike starts next to the campground shower house. At mile 0.1, turn left at the Deer Run Trail loop junction and then cross one of the dirt forest roads, climbing gradually uphill through a thick forest. The variety of trees provides a good opportunity to use your tree identification skills. Craggy old cedar trees, with gnarly branches devoid of leaves, lend the forest an ancient feel. Watch for them along the switchbacks as you climb, and try to spot them reaching out over the bluffs along the Meramec River.

After only a half mile, take in your first view of the river. This area is popular with paddlers and floaters. Look for them dotting the sandbar below.

Head down the hill, and at 0.8 mile recross the forest road. A tenth of a mile later, walk over a pretty wooden bridge. Continue through the dense forest along an unnamed creek, where the kids can seek out mushrooms, wildflowers

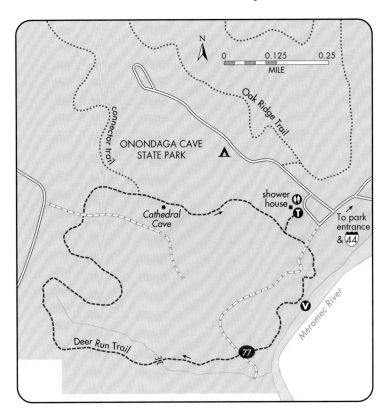

such as coneflowers, and maybe a snake. Bear warnings are posted in the campgrounds, but it's very rare to see one in the woods here. You're more likely to see a bear in the middle of a campground, where there is a lot of tasty food trash for them to dig into.

At mile 1.5, check out the forest valley with its thick canopy and dense carpet of leaf litter. Unfortunately, the red cedars that you saw near the river views are invasive. Around mile 1.7 is a glade where, in 2016, park naturalists started removing the cedars and were getting ready to use controlled burns to encourage plants native to the glades to come back. At mile 1.8, cross another dirt road, then descend and pass a white-blazed connector trail at mile 1.9. Another tenth of a mile later, a concrete hut marks the tour entrance to Cathedral Cave, an underground wonder that you can tour with park naturalists; ask at the visitor center.

From the cave door, you'll have a few more mild ups and downs, taking you through a flowering dogwood grove and then back to the loop junction by the campground.

TOUR THE CAVE STATE'S UNDERGROUND SCENERY

Onondaga Cave is one of the reasons Missouri is known as the Cave State. It has a stunning range of large and well-preserved speleothems, or deposits, such as stalactites, stalagmites, draperies, soda straws, and cave coral. The walk through the cave is about a mile, with some elevation changes but do-able for walkers of all ages. Sturdy shoes are a must.

This may be one of the most scenic cave tours in the state. And the educational value of the tour makes it a good one for grade-school-age kids. They love soaking up geologic lingo and learning about the history and ecosystems that make this cave special. The tour is full of "oh wow" visuals like the Big Room (yes, that's its name), which is as long and wide as a football field and forty feet high.

Like other caves in the Ozark region, Onondaga was formed millions of years ago when shallow seas covered the area. Over time, water eroded the limestone and dolomite around underground cracks, and water-filled passages were formed. When the oceans drained, these air-filled caves remained. European settlers first explored Onondaga Cave in the 1880s. Nearly a century later, the cave and surrounding acreage were purchased by The Nature Conservancy and subsequently transferred to the Missouri Department of Natural Resources.

Trained guides provide frequent tours of Onondaga and Cathedral caves during spring and summer. Check the state park website for schedules and fees.

Onondaga Cave is full of incredible rock formations.

Hughes Mountain is known for this unusual rock formation called Devil's Honeycomb.

78 HUGHES MOUNTAIN NATURAL AREA

BEFORE YOU GO
MAP On park website
CONTACT Missouri Department of Conservation
GPS 37.810273° N, -90.715494° W
NOTES Inaccessible to wheelchairs and strollers; no bathrooms or water

ABOUT THE HIKE
SEASON Fall, winter, spring
DIFFICULTY Moderate to difficult
LENGTH 1.5 miles roundtrip
HIGH POINT 1150 feet
ELEVATION GAIN 330 feet

GETTING THERE

Take Interstate 55 to exit 174B, and turn right (south) onto US Highway 67. Drive 27 miles to the State Route 8 exit, and turn right toward Desloge. Drive 2 miles, and turn right (west) onto SR 8. Drive 5 miles, and turn left on State Highway M. Drive 8 miles, and turn left into the parking lot.

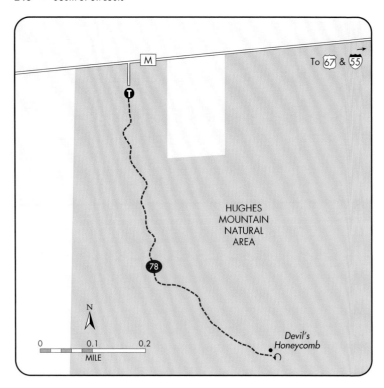

ON THE TRAIL

Devil's Honeycomb is one of the most fascinating rock formations in Missouri. It was formed hundreds of thousands of years ago when violent volcanic activity shifted rocks around; some types cooled faster than others that eroded around it. The forces that created the jagged columns found here are the same ones that formed the more famous Devils Postpile in California—a well-known stop on the Pacific Crest Trail—and Devils Tower in Wyoming, star of the 1977 movie *Close Encounters of the Third Kind.*

This short but scenic hike heads straight south from the parking area, going uphill. In the first half mile, hike through dense brush and forest. At first the trail is mowed between head-high grasses and shrubs. Soon this gives way to a clear dirt trail in a forest of oak, elm, and cedar. Hulking rock formations dot the landscape as you progress up the mountain.

The trail grows steeper the higher it continues up the mountain. At about mile 0.5, it leaves the thick forest behind to reveal the first of several views of the hills to the west. Before long, you start to see the characteristic multihued granite and rhyolite that form the famous "honeycombs. " Climb another third of a mile to further explore the glades and formations at the top of the hill. The hexagonal rocks are most concentrated at the top of the hill, a spot that marks the turnaround point of the hike at mile 0.75. When you're done exploring, retrace your steps back to the parking lot.

Note: Combine this with hike 79, another short but spectacular hike, at Elephant Rocks State Park. From Hughes Mountain, drive west on State Highway M for 3.5 miles, then turn left (south) on State Route 21 for 12 miles. The signed parking lot for Elephant Rocks will be on your left.

79 ELEPHANT ROCKS STATE PARK

BEFORE YOU GO
MAP On park website and at trailhead
CONTACT Missouri State Parks Department
GPS 37.65315238° N, -90.68897294° W
NOTES Rock climbing equipment prohibited; Braille Trail accessible for wheelchairs and strollers; bathrooms and water seasonally at parking lot

ABOUT THE HIKE
SEASON Fall, winter, spring
DIFFICULTY Easy
LENGTH 1mile loop; 1.5 miles with side trip to engine house
HIGH POINT 1275 feet
ELEVATION GAIN 100 feet

GETTING THERE
From Interstate 55, take exit 174B to US Highway 67, and turn right. Drive 30 miles, and take the State Route 32 exit to Leadington. Turn right onto SR 32, drive 10 miles, and turn left onto Cedar Street and State Highway N. Drive 9.5

A hiker atop one of the "elephant rocks" at their namesake state park

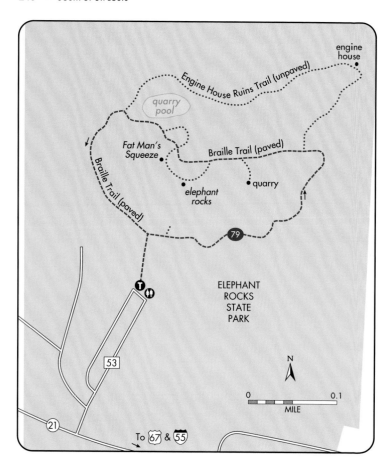

miles, and turn right onto SR 21. Drive 1.5 miles, and turn right onto County Road 53 at the sign for Elephant Rocks State Park.

ON THE TRAIL

As with many of the rich natural wonders in this area, the beauty of Elephant Rocks State Park was discovered because of economic resources. Before becoming one of the state's most beloved state parks, this area was a granite quarry—the stones collected here were used in the streets and buildings of St. Louis and other American cities during their explosive growth in the 1800s. Today we're fortunate that this and other parks have been preserved so we can appreciate the result of geology's work over the last billion years.

This park is named for the huge boulders that, in size and shape, resemble a parade of elephants. The granite masses were born as magma about 1.5 billion years ago. Over time the granite was exposed; then water and ice widened fractures in the granite, turning them into blocks. Millennia of erosion transformed the blocks into the boulders we see today.

The hike at Elephant Rocks is special for a couple of reasons. It showcases one of the most fascinating geologic formations in the state, and it offers its dozen or so interpretive signs in braille as well as English. A sign at the start of the trail describes how people with visual impairments can use the signs and the rope rails to experience the trail.

Begin your hike in the parking area and head uphill. Turn right at the Braille Trail loop junction to hike the trail counterclockwise. Right away kids find a lot of places to scramble up boulders and dash between them. If your time is limited, encourage them to wait until you get around to the middle (north) portion of the trail, where they can discover the path to the elephant rocks themselves, as well as Fat Man's Squeeze.

At 0.25 mile, bear left at a fork. Continue past this to the junction with the unpaved Engine House Ruins Trail at mile 0.4 (see "Fun Side Trip: Engine House" sidebar). Keep left to stay on the paved Braille Trail. At 0.5 mile reach a side trail on the left that takes you to a quarry area with a lot of broken up rocks. The side trail is just 100 feet or so and worth a look. In another tenth of a mile, follow the sign to the left for the path to the big rocks. Climb the short steps up to the flat hill upon which the elephants rest, and take your time exploring this special area.

Next you have the option of walking through Fat Man's Squeeze, a narrow gap along a fracture in the bedrock. Turn right for this brief half-loop that reconnects with the main trail in just a few steps. This is a favorite spot for many kids. Continue on the paved path to get a view of the water-filled pit that was part of the quarry. Just past the quarry pit, the Engine House Ruins Trail intersects with the Braille Trail; stay to the left to complete the paved trail. From here continue on the paved path another third of a mile to the trailhead.

Note: Pair this with another short but spectacularly scenic trail nearby at Hughes Mountain Natural Area (hike 78). From Elephant Rocks, turn right (northwest) out of the parking lot onto State Route 21. Drive 12 miles and turn right (east) onto State Highway M. Drive 3.5 miles and turn right into the parking lot.

FUN SIDE TRIP: ENGINE HOUSE

If your group is up for a half-mile side trip on an unpaved trail, check out the Engine House Ruins Trail, starting at mile 0.4 on the Braille Trail. This is a worthwhile side trip, leading to the remains of a 1890s engine house that serviced trains for the nearby quarry. The trail then wends through the forest of deciduous and evergreen trees, offering a nice taste of this Ozark region's vast forest before linking back to the Braille Trail.

80 JOHNSON'S SHUT-INS STATE PARK: SHUT-INS TRAIL

BEFORE YOU GO
MAP On park website and at visitor center
CONTACT Missouri State Parks Department
GPS 37.539651° N, -90.844117° W
NOTES Dogs prohibited; first 0.25 mile paved and wheelchair accessible; bathrooms, water, and store at trailhead

ABOUT THE HIKE
SEASON Summer to splash in shut-ins, year-round for rest of trail
DIFFICULTY Easy to shut-ins; difficult for entire loop
LENGTH 0.6–0.9 mile roundtrip to shut-ins; 2.5 miles loop
HIGH POINT 950 feet
ELEVATION GAIN 520 feet

GETTING THERE
From Farmington, drive 11.5 miles on State Route 221 southwest, and merge onto State Highway N. Drive 5 miles, and turn right onto SR 21. Drive 0.5 mile, and turn left onto State Highway N. Drive 12.5 miles, and turn left at the park entrance, following signs to shut-ins parking.

ON THE TRAIL
Johnson's Shut-Ins may be the most well-known and popular natural landmark in the state of Missouri. The rocky remnants of the region's volcanic past provide spectacular scenery and, in tandem with the East Fork Black River, a natural waterpark. Carving one of the deepest river valleys in the region, the water has eroded the sedimentary rock, leaving harder rhyolite behind. The result is rounded spires of rock that gather at jaunty angles and trap or "shut in" pools of water. People gather here by the thousands throughout the summer to splash and swim.

The first portion of this hike is an easy walk of about a third of a mile to the first toe-dipping location. The loop hike continues from there, stair-stepping down to the Black River and returning along the mountainside. The more adventurous can push past this hike, taking advantage of trails that crisscross the hills above the river valley.

This hike begins at the main parking lot for the shut-ins, next to the park store. Look for the blue-blazed Shut-Ins Trail. The first 0.3 mile is level pavement, designed for wheelchairs. If your goal is the shorter hike for water play, walk to this point and turn left at the well-signed access point for the shut-ins. Once at the water, you can explore the shut-ins, which puts your one-way distance at about 0.45 mile. Plan to stay at least thirty minutes before retracing your path to the parking lot.

Just past the shut-ins access, the Shut-Ins Trail turns into a boardwalk that's still appropriate for wheelchairs, which offers plenty of opportunities for views

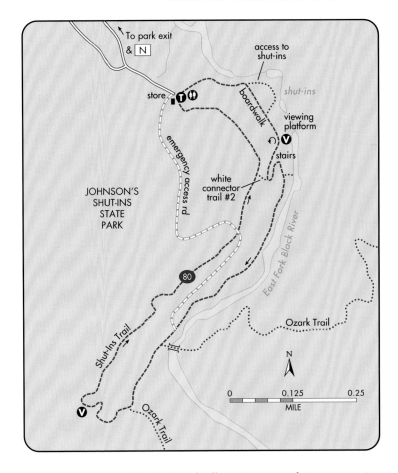

of the pools and waterfalls. The boardwalk continues to mile 0.4 at a viewing platform, and then those in wheelchairs will have to turn back as the stairs begin—about 200 of them, up, up the mountain with the river flowing below. After 0.5 mile the stairs start to go down, and a trail on the left leads down to a large pool. The boardwalk trail continues to hug the river, with the sounds of the rushing water and the delighted shouts of kids and adults splashing in the river carrying across the valley.

The boardwalk portion of the trail ends with another platform over a vivid blue pool, and then at mile 0.6 the trail heads steeply up the hill to the right. It's rooty and rocky, giving a taste of what's to come on a trail that's as tough as any in the St. Louis area. The trail goes up and down, with many switchbacks; remind kids not to take shortcuts, because it causes erosion and

Daddy and daughter creek crossing at Johnson's Shut-Ins State Park

damages the forest. On the left, get a good view of the cliffs that you just came down.

The trail becomes flat and sandy at 0.75 mile along the river's edge. For about a tenth of a mile, the cliffs and boulders on the right and the high mountains across the river to the left provide beautiful vistas all around. Then enter a picturesque forest with evergreen and deciduous trees intermixed and a large variety of wildflowers, including brown-eyed Susan and beggar's lice (which is much prettier than it sounds, even in late summer and fall).

At 1.1 miles is an intersection with an emergency access road. Stay on the blue-blazed Shut-Ins Trail as it heads slightly to the left. For a bit it's wide and smooth as it gets close to the river again. At 1.2 miles, a fire ring is tucked into a nice spot overlooking the river. Next, the trail veers to the right, briefly joining the Ozark Trail. At mile 1.4 the trail starts going up the side of a steep mountain and becomes a challenging series of scrambles up and over boulder and stone steps. Take your time and help kids who are easily frustrated; it can be almost like figuring out a puzzle to determine where best to next put your foot or hand to get over this stretch. Soon you are rewarded with views over the valley. As the trail veers left, watch for the blazes. Continue across a glade, turning around periodically to check out that view.

The trail starts to descend at mile 1.5, but then shifts to steep uphills in the next quarter mile. On the left, view more scenic cliffs and beautiful mixed forest characteristic of the Ozarks.

Stay right at mile 1.9 where the emergency access road intersects with the trail again. Continue to follow the blue blazes to stay on the Shut-Ins Trail. The path here gets wider but is still rocky. At mile 2.25 pass white connector trail #2, remaining on the blue-blazed trail. At mile 2.5, return to the paved trail where you turn left to return to the trailhead.

81 JOHNSON'S SHUT-INS STATE PARK: SCOUR TRAIL

BEFORE YOU GO

MAP On park website and at visitor center

CONTACT Missouri State Parks Department

GPS 37.556164° N, -90.839277° W

NOTES Accessible for some jogging strollers; mosquito populations can be high; no water or bathrooms at trailhead, but a store, bathrooms, and water fountains at visitor center

ABOUT THE HIKE

SEASON Year-round

DIFFICULTY Easy to moderate

LENGTH 1.75 miles loop

HIGH POINT 900 feet

ELEVATION GAIN 230 feet

GETTING THERE

From Farmington, drive southwest for 11.5 miles on State Route 221, and then merge onto State Highway N. Drive 5 miles, and turn right onto SR 21. Drive

When kiddo is sick of walking and the carrier, a shoulder ride is a fun option.

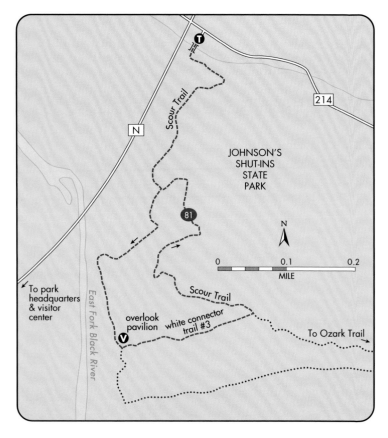

0.5 mile, and turn left onto State Highway N. Drive 12.5 miles, and turn left onto County Road 214. The trailhead parking lot for the Scour Trail is on the right.

ON THE TRAIL

If you want an easier hike than some of the rough and hilly trails elsewhere in this region, check out the Scour Trail. You'll still get a lot of pretty scenery, and you'll have the opportunity to learn firsthand about the history of what is possibly the most popular park in the state.

In December 2005, the Taum Sauk Reservoir breached, sending 1.3 billion gallons of water gushing down Proffit Mountain. Tons of trees, rocks, and debris were swept down the mountain, stripping bare a 1.5-mile, hundred-foot-wide stretch of forest. The park's popular campground was destroyed, but miraculously no one was killed.

GREAT GETAWAY: JOHNSON'S SHUT-INS

The St. Francois Mountains are some of the oldest mountains in the United States, formed by volcanic activity 1.5 billion years ago. The Appalachians, 460 million years old, and the Rockies, 140 million, are babies in comparison. As a result, these mountains, part of the Ozark range, are small in stature (the state high point, Taum Sauk Mountain, measures 1772 feet) but retain a rugged beauty. The area around Johnson's Shut-Ins State Park is one of the most wild and scenic near St. Louis, with hundreds of square miles of land set aside in parks, preserves, and protected forests.

This natural beauty, plus the pools and falls of the shut-ins the park was named for, has been drawing visitors here for generations. Other nearby parks, like Taum Sauk Mountain (hike 82) and Elephant Rocks (hike 79) state parks, are famous in their own right and make this whole region an outdoor playground.

Lodging: Potosi and Farmington, both on the way from St. Louis, offer several basic hotels. Bed-and-breakfasts are scattered about the hills, as well as some vacation cabins.

Camping: Johnson's Shut-Ins State Park has about eighty campsites and six cabins, making it the best bet for lodging in the area. The campground here is known as one of the best in the state park system, having been rebuilt in a new location after the 2005 reservoir breach flooded the park. Campsites can be reserved on the state park's website up to six months in advance—and if you plan to camp on a summer holiday, you'll need to plan that far in advance. Taum Sauk Mountain State Park also has a small campground. Several private campgrounds and RV parks are open seasonally near Lesterville, just fifteen minutes south of Johnson's Shut-Ins.

Attractions: Just twenty minutes northeast of Johnson's Shut-Ins, Pilot Knob is home to Civil War battle history at Battle of Pilot Knob State Historic Site. In September 1864, Union soldiers fought off Confederates seeking to retake Missouri's government at Jefferson City. About 1000 Confederates and 100 Union soldiers died in the battle. Many were buried in unmarked graves in the area. At the site you can learn the story of the battle, see period weapons like cannons, and take a half-mile hike of the grounds. Every three years a group of Civil War enthusiasts stages a full reenactment of the battle. See www.battleofpilotknob.org for more information.

Float trips are a popular activity, with several outfitters based in Lesterville. In Bonne Terre you'll find bowling, bumper boats, restaurants, and other family-friendly activities. Nearby Bonne Terre Mine has underwater boat tours and a bed-and-breakfast.

WALKING THE OZARKS

As through-hikes go, the Ozark Trail doesn't get the attention that the much longer Appalachian and Pacific Crest trails do, but it's a significant and growing trail in its own right.

The Ozark Trail was born in the 1970s, the brainchild of a number of governmental agencies, environmental groups, and landowners. They envisioned a trail that would allow hikers to walk from Castlewood State Park (hikes 21 and 22) more than 300 miles to the Arkansas border. It would stretch from the Ozark border regions on the outskirts of the St. Louis area through the Missouri Ozarks, and then meet up with a trail in Arkansas to make a 700-mile through-trail.

Today there are nearly 400 miles of trail in sections of the southeast part of the state, with the longest continuous stretch now 230 miles long, from Onondaga Cave State Park (hike 77) to the Middle Point Eleven Point River in Oregon, Missouri.

Much of the trail is maintained by volunteers. You can help. Find out more at www.ozarktrail.com.

The reservoir was repaired and the utility company paid millions to rebuild the campground (now located a few miles away in a separate section of the park) and the visitor center. A warning system was built in case the reservoir ever breaches again; signs throughout the park alert visitors of what to do in case sirens go off.

The plants in the area that was scoured by the flood have regrown to a large degree, but it's still obvious where the deluge took place. Trees in the scour path are clearly much younger and smaller than those in the thick forest that reaches up the hill on either side of the scour channel.

Start the hike by heading south from the parking lot and crossing the bridge over a stream. This is an offshoot of the East Fork Black River, which created the shut-ins the park is known for. Once you cross the bridge you'll be on the Scour Trail, which is blazed in red. The path here is wide and level; you notice right away how easy it is to traverse if you've done any of the other hikes in the area, like Taum Sauk Mountain (hike 82) or the Shut-Ins Trail (hike 80). The forest here is dense, featuring lots of variety in the trees, flowers, and rocky outcrops. After a third of mile you reach the loop portion of the Scour Trail; turn right to head down toward the scour overlook.

In this section the trail has more ups and downs and crosses a couple of washes, but is still a relatively easy walk. At 0.75 mile the trail reaches the scour overlook, which features a pavilion with some informative plaques about the scour. The view ranges across the scour, up the hill to where it started, and down the hill to the visitor center. From here, continue 0.1 mile on the Scour Trail to explore the creek bottom, just down the hill from the pavilion.

Once your group has explored this area, retrace your path to the overlook and turn right, following the signs for the white connector trail #3. This trail leads you through the forest for a quarter mile before reconnecting with the Scour Trail. Turn left. In this section you may be sharing the path with backpackers taking the Ozark Trail (see "Walking the Ozarks" sidebar). Overnight hikers often hike the 12 miles between here and Taum Sauk Mountain, the state's highest point.

Continue up the trail through the woods, taking note of the cliffs on the side of the trail around mile 1.3. In another 0.1 mile the loop closes. Turn right and return to the parking lot.

82 TAUM SAUK MOUNTAIN STATE PARK

BEFORE YOU GO

MAP On park website
CONTACT Missouri State Parks Department
GPS 37.572886° N, -90.728185° W
NOTES Accessible for wheelchairs only to state high point; bathroom at trailhead

ABOUT THE HIKE

SEASON Year-round
DIFFICULTY Difficult for loop; difficult for roundtrip
LENGTH 3 miles loop; 5 miles with roundtrip to Devils Tollgate
HIGH POINT 1772 feet (highest point in Missouri)
ELEVATION GAIN 650 feet

One of the many gorgeous views on the trail to Mina Sauk Falls

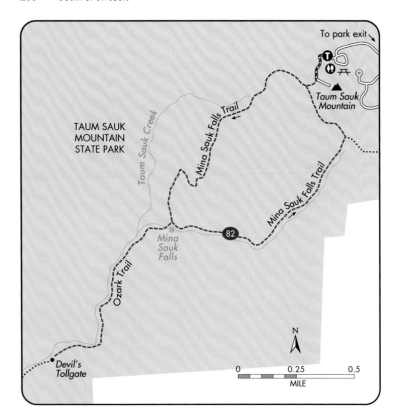

GETTING THERE

From Farmington, drive southwest for 18 miles on State Route 221, and turn left (south) on SR 21. Drive 6 miles, and turn right onto State Highway CC. Drive 4 miles, and turn left on High Point Trailhead. Follow signs to parking for state's high point.

ON THE TRAIL

Missouri's highest point and its tallest waterfall make this a hike of superlatives. It's not an exaggeration to say that this is one of the most beautiful in the region—or two, with its loop and roundtrip sections.

Start the hike from the parking lot with an easy 0.2-mile walk on the Mina Sauk Trail, a paved path to the state high point, Taum Sauk Mountain. The elevation marker is surrounded by forest and doesn't have a dramatic peak, but there are impressive views from the drive to the location and on the hike to come.

Once you're done checking out the geologic survey marker that marks the Missouri high point, head west to the dirt trail. At mile 0.25, at the junction of the Mina Sauk Falls Trail loop, take a right (northwest) to climb down the mountain toward the falls. This section of the hike is characterized by glades interspersed with forest and views of the surrounding hills that showcase the beauty of this, one of the country's oldest mountain ranges.

At 1 mile the trail heads into deep forest and sharply downhill. Watch your step as you enjoy the rock formations and thickening forest. At mile 1.5 you stand at the top of Mina Sauk Falls, the highest waterfall in Missouri, which drops 132 feet over a series of ledges into Taum Sauk Creek. Here too is the intersection with the Ozark Trail (see "Walking the Ozarks" sidebar, in hike 81).

If your group is up for a 5-mile roundtrip hike, bear right to head down the hill. After picking your way down the rocks alongside the falls, head west along the Ozark Trail toward Johnson's Shut-Ins. The trail goes gradually downhill for about a third of a mile, leveling out as you hike along Taum Sauk Creek. The near-constant presence of the creek makes for a verdant and gorgeous walk. The trail is thick with wildflowers in the spring. One mile from the junction with Mina Sauk Falls Trail, you reach Devil's Tollgate, where the trail slides between two thirty-foot-high slabs of volcanic rhyolite, making for quite a dramatic scene. After everyone slithers through the gap a few times, return to the loop junction.

Back at the falls, head up the hill and turn right to continue on the Mina Sauk Falls Trail loop (which joins the Ozark Trail for a while), making your way back up the mountain. Take your time on this rough hike, enjoying the forest and the rock formations. At mile 2.5 come to a junction where the main section of the Ozark Trail turns off to the right. As you take in the different colors and shapes made by erosion and lichens, keep an eye out for collared lizards; they are about the size and shape of the bearded dragons that are popular as pets, but are more colorful. The lizards like to hang out on warm rocks from April to October. Turn left (northwest) to go 0.3 mile to the paved trail and another 0.2 mile to your car.

"We made it!" Devil's Tollgate, hike 82, is an amazing destination.

RESOURCES

PERMITS AND CAMPING

Shaw Nature Reserve (hikes 59 and 60) charges a fee for entry. The rest of the hikes in this book require no fee or permit for day use. Wilderness camping is allowed in most state parks without a permit. Car camping is allowed in established campgrounds in some state parks by permit.

MANAGING AGENCIES

Phone numbers are listed for the park office or visitor center if there is one on site. If a local park phone number is not listed, refer to the agency or regional office. Parks without a visitor center, ranger station, or park office do not have addresses listed below.

US Government Agencies
US Fish and Wildlife Service
www.fws.gov
Two Rivers National Wildlife Refuge
www.fws.gov/refuge/Two_Rivers/
618-883-2524

US Forest Service
www.fs.fed.us

Shawnee National Forest
www.fs.usda.gov/shawnee
618-253-7114

State Agencies
Illinois Department of Natural Resources
www.dnr.illinois.gov

Eldon Hazlet State Recreation Area
20100 Hazlet Park Road
Carlyle IL 62231
618-594-3015

Fults Hill Prairie Nature Preserve
618-826-2706

Giant City State Park
618-457-4836

Horseshoe Lake State Park
618-931-0270

Pere Marquette State Park
13112 Visitor Center Lane
Grafton, IL 62037
618-786-3323

Piney Creek Ravine State Natural Area
4301 South Lake Drive
Chester, IL 62233
618-826-2706

Stemler Cave Woods Nature Preserve
618-295-2877

Illinois Historic Preservation Agency
http://www2.illinois.gov/ihpa
217-785-7930

Cahokia Mounds State Historic Site
https://cahokiamounds.org
618-346-5160

Missouri Department of Conservation
http://mdc.mo.gov, 636-441-4554

August A. Busch Memorial
  Conservation Area
2360 Highway D
St. Charles, MO
636-441-4554

Columbia Bottom Conservation Area
801 Strodtman Road
St. Louis, MO
314-877-6014

Engelmann Woods Natural Area
636-441-4554

Forest 44 Conservation Area
636-458-2236

Frank, Emma Elizabeth, and Edna
  Reifsnider State Forest
573-751-4115

Hickory Canyons Natural Area
573-290-5730

Howell Island Conservation Area
636-441-4554

Hughes Mountain Natural Area
636-441-4554

LaBarque Creek Conservation Area
636-441-4554

Long Ridge Conservation Area
636-441-4554

Meramec Conservation Area
636-441-4554

Myron and Sonya Glassberg Family
  Conservation Area
636-458-2236

Pickle Springs Natural Area
573-290-5730

Powder Valley Conservation Nature
  Center
11715 Cragwold Road
Kirkwood, MO
314-301-1500

Rockwoods Range
636-441-4554

Rockwoods Reservation
2751 Glencoe Road
Wildwood, MO
636-458-2236

Russell E. Emmenegger Nature Park
314-822-5855

St. Stanislaus Conservation Area
314-877-6014

Valley View Glades Natural Area
636-441-4554

Victoria Glades Conservation Area
636-441-4554

Weldon Spring Conservation Area
636-441-4554

Young Conservation Area
636-441-4554

Missouri State Parks Department
https://mostateparks.com
800-334-6946

Castlewood State Park
1401 Kiefer Creek Road
Ballwin, MO 63021
636-227-4433

Cuivre River State Park
678 State Route 147
Troy, MO 63379
636-528-7247

Don Robinson State Park
636-257-3788

Dr. Edmund A. Babler Memorial
    State Park
800 Guy Park Drive
Wildwood, MO 63005
636-458-3813

Elephant Rocks State Park
573-546-3454

Ha Ha Tonka State Park
1491 State Road D
Camdenton, MO 65020
573-346-2986

Hawn State Park
12096 Park Drive
Sainte Genevieve, MO 63670
573-883-3603

Johnson's Shut-Ins State Park
148 Taum Sauk Trail
Lesterville, MO 63656
573-546-2450

Lake of the Ozarks State Park
403 Highway 134
Kaiser, MO 65047
573-348-2694

Mastodon State Historic Site
1050 Charles J. Becker Drive
Imperial, MO 63052
636-464-2976

Meramec State Park
670 Fisher Cave Drive
Sullivan, MO 63080
573-468-6072

Onondaga Cave State Park
7556 Highway H
Leasburg, MO 65535
573-245-6576

Robertsville State Park
902 State Park Road
Robertsville, MO 63072
636-257-3788

St. Francois State Park
8920 US Highway 67
Bonne Terre, MO 63628
573-358-2173

Taum Sauk Mountain State Park
Highway CC
Ironton, MO 63656
573-546-2450

Washington State Park
13041 Missouri Highway 104
De Soto, MO 63020
636-586-5768

COUNTY AGENCIES
St. Louis County Parks and Recreation Department
www.stlouisco.com
    /ParksandRecreation
314-615-5000

Faust Park
314-615-8336

Greensfelder County Park
4515 Hencken Road
Pacific, MO 63069
636-458-3801

Laumeier Sculpture Park
12580 Rott Road
St. Louis, MO 63127
314-615-5278
www.laumeiersculpturepark.org

**St. Charles County Parks and
Recreation Department**
www.sccmo.org/232/Parks-Recreation
636-949-7535

Broemmelsiek Park
1795 Highway DD
Defiance, MO 63341

Indian Camp Creek Park
2679 Dietrich Road
Foristell, MO 63348

Klondike Park
4600 Highway 94 South
Augusta, MO 63332

Quail Ridge County Park
560 Interstate Drive
Wentzville, MO 63385

OTHER AGENCIES
City of Arnold, Missouri
Strawberry Creek Nature Area
www.arnoldmo.org
636-296-2100

Missouri Botanical Garden
Shaw Nature Reserve
307 Pinetum Loop Road
Gray Summit, MO 63039
636-451-3512

Village of Valmeyer, Illinois
Salt Lick Point Land and Water
  Reserve
http://valmeyerillinois.com
618-935-2131

Wildwood Department of Parks and
Recreation: Bluff View Park
www.cityofwildwood.com/154Parks
  -Recreation
636-458-0440

ORGANIZATIONS FOR TRAILS AND HIKING
Hiking and Backpacking with Kids
  Near St. Louis Meetup
www.meetup.com/Hiking-and
  -backpacking-with-kids-near-St
  -Louis-MO

Hike It Baby
https://hikeitbaby.com

Great Rivers Greenway
https://greatriversgreenway.org

Rails to Trails Conservancy
www.railstotrails.org

St. Louis Orienteering Club
http://stlouisorienteering.org/

OTHER
Forest Park Forever
www.forestparkforever.org

GEAR AND CLASSES
Alpine Shop
Kirkwood Chesterfield and
  O'Fallon, IL
www.alpineshop.com

REI Brentwood
www.rei.com

ACKNOWLEDGMENTS

I'm deeply grateful to my husband, Nathan. He supported me every step of the way in the creation of this book, from tagging along on most of the hikes to doing the bulk of the toddler-carrying in the varied conditions of Missouri's four seasons. He watched the kids while I wrote and edited and drew maps. And he was my encouraging cheerleader at every stage.

Thanks to my wonderful son, Arthur, who loves hikes long and short, reminiscing about past conquests, and dreaming with me about future big trails. Thanks to my sweet son, Noah, for hiking with the family even when he would rather be doing something else. And thanks to my joyful daughter, Helen. I cherish the appreciation you all have for trail wonders big and small.

Thanks to Kate Rogers and Laura Shauger at Mountaineers Books for believing in me. Laura's guidance and encouragement were invaluable. Thanks to Pm Weizenbaum for her incredible commitment to making this book the best it could be with her attention to detail and thoughtful consideration of every word.

I'm grateful to the rangers and land managers at all the state parks, county parks, open spaces, forests, and other parks where these hikes take place.

Thanks to the families that have been so important to our adventures in the St. Louis area: the Dirnbergers, the Joneses, the Griggses, the Pankaus, and the Atkinses. Big thanks to Kurt, Molly, Chappy, David, Ryan, Ben, and the rest of the St. Louis Writers Meetup.

Finally I acknowledge Nate Binkert (1977–2017), one of the most dedicated outdoorsmen and finest humans I've ever known, and thank his wife Amity Binkert, as true and beautiful a friend and fellow adventurer as one could ever find, for her encouragement since I first conceived this project.

INDEX

Opposite: *Dramatic cliffs define Fults Hill Prairie Nature Preserve.*

ABOUT THE AUTHOR

Kathy Schrenk writes fiction and nonfiction and is an outdoor enthusiast. In 2014 she started the Hiking and Backpacking with Kids Near St. Louis Meetup, which now has more than 2000 members. She's been writing professionally her entire adult life, including ten years as a newspaper reporter in Illinois and California. Her love of the outdoors was kindled in the redwood forests of Northern California, where she has hiked, biked, and camped with kids of all ages. In 2008 she joined the board of directors of Restore Hetch Hetchy, an organization focused on the goal of removing the reservoir that sits in the Hetch Hetchy Valley inside Yosemite National Park; in *The Yosemite,* John Muir called the valley "one of nature's rarest and most precious mountain temples."

Liz Schrenk

Since moving to Missouri in 2013, she has been awed by the variety of outdoor experiences to be had in the St. Louis region. She hikes most weekends with her husband, Nathan, and their three kids: Arthur, Noah, and Helen.

MOUNTAINEERS BOOKS including its two imprints, Skipstone and Braided River, is a leading publisher of quality outdoor recreation, sustainability, and conservation titles. As a 501(c)(3) nonprofit, we are committed to supporting the environmental and educational goals of our organization by providing expert information on human-powered adventure, sustainable practices at home and on the trail, and preservation of wilderness.

Our publications are made possible through the generosity of donors, and through sales of more than 800 titles on outdoor recreation, sustainable lifestyle, and conservation. To donate, purchase books, or learn more, visit us online:

MOUNTAINEERS BOOKS
1001 SW Klickitat Way, Suite 201• Seattle, WA 98134
800-553-4453 • mbooks@mountaineersbooks.org • www.mountaineersbooks.org

Leave No Trace strives to educate visitors about the nature of their recreational impacts and offers techniques to prevent and minimize such impacts. Leave No Trace is best understood as an educational and ethical program, not as a set of rules and regulations. For more information, visit www.lnt.org or call 800-332-4100.

OTHER MOUNTAINEERS BOOKS TITLES YOU MAY ENJOY!

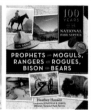